care to persons in diverse settings. Chaplains are called to be fluid and open in their approach to ministry to people from various backgrounds. Chaplain Baker captures this well in his writings."

— **Chaplain Michael L. McCoy**
former National Director of Chaplaincy in
the US Department of Veterans Affairs

"Baker brings his beginnings as a USN Academy plebe through his retirement as the sixteenth Chaplain of the US Marine Corps to this insightful primer on chaplaincy. *Foundations of Chaplaincy* is both a discourse on the chaplaincy field and a 'how-to' course on the professional world of chaplains, who live in the tension between allegiance to their own faith tradition and assuring the free exercise of all persons in a secular, pluralistic environment. The four functional capabilities of chaplains to 'provide, facilitate, advise, and care' inform chaplains and management alike how this tension is lived out with integrity. Information and insight are peppered with practical stories and biblical examples. Prospective through experienced chaplains can all benefit from absorbing the wisdom of this text."

— **Jan McCormack**
Denver Seminary

"Chaplaincy is one of the most interesting and innovative forms of ministry. It finds its roots within the established church, but takes the ministry of care, compassion, and presence into the world in a diversity of healing ways. But what exactly is chaplaincy? What do chaplains do? Why should anyone care? In this interesting and timely book Alan Baker lays out the essence of the tasks of chaplaincy in a way that is clear, accessible, and open to a broad range of people inside and outside of faith communities. Anyone who wants to know about and understand the importance of chaplaincy should read this book."

— **John Swinton**
University of Aberdeen

FOUNDATIONS OF CHAPLAINCY

A Practical Guide

Alan T. Baker

WILLIAM B. EERDMANS PUBLISHING COMPANY

GRAND RAPIDS, MICHIGAN

Wm. B. Eerdmans Publishing Co.
4035 Park East Court SE, Grand Rapids, Michigan 49546
www.eerdmans.com

Published 2021
Printed in the United States of America

27 26 25 24 23   4 5 6 7

ISBN 978-0-8028-7749-9

Library of Congress Cataloging-in-Publication Data

Names: Baker, Alan T., 1956– author.
Title: Foundations of chaplaincy : a practical guide / Alan T. Baker.
Description: Grand Rapids, Michigan : William B. Eerdmans Publishing Com-
    pany, 2021. | Includes bibliographical references and index. | Summary:
    "A comprehensive introduction, overview, and reference book for the min-
    istry of chaplaincy"—Provided by publisher.
Identifiers: LCCN 2020036695 | ISBN 9780802877499 (paperback)
Subjects: LCSH: Pastoral care. | Chaplains.
Classification: LCC BV4375 .B35 2021 | DDC 253—dc23
LC record available at https://lccn.loc.gov/2020036695

*For my mentors Charles Carter and Harold "Shorty" Brown,
who gave me hope and inspired a generation
through their ministry of presence*

Contents

Contents

Introduction

What Is Chaplaincy?

Welcome to the most exciting and fastest-growing segment of specialized ministry: chaplaincy. It is distinct from mainstream pastoral models because the focus is delivering a "ministry of presence" to people outside of a church. While local-church models typically reinforce a wagon-wheel approach, where the pastor remains at the center and the outside community follows the spokes inward, chaplains invert the wagon-wheel model by providing their presence where people live and work along the outer wheel rim. In our current culture, "as fewer people identify with a specific religion or attend religious services, Americans may be more likely to meet a chaplain than a local clergy person at a congregation."[1] Chaplaincy is ministry in motion. It is filled with quick-moving fire trucks, police cars, and military Humvees. It sails over the ocean on cruise liners and aircraft carriers. It paces hygienically clean operating rooms and grimy factory floors. It ministers to those behind bars as well as those taking the bar exam. Chaplains walk the sidelines of the football field and tread the battlefield.

No other religious vocation offers the vibrancy of chaplaincy. This model emphasizes roadside ministry over residential ministry. It is constantly evolving, immensely challenging, fast paced, and deeply fulfilling. Yet chaplaincy is not about the context of a chaplain's geography or the rewarding variety of vocational settings. For chaplains, it is all about looking into the faces and hearts of humans like yourself. It is laboring with and loving fellow sojourners traveling alongside you as together you experience the journey of life.

More than anything else, chaplaincy is being present among those you serve: crying, laughing, worshiping, celebrating, mourning, storytelling, and comforting. Chaplaincy first sends you *out* to places and then draws you *in* toward people. Chaplain positions are filled by people who are encouragers, caregivers, helpers, advocates, and listeners. Core to the chaplain is a commission to bear the image of God, despite your own obvious imperfections and brokenness, to the faces and hearts of those who otherwise may never enter a house of worship except for a wedding or a funeral.

Chaplains are innovators in their organizations. They inspire others to become better versions of themselves. Chaplains bring meaningful change to institutions due to their commitment to people within the organization. They are chartered by their organization to stand as both bridge and buffer between the institution and its people. At times, you encourage those entrusted to you to "keep the long look" and help them not to wane either in their character or in hope. At other times you serve as a buffer between the organization and its people, ensuring that those entrusted with power will listen to what they must hear. You do this in spite of, and often in trepidation of, personal consequences to yourself. The beauty and wonder of your calling as a chaplain are that the institution expects no less from you. You are recognized as someone who cares for everyone, even when others cannot. You are entrusted with bearing the presence of God into malevolent and hostile situations. You are called upon to advocate for those who suffer. You are concerned for those who are ill or injured. You serve the dying and honor the dead.

God is the strength of chaplaincy because it takes God's specific calling to want to serve beyond the walls of a house of worship. If you sense your feet leading you toward people where they work, play, suffer, heal, laugh, cry, and even die, then chaplaincy is worth your consideration.

Who Should Read This Book?

This book explains the essentials, summarizes the expectations, and serves as a reference handbook for chaplaincy and thus will be of benefit whether you are approaching chaplaincy as a seminary student or a prospective chaplain, or are a current chaplain or professor. In the following pages, you will gain clarity on the common fundamentals of chaplain ministry. The goal of this primer is to prepare you for any chaplaincy, no matter the setting. This book will launch you into an orbit shared by current and former chaplains, upon whose shoulders you may soon stand. Its chapters provide guidance and suggestions on how to establish your credibility within the organization and among the people you serve.

This text is also valuable for faith group leaders, such as ecclesiastical endorsers, who *send* and support chaplains. It is equally valuable for government, corporate, nonprofit, and other organizational leaders who *receive* and supervise chaplains. The work of chaplaincy should not be a mystery to the public or private sector. Chaplains currently serve throughout diverse institutions. Both the chaplain's ordaining faith group and the chaplain's employing organization should know what to expect from their chaplain.

Chaplains are sent from a variety of faith traditions and collaboratively work alongside each other within the same institution. Pastors, ministers, and priests serve alongside rabbis, imams, and swamis. This textbook is written from the perspective of a Protestant Christian chaplain; readers from other faith traditions will not identify with its specifically Christian theological content but are warmly invited to glean practical advice for chaplaincy work.

What Do Chaplains Do?

Here is a quick quiz. See if you can find a thread of similarity in the following statements:

> "I've finally made it. The promotion is guaranteed. There will soon be enough cash on hand to pay off the house. Maybe there will even be a little extra. All of this is wonderful, yet I still hate my job."

> "My mom just got a big raise and can finally pay for my college tuition. I will graduate debt free and find a career. All of this is wonderful, but my professor caught me cheating yesterday on the final."

> "My sister is so arrogant about her new promotion. She still thinks I'm scum. I will never experience life as she can now. All of this is wonderful, except I'll be an old man by the time I finish this sentence and get out of the slammer."

> "My neighbor brags about her promotion the same day a hospital bed replaces my sofa. Hospice returns tomorrow. My life would be wonderful, except my husband is dying in our living room."

Not one of these people is connected to a faith community. Yet all of them most likely have access to a chaplain, even if they may not realize it. There are workplace, campus, prison, and hospice chaplains available to help them. Chaplains bear a unique identity as highly committed, well-trained clergy called by God to bring specialized ministry to these people as well as to the chaplains' institutions.

Prospective chaplains initially prepare for chaplaincy by developing five interwoven competencies: as minister, pastor, intercessor, healer, and teacher.[2] Once these professional requirements are forged in seminary and through practical ministry experience, you are ready to begin your work as a chaplain. New chaplains then focus on delivering four core functional capabilities common to all chaplaincy contexts: provision, facilitation, care, and advice. These four unifying pillars of chaplaincy remain consistent regardless of your organizational context or geographic setting. Chaplaincy is comprised of (1) providing ecclesiastical services according to your faith tradition, (2) facilitating the religious expectations and requirements of others, (3) caring for all, and (4) advising leaders within an organization. The upcoming chapters will explore these four essential principles in depth.

Provide

Chaplains provide religious ministry according to their faith tradition. As a chaplain, you are educated and endorsed to meet specific faith-group needs, including the performance of worship services, sacraments, rites, ordinances, religious counsel, biblical studies, and religious education. You provide ministry to those aligned with your faith group's theology. This is the aspect of chaplaincy that most resembles a traditional church pastor; however, the context makes it a wildly different ministry.

Facilitate

Chaplains facilitate ministry for people practicing different faiths. Facilitation of the diverse religious requirements of others within your institution is a unique ministry of chaplaincy. Organizations look to their chaplains for expertise in facilitating faith-based support of individual or group requirements as well as responding to employee requests for accommodation of their religious practices. You facilitate those who don't identify with you but nevertheless have specific religious requirements, expectations, and needs.

Care

Chaplains care for everybody. This is the essence of chaplaincy, and the one activity that everyone receives from their chaplain. Chaplains are specially qualified to deliver pastoral care, counseling, and coaching to members at all levels within their institution. Most opportunities to care for others reach beyond a faith-specific context. Those who come to you for support do not typically recognize you as their worship leader. They may know you are a religious person, but they will likely not understand or care about your religion. They simply see you as a professional who cares about people.

Advise

Chaplains are advisers to others within the organization. Organizational leaders expect chaplains to be subject-matter experts on religion and its influence both internally and beyond. In response, chaplains assist the organization to strengthen the development of leadership at all levels. Chaplains serve as principal advisers on faith to organizational leadership. They also deliver advice to individuals at every level within the organization regarding moral, ethical, spiritual, interpersonal, and humanitarian concerns.

If you are exploring chaplaincy as a potential calling, please read this book while praying about where God might be leading you. I hope these pages will provide an inspiring glimpse into the pivotal role of chaplaincy. For those currently serving as chaplains, I want to thank you for your unwavering commitment to your faith that is foundational to your calling to serve in the ministry of chaplaincy. May this book encourage you to further explore your calling and discern God's "still, small voice" upon your ministry. My goal is to provide you, as reader, the heart and soul of chaplaincy so that you may flourish in this ministry. You hold in your hands a framework for understanding and practicing chaplaincy. May you be inspired along the way.

CATEGORIES OF CHAPLAIN FUNCTIONAL CAPABILITIES

Initiative of chaplain:	For whom?	What happens?
Provide	People identifying with your religion/ ministry	Based on your professional credentials, ecclesiastical endorsement, and employment to meet faith-group specific needs, including worship services, rites, sacraments, ordinances, religious counsel, Scripture study, and religious education.
Facilitate	People identifying with another religion/ ministry	Ensuring support for the variety of diverse religious needs of all people within the organization. Accommodation of these individual and collective religious ministry requirements includes scheduling, contracting, and coordinating lay leaders, volunteers, and other religious organizations.
Care	All people within the institution	Delivering institutionally appropriate care, counseling, and coaching to people outside a faith-group context. Care is hallmarked by confidentiality and genuine respect for others. It is most effective in the context of shared experiences within the same organization and is built on strong relationships.
Advise	People serving in leadership and management	Assisting organizational leadership by providing advice at all levels of management. Chaplains are principal advisers in religion, ethics, and humanitarian matters. Chaplains also provide advice on developing relationships and increasing cooperation with surrounding communities.

CHAPTER 1

The Foundations of Chaplaincy

> In thanksgiving to the living God for all ministers who
> have borne the hot coal of his Word upon their lips and
> in their lives.
>
> —*Inscription at Washington National Cathedral*

1.1 The Call *to* Ministry and the Call *of* Chaplaincy

In a perfect world, all would embrace their vocation and flourish in it. God's plan for Adam and Eve was to place them "in the garden of Eden to work it and keep it" (Gen. 2:15).[1] In the beginning, Adam and Eve thrived in their God-given occupation. But now, due to the Fall, our sinful nature obscures the truth and we no longer feel same absolute assurance of our calling as Adam and Eve did. However, God still calls us to work in his world.

Those in professional ministry are most satisfied when they feel a genuine sense of God's calling toward their vocation. This is especially urgent and significant for chaplain ministry. Chaplains serve on the frontier of the church and are typically distanced from the center of the very faith community that endorses them for chaplaincy. As a chaplain, your ministry seeks a firm foundation that confirms your calling by God to this special work. You will not only need to rely on this foundation in times of stress, but you also will be frequently called upon to articulate and justify your calling to the people and institutions you serve. Therefore, the decision to enter chaplaincy requires a discernment process, starting with an assessment of your motivations, which are always complicated.

Motivation and Calling

Theologians continue to ponder the connection between human motivation and divine calling. Chaplains are fueled by a divine call to extend

7

compassion outward toward others. This vocation is best demonstrated by a horizontal extension of ministry to others. Frederick Buechner captures the thought in his definition of vocation: "The place God calls you to is the place where your deep gladness and the world's deep hunger meet."[2] He sees connective tissue between our inner Spirit-inspired passions and external opportunities to exercise our gifts in a productive way. Buechner understands that we are all searching for a purpose that only God can give.

> I think it's good advice for most seminarians to start in the parish setting, but maybe there are some for whom chaplaincy is the right place to begin. I especially think of women, who do not have as many opportunities open to them in parish ministry, and chaplaincy is where they feel called. Experiencing parish ministry is important, but establishing a connection to the church is essential to chaplaincy.
>
> —*Correctional/Prison Chaplain*

Os Guinness further unpacks calling and motivation: "Calling is the truth that God calls us to himself so decisively that everything we are, everything we do, and everything we have is invested with a special devotion, dynamism, and direction lived out as a response to [God's] summons and service."[3] Guinness offers these comforting words as he provides direction to our activity: "We are not primarily called to do something or go somewhere; we are called to Someone."[4] Our motivation is focused toward responding to God's initiative. He invites us into relationship with him and not into our activities. Instead of identifying yourself by saying, "You are what you do," calling says, "Do what you are."[5]

These working definitions of calling move us toward greater confidence and resolve as we develop a sense of our own vocation. It may be helpful to imagine calling as a balanced teeter-totter, with giftedness on one end and stewardship of talent and energy on the other. The risks of getting this teeter-totter off balance are high. If we allow our giftedness to lead us away from stewardship toward selfishness, we may fall into the trap of believing we are entitled and not simply entrusted with the gifts God has bestowed in us and through us toward others.

There is a healthy way of discerning calling, which is a two-part process. The first criterion of evaluating a potential call *to* vocational ministry is through *affirmation*. The second criterion is the actual call *of* ministry through *confirmation*. While both are required, they are not necessarily sequential. In the process of discernment, affirmation and confirmation are spun together like strands of rope providing strength and confidence as you grasp your calling.

Affirmation and Confirmation

Affirmation comes from people you trust, who live around you, who see you as you are Monday through Saturday as well as Sunday. These people are close to you. They communicate to you that you are setting your life's purpose in the right direction. In the Bible, a terrific example of affirmation is Paul's commendation of Timothy: "I hope in the Lord Jesus to send Timothy to you soon, so that I too may be cheered by news of you. For I have no one like him, who will be genuinely concerned for your welfare" (Phil. 2:19–20). Paul was seeking to minister to the Philippians through Timothy. He was also affirming Timothy as a minister so earnestly concerned for their welfare that there was, in Paul's estimation, simply no one like him. Through Paul's affirmation, Timothy's own calling became clearer. He became aware of his gifts and more confident in his practice of those gifts.

On the other hand, confirmation is something that grows as you spend time doing what you are doing. It is putting your shoulder to the wheel and leaning hard into the opportunities that attract you. Yet instead of bruising your shoulder, you discover your muscles growing stronger in the process. It is measuring, both through anecdotal evidence and quantitative comparisons, whether the use of your talents is growing or shrinking. A biblical example of measurement comparisons is found in this parable: "The master of those servants came and settled accounts with them. And he who had received the five talents came forward, bringing five talents more, saying, 'Master, you delivered to me five talents; here I have made five talents more.' His master said to him, 'Well done, good and faithful servant. You have been faithful over a little; I will set you over much. Enter into the joy of your master'" (Matt. 25:19–21). The supervisor found greater value in talents that were exercised. Talents are measured on the basis of their investment. A valuable talent is worthless if unused. Confidence in your calling to chaplaincy is confirmed as your ministry strengthens over time.

As you discern confirmation of a valid call, reflect whether your aspirations are legitimate, measurable, and reasonable: "For which of you, desiring to build a tower, does not first sit down and count the cost, whether he has enough to complete it? Otherwise, when he has laid a foundation and is not able to finish, all who see it begin to mock him, saying, 'This man began to build and was not able to finish'" (Luke 14:28–30). The confirmation of the tower-builder is not whether he commenced the project but whether he completed it. Was it a soundly built structure? Did it do what he intended it to do? Was its purpose to be a landmark, a lighthouse, or a fortress? Did he build the top of the tower facing outward toward unknown enemies, or did he build a safety tower facing inward so that the smoke of a building fire could be spotted? Whether you are constructing a tower on the border or preparing for chaplain ministry on the frontier, confirmation looks at the result of your experience. Did your experience teaching a religious-education class have positive effects on you, your family, and the participants? Did your preparation and delivery of a sermon bother you or bless you?

When I first considered chaplaincy as a path for my future, my adviser recommended I enroll in Koine Greek before resigning my undergraduate teaching position to become a full-time seminary student. With fear and trepidation, I enrolled in Greek at a nearby Bible college and quickly realized what over-commitment looked like, as I now had classes to teach and classes to take. My mind flooded with rationalizations: I didn't have time for this course. The commute was long. Students were robbed of my prep time. There was too much vocabulary to learn. Yet I unexpectedly thrived. As I developed an un-natural passion for learning an ancient language, I realized I couldn't have developed this delight for Greek on my own. I sensed my joy was a gift of confirmation from the Lord, and a good grade at the end of the first semester validated this confirmation with a quantifiable metric. I was heading in the right direction.

—Prospective Chaplain

Another way of looking at the difference between affirmation and confirmation is by viewing your intent before you begin a project and then reviewing the consequences of your labor. Affirmation is the front door. It focuses on your intent. People you trust affirm your calling alongside the peace that comes from the Holy Spirit. Trusted people look at your intentions and affirm them. Confirmation is the back door. It looks at the result of your potential calling through your activity.

Affirmation of your calling may not always come from family or faith-filled people. There are many sources of affirmation. The key is a trusted source. For example, when I became a Christian aboard my first ship, my desires changed and my interests were redirected. Not long after my conversion, my reckless roommate told me I was no longer much fun. I received his charge with laughter because he inadvertently affirmed that the Holy Spirit was moving my life in a new direction.

Affirmation is proactive, and confirmation is a reactive response to the impact you've experienced in ministry. You go into the wilderness of society, putting one foot forward—starting seminary toward the chaplain ministry you feel called to do—and then you assess how it goes. Like a slalom racer, you must pass through a number of gates as you confirm your ministry: your experience at seminary, your graduation from seminary, your ordination by your faith group, your acceptance to become a chaplain, each annual evaluation by your organization, and your joy in life that you experience along the way.

> When I transitioned from chaplaincy, I struggled to pursue another calling. I really missed chaplaincy, but it was time to retire. Then I received a timely note from my daughter: "Dad, pray to be spent. Give all you can. Don't die with anything in the reserves. Don't retire knowing you could have done more. God has raised you up with the experiences you have not to waste. When you look for your next position, ask yourself: Can someone else do the job just as well as you when you can do something no one else can do?" My daughter gave me the gift of affirmation. As a result, my calling migrated from chaplain to chaplain advocate.
> —*Ecclesiastical Endorser of Chaplains*

Chaplaincy is a process of calling followed by commissioning. Whereas the calling comes from God, commissioning comes from the hiring organization. In the US military, it is not only expected but also required that all new chaplains be commissioned as officers to the specific role of chaplain. These are individuals previously earmarked and set aside by their faith groups as clergy who are now moving to a commission within a specialized ministry of chaplaincy. N. T. Wright confirms this two-step process in the ministry of Paul: "[Paul] is also making it clear that his call and commissioning have placed him in the ancient prophetic tradition, whether of Isaiah, Jeremiah, or Elijah himself."[6] Transformed, Paul moved from persecutor to proclaimer. Prospective chaplains move from being called by God, to being confirmed by their faith group, and finally to being commissioned by an institution.

While ordination happens only once in a chaplain's ministry, a chaplain is commissioned to a specific role each time he starts employment with a particular organization. When a chaplain departs from an organization, he is no longer commissioned to that role, though he remains ordained. He can receive another commission upon subsequent employment. Commissioning is exemplified in the Bible when Joshua succeeds Moses. As part of the transfer of authority, Moses "took Joshua and made him stand before Eleazar the priest and the whole congregation, and he laid his hands on him and commissioned him as the LORD directed through Moses" (Num. 27:22–23). A chaplain must confirm his calling before being commissioned. If someone is commissioned without a calling, then many people within the organization, including the chaplain, will suffer.

The concept of *commissioning* means a minister has an identifiable beginning point in chaplaincy. It could be a military commission certificate or an appointment letter presented by the hiring institution. A commission also has an expected ending, when the minister no longer serves the organization as a chaplain. The end date, whether due to reassignment, retirement, or resignation, signifies the completion of the commission. You may retain your calling to ministry, but you will serve in a different venue.

There are many ministry opportunities and contexts. Ask yourself if God is calling you to serve in the unique context of chaplaincy. No matter how much you might be motivated, not every opportunity in front of you is a calling. Discern your calling through affirmation and confirmation. Chaplaincy may be where God is commissioning you to exercise your unique gifts in a deeply meaningful way.

Building Below the Waterline

Before we look at chaplaincy in depth, there is another aspect of calling for you to explore. In the book *Building Below the Waterline: Shoring Up the Foundations of Leadership*, Gordon MacDonald explores a "menu of motives"[7] that are not made by God. MacDonald includes our need for approval, validation from achievement, hubris born from success, and an undisciplined pursuit for more. He knows better than most pastors the need to discern our motivations: "I am no stranger to failure and public humiliation. From those terrible moments of twenty years ago in my own life I have come to believe that there is a deeper person in many of us who is not unlike an assassin. . . . If you have been burned as deeply as I (and my loved ones) have, you never live a day without remembering that there is something within that, left unguarded, will go on the rampage."[8] His ministry imploded because of his self-centered impulse. But God graciously restored his calling and gave him another commission. Whereas MacDonald once served out of his words and deeds, he now ministers from his wounds. Chastened by his experience, MacDonald is very attuned to the ways in which pastors and other Christian leaders are tempted to derail and crash.

He repeats an analogy throughout his book, borrowed from Washington Roebling, chief engineer of the Brooklyn Bridge. It was part of Roebling's annual report to the bridge company in June 1872. To the casual observer, the building of the Brooklyn Bridge seemed slow, which is not a well-received word in Manhattan. New Yorkers tend to appreciate speed and acceleration, so the public was frustrated at the bridge builders. Roebling responded: "To such of the general public as might imagine that no work has been done on the New York tower, because they see no evidence of it above the water, I should simply remark that the amount of the masonry and concrete laid on that foundation during the past winter, under water, is equal in quantity to the entire masonry of the Brooklyn tower visible today above the waterline."[9]

MacDonald's point is that you have to build below the waterline before you see visible and tangible evidence of the work above the surface. This is important to consider as you ponder your calling and potential commission as a chaplain. Opportunities like seminary, professional conferences, journals, and workshops emphasize leadership themes such as developing vision, core competencies, strategies, and increasing individual and institutional capacities. This is all beneficial, yet the majority of these opportunities are focused above the waterline. They appeal to our public persona and not our private self. As MacDonald says, "Leaders blessed with great natural skills and charisma may be vulnerable to collapse in their character, their key relationships, and their center of belief because they never learned that one cannot (or should not) build *above* the waterline until there is a substantial foundation *below* it."[10] Let us now begin construction of the foundational pillars of chaplaincy below the waterline.

1.2 Biblical Basis for Chaplaincy

Evidence of chaplaincy appears in the Old Testament. Ancient Israel, we remember, was a theocracy, which is quite different from the way most modern countries distinguish between church and civil government. In Deuteronomy 20:2–4, priests are traveling into battle with the army: "When you draw near to the battle, the priest shall come forward and speak to the people and shall say to them, 'Hear, O Israel, today you are drawing near for battle against your enemies: let not your heart faint. Do not fear or panic or be in dread of them, for the LORD your God is he who goes with you to fight for you against your enemies, to give you the victory.'" That is a powerful word boldly proclaimed by a chaplain against the enemy.

My personal experience as a contemporary Christian chaplain was quite different. When I was in combat serving US Marines, I did not pray for victory of one side over the other. Instead, I would pray for peace on both sides and preservation of life. Never did anyone complain about my prayer for peace. Unlike the Old Testament prayer for the execution of God's righteous judgment, current chaplaincy stands squarely on the side of human flourishing. We want people to treat one another humanely and with dignity despite disease, wars, poverty, pain, and suffering. Jesus's ministry in the New Testament serves as an ideal for chaplains, and Jesus himself models three foundational pillars of chaplaincy: (1) being intentional through movement and direction, (2) embracing diversity through connection and compassion, and (3) seeking transformation through presence and service.

Being Intentional through Movement and Direction

The biblical basis for chaplaincy can be built, in part, on a particular experience that Jesus had with a Samaritan woman in John 4. It starts with movement and direction. Jesus is not moving toward Jerusalem, as the center of religious activity, but away from it: "Now when Jesus learned that the Pharisees had heard that Jesus was making and baptizing more disciples than John (although Jesus himself did not baptize, but only his disciples), he left Judea and departed again for Galilee. And he had to pass through Samaria" (John 4:1–4). As mentioned earlier, chaplaincy is focused outward from the boundaries of the church. Christian chaplains imitate Jesus by moving toward the frontier while simultaneously maintaining the standards and practices of their faith.

The proactive movement and intentional direction echo Jesus heading out of his own place and moving through foreign territory: "So he came to a town of Samaria called Sychar, near the field that Jacob had given to his son Joseph. Jacob's well was there; so Jesus, wearied as he was from his journey, was sitting beside the well. It was about the sixth hour" (4:5–6). Jesus, in the process of heading toward Galilee, stops and sits in a very public and visible location. His attire and accent are from a foreign culture. He is soon spotted as not being a member of the local Samaritan village. Some citizens might have avoided him. The situation seemed culturally and socially charged to ignite: What is a Jew doing in Samaria? That question could translate through time into today: What is a chaplain doing in a prison? What is a religious professional doing inside a factory?

Jesus shows us the next step in forming a biblical basis for chaplaincy.

He quickly diffuses the uncomfortable and builds a bridge. He catches the attention of a nearby resident. His choice is unique and intentional. This person isn't the governor, the mayor, or a public official. This person is needy. She is a survivor of deep cultural and social wounds. She is simply hoping to draw water from the well and get home as quickly as possible.

Not only does Jesus practice his ministry by intentionally moving toward those in need of care. He also preaches what he practices. Chaplains also take initiative and provide service over convenience. The direction of their ministry moves them to people rather than waiting for people to come to them. A chaplain presumes no one will visit her, but she must visit everyone.

A chaplain practices intentional initiation. The Christian chaplain is committed to proclaim God's redeeming love to a world that will most likely never step through the doors of a church. Therefore, the chaplain exits the doors into the world. The direction is outward. Taking initiative to meet people in their pain and suffering requires courage and compassion. Accompanying people on their journey will likely bring both hardship and joy. Just as Jesus was weary from his journey away from Jerusalem, chaplains need reservoirs of refreshment when away from their church and faith community. Courage, compassion, hardship, and joy are entwined together as a chaplain embraces the practice of intentionally being focused outward.

Embracing Diversity through Connection and Compassion

The story continues in John 4:7–8: "A woman from Samaria came to draw water. Jesus said to her, 'Give me a drink.' (For his disciples had gone away into the city to buy food.)" Jesus proactively seeks those who suffer and then creates space for conversation. Chaplains also seek the suffering and create opportunities for connection. Jesus, like a prototypical chaplain, is initiating dialogue with the intent of growing deeper in conversation. He engages the Samaritan woman, and she responds in verse 9: "The Samaritan woman said to him, 'How is it that you, a Jew, ask for a drink from me, a woman of Samaria?' (For Jews have no dealings with Samaritans.)"

In commencing this dialogue, Jesus compassionately addresses deeper issues of cultural diversity and accompanying religious differences. Chaplains understand that diversity and inclusivity strengthen organizations by avoiding the costly downside of conformity. Cohesive groups may unintentionally create pressure to avoid controversial issues or alternative solutions. The term "groupthink" is often used when leaders discourage innovative thinking or individual creativity. By the very nature of chaplaincy, chaplains are committed to diversity and inclusion because chaplains facilitate the plurality of faiths represented throughout an organization. Chaplains have a deep respect for others and a compassionate commitment to their well-being.

By Jesus's initiation and her response, their conversation and relationship grow deeper. His request to her is an invitation for her to do something helpful. Although we don't know whether she actually brings him a cup of water, we do know his request is followed by his offer to give her something of value: "If you knew the gift of God, and who it is that is saying to you, 'Give me a drink,' you would have asked him, and he would have given you living water" (4:10). We will soon explore how this offer becomes the nucleus of their connection.

Another biblical example of embracing diversity through connection and compassion is the way Paul respectfully engages the pluralistic environment of a very diverse Athenian culture in Acts 17. Prior to his Areopagus address, Paul had developed a solid pastoral identity and profound understanding of his own faith. He was now prepared to share with others, who received his explanation as "strange things to [their] ears" (Acts 17:20). Yet he connects with this diverse group with compassion and respect.

Pauline theologian and New Testament scholar N. T. Wright suspects that Paul "spoke for two hours rather than two minutes. His speech would form a book in itself, but Luke has no space for such a thing within his own work. He has boiled it down to the bare bones."[11] The point here is that Paul not only developed a high sense of pastoral identity, he also studied the philosophy and understood the diverse worldviews of those who would oppose him. His ability to understand the culture surrounding him resulted in greater compassion toward those hearing him.

Just as Paul demonstrated in his ministry to the Athenians, compassion and respect for all those you encounter are critical. Remember this when you seek to serve people: it is *their* gift extended toward *you* for you to be present there. You have their attention only after their invitation. To embrace diversity through connection and compassion, you must respect where people are coming from, which requires (1) a high appreciation of your ministry context, (2) a deep understanding of your own faith and pastoral identity, (3) a growing patience to wait for an invitation to respectfully share your faith, (4) an ability to draw analogies from your ministry context that can support and illustrate your convictions, and (5) a hope to win an opportunity to talk even while knowing it may never come.

Without an invitation, you violate trust if you share your religious beliefs. This part of the ministry of presence is opposite from the local church model of delivering ministry by proclaiming Christ at all times. Why is there a difference? Because people attend church voluntarily. People don't volunteer to be in prison, or in hospice, or in a hospital bed, or on a battlefield. This is why diverse beliefs need to be valued and honored. Toss aside your own agenda and be present to the people you serve.

Seeking Transformation through Presence and Service

Chaplains invite others to share not only what they do but, more significantly, who they are. Chaplains learn names and listen to stories. Listening with a nonanxious presence is valued. Prison is a lonely place for new inmates. College is a lonely place for freshmen. Boot camp is a lonely place for recruits. Sometimes they come to speak to the chaplain because they know they will be listened to and not judged.

> I'll never forget the time an older inmate was called to my office to receive the news of a death in his family. After I allowed him to speak with family by phone, I inquired about his family and his time in prison. I learned that he was not a religious man and realized that being in the chapel with a chaplain was foreign territory for him. At the conclusion of our time together, he rose to leave, and I extended my hand to shake his. He shook my hand firmly and sincerely thanked me. As he headed for the door to leave, he abruptly turned around and with a smile on his face, he said, "You know, I've been incarcerated for fifteen years, and you are the first staff person to shake my hand." The statement made me realize the line that is drawn between staff and inmates, and I thought of the old rabbi I worked with at my first prison in New York, who advised me that I would need to learn to walk the line between justice and mercy.
>
> —*Correctional/Prison Chaplain*

Just as the Samaritan woman and Jesus appreciated their connection, chaplains and others explore how they connect in community. The good work of chaplaincy radiates a ministry of presence back to the person by asking, "How can I serve you?"

Jesus moves toward meeting the Samaritan woman's deeper need by inviting her to ask what he can do. He is invitational, and a deeper level of conversation with the Samaritan woman can now take place when she asks: "Sir, you have nothing to draw water with, and the well is deep. Where do you get that living water? Are you greater than our father Jacob? He gave us the well and drank from it himself, as did his sons and his livestock" (John 4:11–12). She is now fully engaged in conversation with Jesus. Moreover, their talk has faith as its foundation. His response communicates her value and his respect for her: "Jesus said to her, 'Everyone who drinks of this water will be thirsty again, but whoever drinks of the water that I will give him will never be thirsty again. The water that I will give him will become in him a spring of water welling up to eternal life'" (4:13–14). She inquisitively pursues his invitation in verse 15, "Sir, give me this water, so that I won't get thirsty and have to keep coming here to draw water."

> There is something very special about walking alongside someone as an understanding companion without demanding they act a particular way or wishing it were different. I have found that I am able to speak truth to families with wisdom, clarity, and compassion that help them cope with anticipated loss, unfinished business, and grief. That allows me to be fully present to a patient and their experience as they wrestle with end-of-life issues.
>
> *—Hospice Chaplain*

Other passages in the Bible also affirm the value of seeking transformation through intentionally initiating a ministry of presence to serve the suffering. Jesus speaks of the power of presence and service in the Gospel of Matthew: "For I was hungry and you gave me food, I was thirsty and you gave me drink, I was a stranger and you welcomed me, I was naked and you clothed me, I was sick and you visited me, I was in prison and you came to me. . . . Truly, I say to you, as you did it to one of the least of these my brothers, you did it to me" (Matt. 25:35–36, 40). Jesus aims his ministry focus like a laser at the "least of these," the outliers with obvious limitations. These include the grieving, homeless, abandoned, imprisoned, wounded, diseased, traumatized, addicted, dying, and people with physical or intellectual developmental disabilities. This is the center focus of the chaplain's ministry bull's-eye.

The center focus expands outward from the core to include two more groups of people who need a chaplain. Think of the rings around a bull's-eye. The middle ring comprises the majority of folks who work at the organizations, companies, and institutions—the average Joes and Janes who won't be selected to appear on *American Idol*. These are people who work their jobs and raise their families and live their lives, who also face chaplain-sized struggles.

The outer ring includes the powerful and privileged, who are often disconnected from healthy relationships and access to hearing truth. Some powerful leaders create a climate of fear; they don't want to hear bad news, so people steer clear. Many privileged people suspect that every conversation will become a request for more of their resources. Their practice of avoidance, coupled with a fear of vulnerability, makes them surprisingly accessible to chaplains seeking human transformation through a ministry of presence. For example, a ship's commanding officer has the loneliest job on the entire vessel. Where could he go to decompress after a hard and long day at sea? Everyone on the ship is subordinate and accountable to him. When he looks outside the ship, his peers are the same rank on similar ships competing with him for efficiency awards or accolades. It's hard to be vulnerable in a competitive culture, especially at the top.

Chaplains minister to everyone and value the innate worth of *all* people because all are born in the image of God:

> So God created man in his own image,
>   in the image of God he created him;
>   male and female he created them. (Gen. 1:27)

And chaplains also understand that because of sin, all humans suffer. Sin and suffering are equal opportunity destroyers. Chaplains are in position to invert the common cultural view of valuing the outer ring privileged over the center ring disenfranchised. Chaplains who consistently seek the suffering as center target bring great value to the institution and to "the least of these."

Transformation comes through service as well as presence. In Matthew 25, Jesus is clear that spiritual care includes practical service, such as providing food, water, shelter, and clothing. Spiritual care is not theological jargon and religious rituals. Jesus understood that unless basic survival needs are met, people are rarely in any position to want or appreciate fellowship with others. Serving the suffering is where the chaplain spends the majority of her time, whether on the battlefield, in the boardroom, or outside the classroom. The apostle Paul sees the connection between providing for practical needs and spiritual care. He describes his practice of serving the powerless in his address to the Ephesian elders: "You yourselves know that these hands ministered to my necessities and to those who were with me. In all things I have shown you that by working hard in this way we must help the weak and remember the words of the Lord Jesus, how he himself said, 'It is more blessed to give than to receive'" (Acts 20:34–35). Organizations are healthy when they have chaplains who bring not only their head and heart but also their hands into the service of chaplaincy.

During an institution lockdown at the prison, it's important for the chaplain to make rounds in the housing units to speak to inmates who are locked in their cells, and also to check on staff who are usually busy conducting mass shake-downs. If there is a staff shortage, it may be an opportunity for the chaplain to assist with making sack lunches for inmates during a lockdown. These are straightforward ways to serve.

—Correctional/Prison Chaplain

Acts of service do not require a seminary degree. They are inspired by the Holy Spirit and come from the heart and not the head. Chaplains allow God's presence to move through them toward others. Chaplains model transformation through their presence by activities such as handing out meals to hurricane refugees, coordinating teams to build a Habitat for Humanity home, siphoning gas out of their car to share with a stranded employee, or offering directions to visitors new to their organization. Good works accompany great faith: "If a brother or sister is poorly clothed and lacking in daily food, and one of you says to them, 'Go in peace, be warmed and filled,' without giving them the things needed for the body, what good is that?" (James 2:15–16).

When service isn't the obvious need, transformational response may come from your presence. We see Jesus asking for presence from his disciples in the Garden of Gethsemane: "Remain here, and watch with me" (Matt. 26:38 RSV). Chaplains also bring value to those who suffer by being present. They can avoid the failure of Peter, James, and John by staying alert. Unlike Job's friends, chaplains don't need to find it necessary to explain suffering. The greater gift is to be alongside and offer silent prayer.

There is incredible power in being present. I teach my chaplains about the fact that "we make our feet stick in places where most people (understandably) would want to run." Sometimes all and *everything* we can offer to someone in pain is compassionate presence. Words often fail. Prayers are sometimes the *last* things that people want to hear. Sometimes we cannot "make it [grief, pain, loss] stop," as one physician once asked me to do. We simply accompany the wave of whatever "it" is on the journey.

—Hospital Chaplain

Many prospective chaplains don't like the idea of being in the uncomfortable path of other people's suffering, because they fear unanswerable questions about faith: Why did God do this to me? Why did God punish my innocent son by taking his life? Instead of withdrawing from these faith-challenging moments, chaplains contribute value by moving toward the pain and praying for a transformational, faith-changing moment. It is the place of greatest risk because chaplains don't have the answers. However, vulnerable people need the comfort that chaplains can provide. Comfort often comes not in the answer but in the safe presence of one who understands the question. This is a wonderful gift due to the access institutions give their chaplains; it is also core to a chaplain's ministry of emotional, spiritual, and physical presence. Chaplains invite those suffering to share their stories and struggles. Chaplains create a safe space for sustaining a sacred conversation immune from distractions.

> In the trauma bay, when a patient arrives at the hospital, it is the job of the chaplain to be the in-between with the physicians and the patient's family. The medical staff needs time to do a rapid assessment on the trauma patient, and the family is asked to wait, often with little information, for that evaluation to be complete. As a chaplain, we understand the necessity of time for medical staff as well as the anxiety of the family. In that space and time, the chaplain is present with the family—often orienting the family on what to expect in the next hour (as far as process, *not* providing medical information). Each family is different in their needs—some need privacy, some need presence. The chaplain must also be mindful of the physical needs of the family members during this time, offering the simple kindness of a glass of water or cup of coffee, directing them to the bathrooms, providing tissue, and assisting with contacting clergy, if requested. This is not a set formula, but rather an art of when to be silent, when to offer support, and when to meet the physical needs of the family. I think of it as hospitality.
>
> —*Hospital Chaplain*

People view chaplains as representatives of God, and so do many institutions. Because of this, chaplains have incredible access to places where others can't go. They don't have to leave the hospital when visiting hours are over. They can visit hospice patients in their homes. They can pray for soldiers on the field of battle. This is a ministry of presence and stillness. It may also be the one time people remember their chaplain. Just as God was heard in the "still, small voice," a chaplain's loudest message may be through the silence of simply being present, still, and available.

1.3 Characteristics, Advantages, and Challenges of Institutional Ministry

The duality of being in two institutions simultaneously is one of the most unique and challenging aspects of chaplaincy. The chaplain is not half clergy and half employee; she is a full member of both the church and the employing organization. Simultaneously participating in both requires adaptability and awareness of their differences.

In the church, full clergy status is required and expected to be maintained. The chaplain's unique faith group determines the educational and experiential requirements for professional credentials and ordination. The chaplain remains fully accountable to her bishop or presbytery or board while serving as chaplain. To sustain connection with its chaplain, the faith group will likely require her to attend conferences periodically and maintain regular correspondence outlining the chaplain's current ministry. The faith group has an enduring responsibility to be proactive in supporting its chaplain.

Just as the faith group is responsible to its chaplain, there is an expectation for the chaplain to remain in relationship with the faith community. As ambassadors maintain strong connection with their appointing country, chaplains also stay connected to their sending faith group. It is regrettable when a chaplain no longer senses a strong connection with her ecclesial body. If this happens, the denomination risks having the chaplain inadvertently misrepresent her faith group. Therefore, it is important for the faith group to identify and articulate expectations both for its organization and for chaplains representing it. Setting expectations from the outset is a common practice that avoids disconnected chaplains and disinterested denominations.

Many faith groups publish a regular chaplain newsletter and distribute it to all chaplains, churches, and denominational staff. This practice sustains awareness of chaplaincy to the larger denomination and communicates the value of chaplains as a unique community among clergy. The newsletter is a simple forum for sharing experiences and announcements as well as communicating denominational support, such as an annual chaplains conference, conference scholarships, travel reimbursements, regional gatherings, and professional opportunities.

Some Christian faith communities spotlight chaplain ministry through an annual chaplain recognition Sunday. Chaplains may be invited to write denomination-wide devotions and articles. Chaplains sense closer connection to their denominations by these invitations, and the church gains clearer appreciation for the unique ministerial settings and challenges of chaplaincy. Chaplains often represent a significant percentage of clergy within a faith group. Unlike most local church pastors, they are employed and funded by external organizations. If a faith group has two hundred chaplains each of whom receives a salary and benefit package of $50,000 to $100,000 per year, the amount of denominational-free funding for chaplaincy is between $10 and $20 million. These numbers usually catch church leaders by welcome surprise.

Institutions employing chaplains tend to be people-centric with a high investment in human resources and human services. In an article published in the *Atlantic*, David Miller, a Princeton professor who studies faith and work, states, "Chaplaincies add value to companies, potentially helping create lower turnover rates, increased levels of focus, and reduction in stress-related illnesses."[12] Organizations seek to sustain high employee job satisfaction in order to retain quality. The ring of people impacted by institutional chaplaincy extends beyond employees, because many of these organizations are deliberately focused on delivering a service to others, such as providing health care for patients, education for students, or incarceration for prisoners. Patients, students, and prisoners are not employees of the organization but are integral end users receiving services, including access to chaplains.

Chaplains frequently wear the same institutional clothing, logos, and name badges as other employees, though they may wear a special device or identifier to assist others in recognizing their unique role. Chaplains are expected to comply with company policies, regulations, and practices along with other employees. Chaplains receive their salary and benefits from their organization, unless contracted by a third party or serving as an independent consultant. Promotions, assignments, salary scales, and continuing-education opportunities are the prerogative of their employer and not their faith group.

Being simultaneously a full member in two institutions has advantages and challenges. Many organizations offer orientation and initial onboarding for new chaplains in order to bridge the transition from church to institution as seamlessly as possible.

For my general orientation into Navy chaplaincy, I attended eight weeks of chaplain basic school. The initial period focused on orienting new chaplains to the unique characteristics of military culture, including nautical terms, shipboard firefighting, and naval history. The latter half deliberately focused on adapting our clergy skills to the military, culminating in the delivery of a worship service aboard a pier-side ship. As students, we were quick to realize not all that we bring into the Navy will be appreciated by the Navy. It was our first night in the barracks. Upon command, we turned off overhead lights and jumped into bunk beds. The next thing I remember is waking up in a panic, jumping out of bed, and running to the door. An alarm was sounding—it was the general alarm of a ship. No one who ever saw a war movie can forget the GONG-GONG-GONG of a general alarm, activated when a ship finds an inbound enemy torpedo. One of our classmates reached for his alarm clock. The sound stopped. Smiling sheepishly, he said, "My parish presented this as my farewell gift." In a not-so-gentle fashion, he heard that he could never use the clock again. In the Navy, his alarm would cause panic anywhere he went. He obviously hadn't watched the same war movies. This is just one entertaining example of how not all that we bring into an institution will be welcomed by the institution.

—*Military Chaplain*

It is essential for prospective chaplains to examine particular characteristics of the secular institution in which they will serve. The better understanding of these values, priorities, and processes, the higher the probability that the services offered by the chaplain will fit the culture of the institution and be appreciated by members within the organization.

Characteristics of Total Institutions

Richard Hutcheson Jr., in his book *The Churches and the Chaplaincy*, embraces the work of sociologist Erving Goffman and his identification of characteristics common to "total institutions."[13] "Total institutions," a term coined by Goffman, seek to fulfill both work and life domains. One example of a total institution is a prison. Goffman summarizes, "In a prison, life is regimented, orderly, and compliance with even the most insignificant directive is required. Prisons control what inmates watch on television, what is available to read, what and when an inmate eats, and even what passes through the mail or the phone."[14] Total institutions are typically places of work or residence where there are many others in a similar situation, separated from their wider community for a defined period of time. These people tend to live in a highly administered context where the food they receive and the rooms they sleep in are determined by the parent organization.

Examples of total institutions served by chaplains include prisons; hospitals; colleges; military installations; assisted-living, memory-care, and skilled-nursing facilities; and institutions for people requiring temporary assistance, such as homeless shelters and postdisaster emergency shelters. A nontraditional example is found in the area of tourism. Sociologists have pointed out that cruise ships share many characteristics of a total institution, though tourists may not be aware that they are being shaped and controlled by an environment designed to subtly influence their choices and behavior.[15] Another example is a commercial airline flight. From the moment one boards the jet, one knows that the flight attendant has full control over what can be served and when one's seat back and tray table must be returned to their full upright position.

Since chaplains are frequently employed by total institutions, identifying the characteristics of such institutions will orient prospective chaplains to the advantages and challenges of institutional ministry.

1. *They are encompassing.* Total institutions seek to deliver a full range of resources with the intent to balance both work and life needs. An all-inclusive resort typically includes lodging, meals, drinks, gratuities, and recreational opportunities for one price. Food-service staff and resort workers may be expected to remain on the resort property to eat and sleep in their own separate area. To capture efficiencies, choices for participants may be limited. The chef may offer five menu items but not ten. The chaplain may offer one Christian worship service but not separate Lutheran, Baptist, and Presbyterian services. Autonomy, to a considerable extent, is sublimated to institutional goals. While participants can make choices, decision making is typically tilted toward institutional goals. People surrender personal control—either willingly at a child-care center or coercively at a memory-care center—in support of the organizational mission. Encompassing institutions frequently have boundaries separating insiders from those outside. The barrier could be physical, such as a fence, a pier, sentries, a check-in desk, or barred windows. The barriers can also be intangible, like policies, regulations, titles, rank, degrees, or unique traditions. The goal is to reinforce cohesiveness among members and a sense of distinctiveness from outsiders.

2. *They are combining.* Total institutions seek to break down barriers ordinarily separating the different spheres of human life. Most people sleep in one place, work in another, and find recreation in yet another location. Each of these spheres is lived not only in different places but often among different people, with different rules, without any unifying theme. In a total institution these three spheres of sleep, work, and play are combined and shared with the same coparticipants. Whether in a for-profit, government, or nonprofit organization, these three spheres are frequently synchronized to a

tight schedule designed to fulfill the aims of the institution. For example, the cafeteria is only open from noon to one. Early birds must wait for the doors to open. Those arriving late must stay hungry until dinner. Or another example, heard over the loudspeaker at summer camp: "Campers, we look forward to seeing everyone at the soccer game tonight. We will be sure to have you in bed early enough for you to attend worship services tomorrow."

3. *They are organized.* Bureaucracies are known for their hierarchy and policy. They tend to be highly organized so as to handle a diversity of needs. Policies are developed to streamline repetitive tasks, such as hiring processes, vacation requests, or promotions. There tend to be many written rules as well as unstated practices. There is typically a clear division of labor to keep both the institution and employees accountable. If you want to see whether a business is heavily bureaucratic, find its organizational chart. The clearer the boxes and lines, the more defined the hierarchy. Bureaucracies are well known for maintaining a chain of command and assigning titles to their employees. Organizations feel compelled to maintain these standards because they safeguard the institution from arbitrariness and capriciousness. This is critically important where there is a divergence between the supervisory group (e.g., doctors, wardens) and the managed group (e.g., patients, prisoners).

4. *They put chaplains in the middle of the food chain.* Chaplains within total institutions are not at the top of the hierarchy. While chaplains try to gain unlimited access to people within the institution, their authority is typically limited to their immediate administrative staff. Chaplains generally receive higher perceived authority from those within the institution than they actually merit. This may be a vestige of a former age that granted higher status to clergy. However, do not expect the common perks provided by a local church, such as a private office, a designated parking space, a professional development account, or expansive decision-making opportunities. Chaplains are in the middle, not at the top. This is a frequent area of tension for those who previously served in the parish setting. It is often difficult to give up one's autonomy to a nonreligious higher authority.

5. *They offer family autonomy.* Total institutions present unique challenges to families. The member of the institution is an insider, but the member's spouse and other family members are outsiders. This is very different from a local church, where spouses are occasionally

viewed as unpaid staff. Many chaplain families enjoy this autonomy and separation from the employee's institution. They can live their lives separate from the chaplain's call to ministry.

6. *They create lifelong affiliation.* Total institutions frequently create affiliations among participants that continue long after the member departs the organization. For example, in the movie *The Blues Brothers*, the character Jake Blues takes on the nickname "Joliet," referring to his long incarceration at Joliet Prison. As another example, universities capitalize on alumni homecomings. People find deep meaning and significance in gathering with former insider colleagues. Witness the durability of institutional self-identification and lifelong affiliation by military veterans: there are currently 12,000 American Legion posts and 6,200 Veterans of Foreign Wars posts. Military and college logos are routinely affixed to car windows as iconic symbols of lifelong affection.

Advantages and Challenges of Institutional Ministry

The characteristics of total institutions set the stage for unique ministry opportunities for a chaplain operating from within the organization. There are benefits for chaplains once they are given institutional insider status. While benefits outweigh challenges, it is also helpful to know what confronts chaplains.

Advantages of Institutional Ministry

1. *You are legitimized.* The longer you remain within an institution, the greater your influence throughout the organization. Your influence is accelerated by adopting the practices and learning the traditions of the institution. Chaplains must commit to wearing the same uniform, obeying the same regulations, eating the same chow, and living under the same conditions as those they seek to serve. Chaplains learn that great leaders eat last.[16] For the chaplain to be legitimized, he could eat last as well. As an alternative, he could help food servers distribute the meal. Offer those in the institution food for the body accompanied by a cheerful word for the soul. As a member of the institution, accept the title of "chaplain" with gratefulness and confidence. There may be various vice presidents within an organization, but there is frequently only one chaplain. Whenever you hear

people address you simply as "chaplain," celebrate because they have legitimized your calling.

When I first served as chaplain to an Army unit, I knew a senior chaplain who was highly respected by the soldiers for his service to them and his deep commitment to their welfare. I asked him how I could best develop legitimacy and a sense of belonging to my new unit. He smiled and, with a wink of experience, simply said, "Carry your own pack." I understood this to mean that a prior chaplain had asked others to carry what he should have owned.

—*Military Chaplain*

---

2. *You lose the element of artificiality.* Another advantage of institutional ministry is the removal of artificiality and possible hypocrisy that frequently exist between clergy and parishioners in the local church. People understandably put on their best behavior when they go to church. Pastors also put on their Sunday best; this is the one opportunity to connect with the entire congregation, and it only happens once a week. Even if this part of pastoral ministry is challenging, it only lasts a few hours each Sunday morning. However, chaplains habitually see their parishioners at their least presentable times as well. Chaplains live with their people not only on Sunday but also on every other day. This makes for a deeper incarnational ministry. Chaplains hear their colleagues talk in the earthiness of everyday language. When the element of artificiality is removed, sermons become more relevant.

A few years back, I went to a retirement party for a director of nursing. As I went through the line to offer my congratulations, she drew me into a giant hug and with tears in her eyes said, "We have been through so much together!" Memories flooded back to me of times when we had helped families through medical crises, when we had dedicated new pieces of equipment, when we had shared meals together at hospital functions, when she often stopped by the office for a cup of coffee. . . . I loved that image. We really have been through it all together.

—*Hospital Chaplain*

---

3. *You share fully the conditions under which your people live.* Chaplains enhance their pastoral ministry when they have a greater awareness of the challenges and problems faced by those they serve. Chap-

lains not only know the stress, boredom, and loneliness of their colleagues, they also experience it. If you are a military chaplain, you know the moral contradiction of supporting those who fight war while you love peace. If you are a police chaplain, you know the pain of losing a fellow officer. If you are a correctional chaplain, you empathize with the prisoner denied parole or losing good conduct time. If you are a hospice chaplain, you hold your patient's hand while hearing last words. If your college wears distinctive clothing, so does its campus chaplain. If your campers are out of food, so is their camp chaplain. If your sports team is out of energy drinks, so is their chaplain. If your people are gripped with fear of impending battle, so are you. Your ministry of presence is often challenging and frequently beyond your normal duties.

4. *You have a natural and continuing contact with both the religious and the unaffiliated.* You have an advantage deeply desired by many local religious leaders: instantaneous contact with those who are not religiously affiliated. For many, you may be the first person they ever talked with about faith. There isn't another ministry that offers a more natural opportunity for a meaningful encounter with functionally nonreligious folks. It seems this is a point at which we find common ground, because all of us are spiritual, even though not all of us are religious. People respect the moxie of confident chaplains. Don't surrender the high moral ground of your calling by trying to fit in. One colleague told me, "A chaplain can *get* dirty, not *be* dirty." Be comfortable with your role. Wear your title well. Be confident in your calling.

Walking into a small but crowded military barbershop, the conversation immediately stopped once the first person said, "Hi, Chaplain." It was as if an alarm had sounded. All eyes turned to me, then immediately looked down. This is a critically important moment for the chaplain to respond. What would you say? Grinning, I quipped, "I thought I was walking into a barbershop, but must have entered the library." Later, I shared a meal with a group of nonchaplain colleagues. They swore and cussed and used the Lord's name in vain so often that I finally said, "You know, you all are using God's name more often than I do during a typical Sunday sermon. I hope to see some of you there to confirm whether I'm right."

—*Military Chaplain*

---

5. *You align your strengths and interests with the population you serve.* Local church ministry serves members of diverse ages. Church staff

develop programs for everyone from preschool kids to senior adults. Chaplaincy is frequently different, as the institution may focus on a particular age demographic. For example, younger people tend to volunteer for the military. Older people might retire to a senior active adult community. Prospective chaplains should consider the age demographics within an institution. Do you have a higher inclination to develop and sustain youth ministry? Then military,[17] college,[18] or camp[19] chaplaincy may be viable opportunities to pursue. Do you have a particular interest in the spiritual care of an older adult and senior living population? You might want to consider chaplaincy at a continuing-care retirement community (CCRC); chaplaincy at a facility for senior independent and assisted living, memory care, skilled nursing, or hospice care; or employment by the Department of Veterans Affairs.[20]

I just transitioned from the church to chaplaincy. In the church, people put up barriers between themselves and their pastor. My commitment in both church and hospital is to meet people and be fully present where they are. In a church setting, I met them in the context of a Christian environment and tradition. Now in a hospital setting, I meet them wherever they are emotionally and spiritually to help them understand their experience through their own worldview. The people coming in here have long stories of living in the world, and I realize I am not their only shot of ever hearing the gospel. Yet I may be their only shot of having someone really sit with them and hear them. I am pairing my worldview to theirs.

—Hospital Chaplain

6. *You have an opportunity to minister to the secular institution itself.* Chaplains frequently have access to everyone in the institution. While not compromising anyone's confidentiality, chaplains can quickly evaluate employee engagement within an organization. This might result in the chaplain offering recommendations for greater institutional health. For example, in the nineteenth century, US Navy chaplains contributed to a number of reforms, including the abolition of flogging and the elimination of a daily ration of grog.[21] Institutions have a strong track record for recognizing the scholarship and commitment to lifelong learning that chaplains bring to their organization. Because of this, many chaplains are invited to minister to people within the

secular institution by teaching. Why not teach a class on public speaking or résumé writing? This becomes a pathway of ministry to the institution and to people who may never see a worship service.

The hospital employs me to help meet the spiritual needs of our patients and their visitors—these encounters are generally short term. It is definitely the focus of my work. In the process, however, I form strong bonds with many staff members over time—ones who may not attend any church, but who will share with me struggles of work, family, interpersonal balance, etc. These staff members may not even realize that I am their chaplain, too. It is a sacred place to be.

—Hospital Chaplain

Challenges of Institutional Ministry

1. *It is a turnstile ministry.* Ministry and programming in a local church are strongly dependent upon people entering the front door and staying. However, due to the turnstile effect of many organizations employing chaplains, the typical parish model for developing and sustaining programs must be modified. Horizons for planning and executing are shorter because participants are typically not long term. Patients are admitted and discharged, prisoners transfer in and out, students matriculate and graduate, soldiers enlist and retire. Students, patients, soldiers, and prisoners cycle through the organization until they graduate or are discharged, transferred, or released. Those receiving benefit from the organization are typically there for a season, unless they are employees of the organization. People arrive at the institution, receive a service or benefit from the chaplain, and then depart the institution. Others come behind them to occupy their classroom, hospital bed, or prison cell. Because of the turnstile effect, chaplain ministry is intentionally proactive. It requires the chaplain to connect quickly with those entering the organization. It also requires chaplains to be familiar with and acknowledge the power of grief as they are constantly surrendering quickly made but frequently deep relationships with patients, prisoners, soldiers, and students.

2. *It is ministry without members.* Whereas churches have a membership process, chapels are nonmembership organizations. Programs

and personnel are typically funded by the parent organization and not chapel attendees. The chaplain may be ordained or licensed by a faith group not represented by any of the parishioners. Chapel attendees are referred to as a "community" and not a "congregation," because membership is not required or expected. They represent a variety of faith traditions with varying degrees of expectations, interests, and loyalties. Like their chaplains, these people represent a faithful community of Christians gathered from a diversity of denominations and backgrounds.

3. *It is ministry without church officers.* Chapels do not have elders or deacons because there is no form of independent governance. Since the chaplain is employed by the organization, the chaplain is accountable to the institutional supervisor in lieu of an elder board. Supervisors may be chaplains not sharing the same faith identity. The Protestant community chaplain may report to a more senior Roman Catholic priest, or vice versa. Supervisors often are not clergy. They may be human resource directors or program directors. Chaplains often seek out faithful attendees within their chapels to provide advice and counsel. Many chapel communities form a chapel advisory committee in order to offer the chaplain feedback on programs, activities, and scheduling. This advisory committee understands that decisions for the chapel program and personnel funding remain with the chaplain's employer.

4. *It is a mobile ministry.* Many chaplain ministries are geographically stable. A campus does not move. A correctional facility remains at a permanent address. Those working there, including chaplains, are immune from issues experienced by organizations operating in a mobile environment common to military, disaster-relief, first-responder, sports-team, and recreational chaplains, who frequently conduct their duties in places where typical community services may not be available. These chaplains travel over many time zones alongside those they serve. Disaster-relief and first-responder chaplains may encounter civil unrest and natural disasters. Sports-team and recreational chaplains may experience unanticipated cultural practices or adverse community reactions. Military chaplains may find themselves in isolation or combat. Unless there are exceptional family concerns, military chaplains are expected to move in order to broaden professional experiences. Overseas assignments typically allow families to accompany their chaplain and experience new cultures.

1.4 Five Ministry Tasks and Competencies

How does one prepare for chaplaincy? It seems both overwhelming and presumptive that chaplains are recognized by their institution, and many of its members, as bearing the presence of God. If chaplains are viewed as visible reminders of God's presence in what are often God-forsaken places and circumstances, then how does a potential chaplain gain adequate competencies? Secular institutions don't have the expertise to determine whether a prospective chaplain has the experience or background necessary to fulfill their expectations. Instead, they rely upon established faith communities, religious organizations, seminaries, and field experience, including Clinical Pastoral Education (CPE), to adequately prepare and certify clergy for their initial experience into chaplaincy.

Yet preparation and certification of ministers for chaplaincy is not solely the responsibility of religious and professional certifying organizations. The prospective chaplain also has the responsibility to personally invest in acquiring ministry tasks and competencies. The greater the preparation, the higher the probability that a chaplain will flourish. Without intentional competency acquisition, a chaplain is likely to fall short. The following ministry tasks and competencies are absolute baseline expectations for any clergy to acquire before heading into chaplaincy. Keep in mind that these five tasks and competencies are prerequisite to chaplaincy. They do not reflect what the chaplain actually delivers on a daily basis. It might be helpful to view these tasks as the fuel loaded inside a launchpad rocket, yet they are not the missile itself. As a rocket cannot fly without fuel, a chaplain cannot adequately fulfill her role without first acquiring these five essential ministry competencies. The rocket flight itself will be addressed in the chapters addressing the four functional capabilities of chaplaincy.

Competencies Developed by Chaplains
Minister   Pastor   Intercessor   Healer   Teacher

Capabilities Expected from Institution
Provide   Facilitate   Care   Advise

Figure 1. Development of Competencies to Capabilities

A prospective chaplain cannot adequately fulfill the four functional capabilities without personally acquiring these five ministry competencies. *Acquisition* of the five following ministry tasks is not the same as *mastery* of the tasks. Organizations with chaplains allow room for their employees to grow and flourish. They don't expect immediate mastery of chaplaincy skills. However, they do expect a religious organization to certify that the new chaplain comes into the institution with solid ministry fundamentals. As you grow in your ministry skills, you will refine your pastoral identity and better understand what you can and can't provide.

Chaplaincy is a sacred calling requiring clergy who are fully qualified, highly skilled, and habitually available to meet the institution's expectations for their chaplains. Organizations presume high standards of professionalism, character, and integrity from those they employ, especially from their chaplains. To be considered for employment as a chaplain, institutions require their clergy to be well grounded in their faith tradition and have a well-defined pastoral identity that is firmly rooted in the chaplain's religious organization.

Naomi Paget and Janet McCormack offer a wonderful overview of these prerequisite ministry tasks in their important book *The Work of the Chaplain*.[22] Although not an exhaustive list of ministerial preparation for chaplaincy, the four competency categories of minister, pastor, intercessor, and healer are forged in seminary and through practical ministry experience. Added to these four is the category of teacher.

Minister

"Minister" is a term specifically referring to the way in which a clergyperson provides religious functions unique to a faith group's expectations and requirements. It represents the truest expression of a clergy's ordination or license. These various functions are frequently distinct to a particular faith group. For example, some religious organizations require their ministers to use a standardized liturgy for baptism. Other faith groups make a specific liturgy optional. Some denominations require a chaplain to submit a certificate of baptism to their faith group headquarters following a baptism. Other denominations keep no systemic record. These are examples of how ministry and "administry" frequently coincide.

In the context of Christian chaplaincy, ministers will most often officiate their religious duties and tasks in unique settings outside the traditional structure of a local church. There could be a worship service in a locker room, in a classroom, or aboard a ship. The location might potentially be controversial, such as a battlefield, or a prison cell, or the US Capitol, or a country where their own faith tradition is in the minority. There is an enormous diversity of settings for chaplains to provide religious duties, which include rituals, observances, sacraments, and rites typically provided in the local faith community. Also included may be occasional services such as weddings, baptisms, dedications, christenings, funerals, and memorial services.

Ministers preparing for chaplaincy must understand the traditions, practices, and ecclesiology of their endorsing faith group. Does the faith group require their clergy to wear an alb or a Geneva gown? Do their clergy wear a stole or a suit? Do their ministers typically have a chalice or cross present during worship services? What version of the Bible is used by the denomination? Does the chaplain's faith group practice infant baptism or believer's baptism? Two overarching questions emerge from these various examples: (1) Does the chaplain's faith group require it? and (2) Why does the chaplain do what he does? Simply responding with "My faith group requires it" may not satisfy those who ask the question, and such an answer misses a valuable teaching opportunity. A chaplain must clearly understand and practice the traditions and ecclesiology of the chaplain's faith group. The chaplain also needs to sustain a conduit back to the church leadership when questions emerge.

At the beginning of my work as a chaplain, I administered a number of baptisms. I reached back to my faith group and discovered a requirement to send them a completed baptism certificate following each baptism. Those I baptized asked why I was sending my denomination a copy of their baptism certificate when they weren't part of the denomination. I was stuck because I too didn't understand why my denomination required the certificate. I offered an unsatisfactory response: "My faith group requires it." I then asked my ecclesiastical endorser, who explained that the denomination retains and safeguards this record of baptism in case the person ever needs evidence certifying the baptism. There was never any expectation for the person receiving baptism to become a member of my denomination.

—*College Chaplain*

Pastor

An ordained minister who recently transitioned from the local church to hospital chaplaincy was completing his second unit of full-time Clinical Pastoral Education (CPE) in a large hospital. Here are his thoughts about the difference between pastoring a local church and serving as a chaplain:

I can't believe how much more access to people I now have than when I was a pastor. I am surprised by this because my concern of moving into chaplaincy was the short duration of personal relationships. It seems the nature of pastoring in a church creates long-term relationships allowing deep connection. I thought chaplaincy would be something I didn't like because I wouldn't connect. But now I get to connect even more significantly. People are more available because of their high level of trauma. The intensity of what they are going through makes them more receptive to a ministry of presence.

By design, chaplaincy reaches out and gives. It doesn't focus inward and acquire. Chaplains extend ministry to the deepest and most painful places on the planet. Pope Francis warned that a priest who "doesn't put his own skin and his own heart on the line"[23] becomes a manager rather than a mediator. "This is precisely the reason for the dissatisfaction of some, who end up sad—sad priests—in some sense becoming collectors of antiques or novelties, instead of being shepherds living with 'the odor of the sheep,'" the pope explained. "This I ask you: Be shepherds, with the 'odor of the sheep.'" Chaplains bear the odor of their sheep. They eat the same food, sleep in the same buildings, bear the same conditions, and wear the same clothes as those they serve.

Oftentimes you're simply alongside those who are suffering. Sometimes you suffer with them: The hospital food isn't tasty, but everyone is eating it. All the mattresses on campus or at camp are too soft. Everyone is getting seasick. It is easy to feel sorry for yourself and indulge in the "victimization" of being a chaplain.[24] As you sit beside the sickbed of a patient, your mind wanders to what you are missing. Instead of realizing the privileged position you have, you end up resenting the patient. Realize how God has entrusted you to listen to the patient's story or offer yourself to be a quiet presence amidst an anxious family waiting to receive news on the outcome of a loved one's surgery.

I feel like I am "on everybody's team and on nobody's team." Chaplains are a part of many teams—administration and staff, families and medical staff, patients and workforce. We never really have a permanent place, yet we are in all places.

– *Hospital Chaplain*

Intercessor

The chaplain as intercessor is a baseline expectation for any organization hiring a chaplain. Intervening on behalf of others includes prayer, advocacy, and liaison. While intercessory prayer competencies are developed in seminary and through spiritual direction, nothing develops advocacy and liaison skills faster than actual experience as a chaplain within an organization. Advocates believe in people and lend support by offering counsel, comfort, and encouragement. They frequently reach beyond these three activities by offering advice and intercession for the disenfranchised and powerless.

> When I served as a military chaplain, I was expected to attend Captain's Mast. Captain's Mast is like an informal courtroom where commanders administratively discipline errant sailors without resorting to a court-martial. Punishment for someone found guilty can range from reprimand to reduction in rank. Aboard ship, the sentence can include confinement on bread and water. I was invited and attended every Captain's Mast. It was not lost on the captain that his chaplain was there as a witness to any decisions regarding punishment. My presence as a chaplain represented mercy. Frequently asked by sailors to provide the commander a character reference or supporting testimony, the chaplain served as a visible and valuable intercessor for the crew. Not every errant sailor received a positive character reference from me. In order to sustain credibility, there must be a high level of institutional confidence in the chaplain's discretion and integrity.
> —*Military Chaplain*

Chaplains serve as intercessors or advocates for the institution as well as the individual. Chaplains help the institution because employees consider them highly credible. They are sensitive to the issues and needs of the employee while simultaneously advocating for institutional integrity and leadership. It is reasonable for a chaplain to explain to a counselee why the institution responds in ways that may not favor the counselee. This is even more apparent when the counselee is a prisoner and not a guard, or a patient and not a doctor. One health-care chaplain exemplifies this challenge of intervening: "In our setting we frequently found ourselves reminding and educating patients about their rights, knowing that it might place us in conflict with the institution."

At times, the chaplain provides a prophetic voice *to* the institution.

Wise chaplains choose their advocacy moments. They understand and believe that some battles are not meant for them to fight. When someone reveals an institutional problem requiring organizational change, it may not be the chaplain who spearheads the charge toward transformation. Chaplains may need to redirect the person to someone with the institutional authority to make decisions leading to growth and change. As an intercessor, you are called to listen. You are expected to pray. You should offer your thoughts. You will offer your time to stand alongside the suffering. Depending on the person and situation, you may advocate in ways similar to Mordecai pressing Esther: "For if you keep silent at this time, relief and deliverance will rise for the Jews from another place, but you and your father's house will perish. And who knows whether you have not come to the kingdom for such a time as this?" (Esther 4:14).

Like Esther, choose wisely in responding to opportunities requesting your advocacy. There are those who seek chaplains simply to support personal ambition or sustain unhealthy performance within the organization. A simple example is malingering or "pretending to be sick when you aren't or pretending to be sicker than you are, particularly when you have something to gain."[25] Malingering may occur when someone comes to you with grossly exaggerated complaints about his situation with a goal of receiving your sympathy and hoping you will intercede as an advocate for him. It may be a counselee's desire to avoid work, skip school, circumvent punishment, get more vacation time, extend sick leave, avoid prison time, or skip a military deployment. In medicine, a malingerer may hold the thermometer near a lamp to falsify a rise in body temperature. Malingering tends to be discreet and difficult for a chaplain to discover. In stressful situations, most everyone is prone to exaggerate challenges. The chaplain does not want to become cynical or doubtful toward her counselees, but intercessors must have discernment.

Ask people you suspect of malingering what they are trying to avoid. They may be seeking to avoid school, work, deployment, prison, or legal obligation. Then ask what they might gain by avoiding it. It might be financial gain, promotion, or time off. These are fair questions and offer the opportunity for chaplains to engage in honest dialogue. If you recognize malingering in someone, even if you can't intercede on the person's behalf, you can nevertheless commit to provide healthy and helpful support. The person may be disappointed, but the person will also respect the chaplain as someone who will listen and support.

The chaplain is an intercessor providing prayer, liaison, referrals, and advocacy for both individuals and the institution itself. This ministry competency is considered a valued tool by the institution and is core to the pastoral identity of all faith groups. Institutions believe their chaplain is the one person in an organization that anyone can approach. This represents a considerable amount of referent authority entrusted to chaplains at all levels of the organization. As clergy move toward their role as intercessor with openness and humility, they will gain a reputation for approachability and discretion.

Healer

Societies and cultures have associated clergy with healing and wholeness since ancient times. We witness it in the first words of Jesus following his healing of a leper: "Show yourself to the priest" (Matt. 8:4). Priests were expected to verify that someone was healthy and had been cured (Lev. 13:49; 14:2). In this context, the priest did not actually perform the healing but simply verified the healing. Chaplains should not be surprised to discover people in their organization who persist in viewing them as modern shamans holding special powers. There is an account of General George Patton calling his chaplain into his office to ask him to provide a prayer to change the miserable weather in the midst of a military campaign during World War II: "Chaplain, I want you to publish a prayer for good weather. I'm tired of these soldiers having to fight mud and floods as well as Germans. See if we can't get God to work on our side."[26]

While chaplains may not have the ability to heal humans or change weather, they serve a God who does. They are also expected to have a commitment to the holistic condition of people. For a chaplain to effectively serve as a healer, she must develop a well-rounded understanding of the soul that encompasses the physical, psychological, emotional, volitional, and spiritual. The most significant commitment toward developing this competency is being physically and emotionally present.

This ministry of presence frustrates many chaplains. There are always more sermons to prepare and more devotions to publish. Task-oriented chaplains find that developing the skill of "being present" is challenging. In this type of ministry, goals are hard to identify, projects don't get completed, and tasks are not accomplished. "Doing" becomes subordinate to "being." Too often we have a need to produce and perform instead of practicing a nonanxious presence.

How does a chaplain develop competencies as a healer? First, by sustaining his own spiritual health and practices. Second, by intentionally seeking opportunities to exercise patience: sit with someone "wasting time" as he waits at the pharmacy for a prescription; find someone in the organization who you observe has a boring job and commit to tag along with him for an hour. This may crush the spirit of the task-oriented chaplain, yet it also invites the Holy Spirit to do what the chaplain cannot do.

By God's grace, I developed spiritual practices to help me focus on God's activity in healing. For example, it's too easy for me to say, "I'll pray for you," and not follow through. I now add the person's name to my prayer list I keep in my pocket. Being project focused and task oriented, I find reading through the Bible once a year to be very satisfying. Prayer and reading offer valuable time to process and prepare for those sacred appointments that God sends my way. I am preparing to be used by the Holy Spirit in ways that will affirm the healing that God is doing in the people around me. And finally, as a chaplain on a college campus, I make a practice of not avoiding students who unexpectedly stop by. I keep a sign above my desk to reinforce what I frequently find hard to practice: "Students are not an interruption of the day; they are the reason for the day."

—*College Chaplain*

In *The Work of the Chaplain*, Paget and McCormack describe a practice they call "loitering with intent." The chaplain honors others by providing a nonanxious presence: "The ministry of presence often looks like standing around the water cooler, circulating among the people, sitting quietly with someone, or having a cup of coffee in the lunchroom. Presence may seem insignificant, but presence is the grace gift that chaplains bring to the human encounter."[27] Make yourself available for others. Bring the gift of a nonanxious presence. Those you serve will perceive when you are anxious. If you are having a bad day as a chaplain, you unknowingly transmit that to people around you, whether you serve a family in hospice, a hospital patient, a prisoner, or a soldier in the field. Remember, people frequently project upon you the role of healer. Some will think, "If the chaplain is having a bad day, then we are really in trouble."

As a healer, being physically present to others when surroundings are threatening is significant. During my first experience as a chaplain following seminary, I served as a ship chaplain aboard a Navy cruiser, and we were steaming in the war-torn waters of the Persian Gulf. One of the local nations, in order to inhibit ship traffic, floated a number of armed mines in the water. These mines were not anchored to the sea floor but were indiscriminately scattered and floating on the water, ready to destroy any ship that accidently touched them. Regrettably, they were small and difficult to see, and they would be hard to avoid. The captain of the ship required two sailors to position themselves on the very front bow of the ship. Each received a set of binoculars and a rifle. Their orders were to use the binoculars to search for mines and then use the rifle to shoot and explode the mine before it hit the ship. As their chaplain, I wanted to practice a ministry of presence. After a lot of prayer, I mustered some courage and walked to the pointy bow to sit with two very anxious sailors. I greeted them and asked if they wanted another set of eyes on the water surface. They thought I was crazy. So did I. This is the first time I remember "loitering with intent" as I tried, through a nonanxious presence, to bring healing and prayer to our shared fears.

—Military Chaplain

Chaplains offer hope over despair, comfort in loss, and God's sufficiency in need. Remember that you are a steward of God's gifts. You serve as his ambassador. As Chaplain Janet McCormack comments, "When people see us as an ambassador for Christ caring for them, not abandoning them when they're scared or stupid or sinful, then they have a chance to figure out that God hasn't walked away from them either, and that's awesome."[28]

Healers are listeners. The chaplain is a listener most of the time and a speaker some of the time. Invite people to share their story without fear of judgment. Offer them a safe and caring environment. The well-known quote attributed to Saint Francis of Assisi, "Preach the gospel at all times. When necessary, use words," is a core attribute for effective chaplaincy.[29] It is no use walking anywhere to preach unless our walking is our preaching and our listening allows God's healing.

I was in the emergency department waiting with a family for test results. In that situation, it is important to let the family lead the conversation. A family member later told the patient about me, "This is Julie, and she sat and talked with me while we waited. She kept me calm." Sometimes the unfolding situation in the patient room is really terrible, and lifesaving measures may be in process. While this can reasonably make a family very anxious, it is important for me to remain a nonanxious presence. Often I will calmly let the family know, "I don't know what the outcome of this afternoon is going to be, but we will get through this together."

—Hospital Chaplain

Teacher

Most faith groups expect their clergy to have a high degree of education. Early Protestant denominations in the United States deeply invested in the education of their clergy. Harvard University is named after Rev. John Harvard, who donated his entire library to prepare Congregationalist ministers. Yale University traces its charter to 1701 when a grant was given "wherein youth may be instructed in the arts and sciences [and] through the blessing of Almighty God may be fitted for public employment both in church and civil state."[30] Princeton was originally a seminary for educating ministers, and the university motto remains *Dei sub numine viget*, which is Latin for "Under God's power she flourishes." Brown University originated to prepare clergy in Baptist churches scattered on the Atlantic seaboard. Rutgers University was founded as Queen's College to supply ministers for the churches, and a professorship of divinity was provided "for the education of youth in the learned languages, liberal and useful arts and sciences, and especially in divinity, preparing them for the ministry and other good offices."[31]

Chaplains may have more degrees and years of study than others in their organization. Their education and certification mean they are often sought as teachers within the organization. Beginning in the early nineteenth century, "chaplains were also assigned to geographical posts for educational duties. The post chaplains, for example, were tasked not only religious ministry but also with teaching basic reading, writing and arithmetic to illiterate soldiers and the children of married personnel."[32] Navy chaplains were expected to teach young officers aboard ship and "were assigned at the Washington Navy Yard as early as 1805 to teach midshipmen the theory of navigation."[33]

A highly respected chaplain who influenced the formation of the US Naval Academy was George Jones. He understood the ministry task and value of teaching. "Chaplain George Jones wrote to the Secretary of the Navy in 1839 decrying the inadequacy of the current shipboard instruction and calling for a landlocked naval academy. When the naval school was finally founded in Annapolis in 1845, Jones operated as a member of the eight-member academic board as head of the Department of English studies and only secondarily as a chaplain. When the school officially became the Naval Academy in 1850, Jones was appointed its first chaplain and that office was separated from any academic responsibilities."[34] Chaplaincy continues to have a significant teaching component. Preparation for chaplaincy should focus on enriching competencies that expand the chaplain's knowledge base. Valued topics for which chaplains frequently offer teaching include stress management, suicide prevention, communication skills, conflict resolution, premarital counseling such as Prepare/Enrich,[35] divorce recovery, cultural diversity, grief support, and spiritual awareness. Teaching opportunities give chaplains access to, influence over, and credibility with those who otherwise may not appreciate or understand other aspects of chaplaincy.

Chaplaincy preparation focuses on developing the competencies associated with the categories of minister, pastor, intercessor, healer, and teacher. Again, it might be helpful to view these tasks as the fuel loaded inside a launchpad rocket, yet they are not the missile itself. As a rocket cannot fly without fuel, a chaplain cannot adequately fulfill the upcoming four chaplain functional capabilities without first acquiring these five essential ministry competencies. If these competencies are developed on the "front end" as part of a chaplain's pastoral identity, then the chaplain is prepared to flourish in the delivery of ministry.

1.5 Four Chaplain Functional Capabilities

The upcoming chapters will develop the core chaplain functional capabilities in great detail. These four unifying pillars serve as the structural principles for chaplains as they deliver ministry and carry the presence of God to people within their organization. All four of these structural principles apply to a varying degree in every context. Religious organizations credential chaplains before organizations employ them, and both religious groups and chaplain employers expect chaplains to be deeply invested in understanding these structural principles of chaplaincy.

1. *Provision.* Chaplains are providers of spiritual care, providers of worship experiences, and providers of the sacred truths. Being a minister is a primary component of the chaplain's role. It is the unique specialization that chaplains bring to institutions. Organizations seek chaplains because no one else can legitimately lead worship and prayers and provide faith-specific counseling. The act of provision depends on a voluntary relationship between the person who is providing and the recipient. This is one of the toughest concepts for new chaplains to learn. Every encounter they have with someone is not automatically a provider/recipient relationship. This is only established if the recipient consents to it.

2. *Facilitation.* Chaplains help organizational leaders determine the religious and spiritual needs of the people within the institution. Yet chaplaincy does not exist only to serve the needs of those who are in the organization, it also enhances the overall effectiveness of the institution. The hospital works better and meets its accreditation demands if it has chaplains. The military is more balanced when its service members receive the spiritual care they need. A prison functions better if prisoners are given access to services that meet their religious requirements and deepen their faith. Part of a chaplain's role is to help the institution facilitate the religious needs of all people within the organization. Even when the chaplain cannot be a provider, she develops the competence to engage in individual faith conversations that help people identify their specific need. This means the chaplain learns a lot about other faith groups. Additionally, she develops an extensive referral list that includes leaders from a wide range of faiths and, when necessary, confidently contacts someone with experience, who then performs the faith requirements of people within her institution. She intentionally explores available community resources so that everyone within the organization receives the attention they need.

3. *Caring.* Giving care includes counseling but is not limited to counseling. Many new chaplains may wonder why counseling is separate from the capability of provision. This is because counseling is not necessarily a religious ministry, even though many pastors affirm it as part of their calling. Chaplains offer counsel to anyone seeking pastoral care. The counselee may likely view the chaplain as a helpful person yet not a religious provider. This means, for example, that Christian chaplains should not presume consent to talk about Jesus when counselees come to talk with them. Most chaplaincy training, such as Clinical Pastoral Education (CPE), provides education in how to counsel any person who may need your ministry, regardless of background. This training doesn't assume that you and the person with whom you are interacting share the same faith perspective. You just happen to be the person who is available at a time of need. The chaplain must always be in a role of active listener, helping the person and honoring the person's faith tradition and life perspective. Perhaps after the immediate crisis has passed it could be appropriate to refer the counselee to another religious resource. But in the moment of crisis, you're the one who is there. It

is the mark of an excellent chaplain to be able to care and counsel within the fullness and integrity of one's faith while at the same time not forcefully imposing that faith upon others. Chaplains practice hospitality by offering a place of relational refuge. Consider the biblical understanding of welcoming the stranger into your home (Matt. 25:35). Care comes in the ministry of presence. Care comes in the silence where no words can bring comfort. Care comes by staying with people. Care does not require words. It requires presence.

4. *Advising.* Chaplains are expected to offer advice to institutional leadership. At times, the advice may pertain to issues external to the organization that may affect people within the institution, such as the impact of religion upon culture as well as the influence of culture upon faith. Internally, chaplains advocate for the specific religious needs of the employee and other beneficiaries. For example, if the prison warden wants to talk to his chaplain about religious needs and resource allocation, the chaplain may respond to the warden with, "We need to shift some things around because our population is changing in these ways . . ."

Our health-care institution is a faith-based organization. Over time we served a much more diverse population than originally envisioned. Our pastoral care department completed a research project and presented it to the CEO. As a result, our institution arranged for a much more varied array of religious services in order to meet the increasing demand of our patient and resident spiritual needs.

—Health-Care Chaplain

These four chaplain core capabilities serve as structural principles for chaplains delivering ministry and carrying the presence of God to people within their organizations. It may be helpful to think of them as four full cylinders. However, these cylinders are not equal in size. Some lengthen over time due to experience. Others grow quickly due to education. Seminaries don't prepare you to deliver ministry in each of these four categories because their curriculum is typically focused on theology, mission, and the local church. On the other hand, an organization seeking to appoint a chaplain would not draw the cylinders to the same length or scale as a seminary. Your personal competencies as a seminary graduate are not yet aligned with the institutional capabilities expected of chaplains.

There is an encouraging trend by seminaries to offer courses on chaplaincy at the master of divinity and doctor of ministry levels. Many seminaries validate chaplaincy alongside other forms of pastoral ministry and demonstrate their commitment by offering courses on chaplaincy. Additionally, seminaries frequently accept CPE as fulfilling a portion of their field education requirement because many faith groups expect a unit or more of CPE prior to licensure or ordination.

When you first become a chaplain, your seminary education gives you strong competencies in the provision of religious ministry. You've likely studied other religions in seminary, so you have emerging confidence in your facilitation of other faiths. You've developed the competency of care as you studied theories of therapy and practiced the dynamics of counseling. Your experience in CPE increased your pastoral ability to care for others. Your competency of advising is reasonably low, because you are not yet familiar with the context of your organizational culture, so you must establish credibility within the organization before you properly offer advice. Upon graduation from seminary and serving in a position at a local church, the prospective chaplain's personal competency profile might look similar to this:

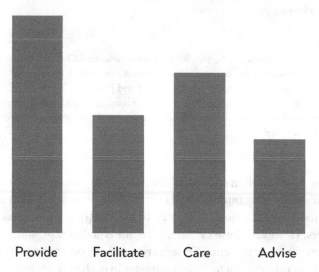

Figure 2. New Seminary Graduate

As new chaplains experience the culture, expectations, and demands of an organization, they form personal competencies in underdeveloped areas. Many organizations provide classes to orient new employees to their culture. Some provide classes specifically for chaplains to practice adapting their ministry skills to a new context. A chaplain grows in confidence when leaders within an institution encourage professional growth. For example, a hospital ethics committee, providing a holistic examination of a patient's situation through an interdisciplinary team of nurses, chaplains, physicians, social workers, and lawyers, would confer higher credibility to their chaplain's participation once they gain confidence in the chaplain's competencies. It is reasonable to expect the cylinders of facilitation and advising to lengthen over time. Therefore, the personal competency profile of an experienced chaplain generally looks more like this:

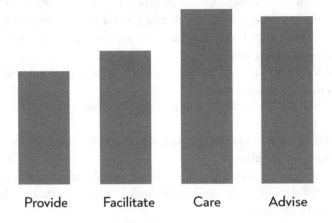

Provide   Facilitate   Care   Advise

Figure 3. Experienced Chaplain

Caring for everyone within the institution, no matter their position of authority or contribution to organizational mission, remains the preeminent capability of chaplains. Chaplains have access to the prison cell and guard tower, nurses' station and bedside, faculty lounge and locker room. Also note the decrease over time in the cylinder titled "provide." In multistaff chaplaincies, there is an organizational tendency to promote proficient chaplains to higher levels of leadership. Whereas the senior pastor in a multistaff Protestant church remains prominent in the pulpit and is commonly featured on the website, bulletin, or outdoor church sign, it is not the same for chaplains. Sermon preparation and preaching are often shared among all chaplains, including new staff chaplains. Senior chaplains often serve as mentors to other chaplains and interface frequently with organizational leaders. Their advising role expands because of their deep experience. Their management role provides them valued access to other leaders within and outside the institution.

Discussion Questions

1. What's your motivation for reading this book? What's your motivation for ministry? How do you discern your motivations?
2. How are you receiving confirmation of your calling? Who are the people in your life giving you affirmation of your calling?
3. How are you currently building below your waterline?
4. For your own benefit, write a page on what you perceive as the significant difference between a chaplain and a civilian clergy member.
5. What ministry issues do chaplains encounter that parish pastors don't typically face?
6. What does it mean to provide ministry and engage in worship within a non-Christian institution?
7. What are six ministry advantages of chaplaincy within a total institution?
8. What five ministry competency areas need development as one prepares for chaplaincy?
9. How does the development of your pastoral identity allow you to facilitate requirements for religious faiths and expressions different from your own?
10. How do you ensure that the spiritual and religious needs of people within your institution are met even when you can't personally provide them?

CHAPTER 2

The Chaplain as Provider

It is a hardship upon the Regiment, I think, to be denied a Chaplain.

—*George Washington*

2.1 Definition of Provide and Perform

Chaplains provide and perform religious ministry. Based upon their theological education and ecclesial credentials, chaplains are endorsed to meet specific faith group requirements; they conduct worship services, administer sacraments, perform rites and ordinances, provide religious counsel, teach the Bible, and offer religious education. Integrating these professional practices—specific to seminary education and distinct to each faith group—requires preparation in a local church. This experience in a congregational context serves to deepen self-assurance and form a pastoral identity.

As prospective chaplains prepare for ministry in the chaplaincy, it is essential that they understand their own unique faith tradition. "Why do you do it that way?" is heard frequently in a chapel where people come from diverse faith backgrounds. Most chapel attendees who ask this question are not criticizing but merely wanting to value their corporate worship experience and grow stronger in their own faith. If the chaplain does not understand why some liturgical part of worship is practiced, the teachable moment vanishes. Therefore, those preparing for chaplaincy must invest in understanding, rehearsing, and practicing their own faith-specific delivery of ministry.

While your faith group provides the format, training, and certification for conducting worship services, your context of delivering this ministry may look vastly different from your home church. As an example, a Methodist chaplain will frequently officiate worship services at a chapel with no other Methodists within the worshiping community. Many chapel attendees identify with no particular denomination. More commonly, worshipers represent an assortment of believers who would rather worship at their home Presbyterian, Lutheran, Church of God in Christ, or Vineyard churches. They attend chapel service because they may not have transportation or convenient access to their own churches. They trust you enough to participate in worship even though they may not fully identify with your faith practices. They communicate, most likely nonverbally, "This is my chaplain, and I willingly participate in the services she officiates." The core functional chaplain category of provision revolves around those who identify with the chaplain and her credentials.

> I provide general Protestant services in order to make an effort to accommodate different tastes. There are some hymns and some gospel music. I get inmates involved in leading prayers and testimonies. I use my faith group's liturgy for communion and prayers. I often wear a robe in order to cover my radio and prison keys while leading worship. I wore the robe because I wanted the prisoners to feel that they were in the house of God and that I was their pastor, not their jailer. I think it worked too. For many of the men Sunday night is what they look most forward to each week. It's an oasis amidst the hardships of prison life.
>
> —*Correctional/Prison Chaplain*

When you serve as part of a larger chaplain staff, you will initially want to observe current chapel worship before participating up front. Do they conduct a worship service similar to one in your local church? Once you enter the chaplain rotation for co-officiating worship, you will likely be alongside chaplains endorsed by other Christian faith groups. Is there a priority to wear standardized attire so you represent a united front? You will likely discuss whether to wear stoles, robes, gowns, albs, uniforms, or business attire. Vestments may be contingent on whether chapel services are conducted in a dedicated chapel, auditorium, classroom, or prison cell. Chaplains may agree to display a cross, a chalice, and candles. They will want to discuss the value of shaping the order of service and liturgy in a way that respects, and does not conflict with, the ecclesiology of each chaplain's faith group. If there are parts within the service that the chaplain's faith group does not recognize, such as reciting the Nicene Creed, then that chaplain should not be expected to lead that section of the liturgy. The order of service should not distract from the gathered community's purpose of worshiping Jesus.

Once you become a chaplain, it is essential to sustain relationships within your faith community. They can support you in discerning whether certain worship activities could potentially compromise the tenets of your faith tradition, violate your denominational standards, or harm your conscience. There may be worship services led by other chaplains in your institution that you cannot, with a clear conscience, co-officiate. Before you decline, make sure you have clearly discussed your conflict with your faith group's ecclesiastical endorser. A chaplain who is not well grounded in the traditions and practices of his faith group is frequently a liability to the hiring organization. Employers expect their chaplains to be experts in providing their own faith group requirements prior to applying for a chaplain position. Neither the institution that employs you nor the faith group that certifies you wants you to compromise the tenets of your unique theology and ecclesiology.

A frequent requirement imposed by chaplain employers upon the faith community of potential chaplains is a certification of their clergy's fitness for chaplain ministry. The document is called an "ecclesiastical endorsement." The endorsement certifies to an employer that a chaplain is in good standing with her faith group. Ecclesiastical endorsements are mandatory if prospective chaplains are considering a federal chaplaincy in the military, the correctional system, or the Department of Veterans Affairs (VA). The endorsement is also expected in health-care chaplaincy prior to board certification.

The Association of Professional Chaplains (APC) is a not-for-profit association that advocates for professional chaplaincy care of all persons in health-care facilities; correctional institutions; long-term care units; rehabilitation centers; and hospice, military, and other specialized settings. This organization of five thousand member chaplains and affiliates sets professional expectations through the Board of Chaplaincy Certification, Inc. (BCCI), an affiliate of APC, with the following statement: "Becoming a certified chaplain isn't an overnight process. It requires a master's degree with graduate-level theological education, Clinical Pastoral Education, endorsement/support from a recognized faith group and demonstrated competency in functioning as a chaplain," and their general qualifications require "documentation of current endorsement or of good standing in accordance with the applicant's spiritual/faith group (received or reaffirmed within last twelve months)."[1]

The ecclesiastical endorsement verifies the professional qualifications of clergy for initial appointment as a chaplain. This form is an essential element of a chaplain's certification and becomes part of a chaplain's employment record. The format of the endorsement varies between types of chaplaincy such as military, civil air patrol, federal prison, state prison, and health care.

One seeking to become a chaplain must initially align with a particular denomination or faith group. Independent local churches may be unaffiliated and nondenominational, so prospective chaplains from independent churches may need to explore ecclesiastical endorsement from religious endorsers who collectively represent various independent churches specifically to endorse their clergy for chaplaincy. Religious organizations and administrative agents that certify nondenominational candidates to be in good standing with their local church body include the Evangelical Chaplains Commission, the Evangelical Church Alliance, and the Chaplaincy of Full Gospel Churches, to name a few.[2]

These organizations meet the endorsement requirements of public law for clergy to serve the government as well as health-care institutions, correction facilities, law-enforcement institutions, businesses, and industries. They typically sustain affiliation with the National Conference on Ministry to the Armed Forces (NCMAF), Endorsers Conference for Veterans Affairs Chaplaincy (ECVAC), Association of Professional Chaplains (APC), Association for Clinical Pastoral Education (ACPE), American Correctional Chaplains Association (ACCA), National Institute of Business and Industrial Chaplains (NIBIC), and the American Protestant Correctional Chaplains Association (APCCA). Finally, they maintain regular liaison with governmental chaplaincies including the military, VA, Federal Bureau of Prisons, Secret Service Chaplain Program, and Federal Bureau of Investigation.

Parachurch organizations—that is, Christian organizations that carry out their mission independent of denominational oversight—do not endorse chaplains. Whereas churches frequently align with denominations, such as the Southern Baptist Convention or the Church of God, parachurch organizations identify themselves in broader terms. These Christian faith-based membership organizations are typically interdenominational and purposefully ecumenical. For example, common parachurch organizations ministering to school campuses include Cru, the Navigators, Young Life, Youth for Christ, InterVarsity, and Youth with a Mission (YWAM). These organizations do not provide ecclesiastical endorsements for chaplains because they do not ordain and license clergy.

2.2 Incarnational Ministry and the Center Set

Incarnational ministry testifies to the life of Jesus by modeling his approach, compassion, and care for others. Chaplains seek to incarnate the example of Jesus's life by modeling a "ministry of presence" to people outside of a church. Incarnational ministry requires deliberate movement and direction. While local church models typically emphasize a wagon-wheel approach to ministry, where the pastor remains at the center and the outside community follows the spokes inward, chaplains invert the wagon-wheel model by providing ministry along the outer wheel rim where people live and work.

Chaplains are participants in God's ministry throughout "all Judea and Samaria, and to the end of the earth" (Acts 1:8). Jesus healed ten men with leprosy "on the way to Jerusalem," along the border "between Samaria and Galilee" (Luke 17:11). A blind beggar received his sight sitting along the road as Jesus "drew near to Jericho" (Luke 18:35). The cash-flush but soul-destitute Zacchaeus didn't meet Jesus in Jerusalem but as Jesus "entered Jericho and was passing through" (Luke 19:1). Just as Jesus spent most of his ministry outside Jerusalem, chaplains are called to serve outside the religious center of the church. The incarnational ministry model practices roadside ministry rather than residential ministry.

Incarnational ministry proclaims the uniqueness of Jesus and the good news of his gospel. Chaplains hope, like Paul at the Areopagus,[3] that some will respond. Chaplains do not need to be pushy because they patiently wait for opportunities to discuss faith. Most often, they find themselves in a position to share Jesus because they care for those alongside them. For example, a hospital chaplain describes using her gift of music "at the bedside as I sing with patients and share the joy, comfort, and peace that music can bring even in times of pain and loss." This seems a perfect example of proclaiming the gospel without words.

Christian chaplains often wear or carry a distinctive symbol identifying them not only as a chaplain but also as a Christian. In the military, it is typically a cross on the uniform. In health services, it may be a name tag identifying them as "reverend" or "pastor." On campus, it may be the Bible they carry in their hands. Whether it is a pin or patch or another symbol, it communicates their Christian faith like a monk's robe or nun's habit. They will discover creative opportunities in responding to others as others first recognize them as a chaplain and then specifically as a Christian chaplain.

Incarnational Ministry Is Not Building Centered

Chaplaincy is not building centered. While chaplains probably have an office, it is typically not the primary place for ministry. Chaplains remember: people don't walk to you; you walk to people. The Christian chaplain's role is to represent Jesus Christ within the chaos of human suffering and bring his mercy and grace to others. Incarnational ministry means that the chaplain's office may not be the best place to meet people. While an office offers the convenience of chairs and privacy, few people have the time or access to visit an office unless it's for a scheduled appointment. Others fear to be seen in the chaplain's office, either because their peers might think they are "needy" or because they identify chaplains with the delivery of bad news.

> As a newly commissioned chaplain sailing on the Atlantic Ocean toward the Strait of Gibraltar aboard a ship of 420 sailors, the Navy wisely assigned a seasoned chaplain colleague to serve on the same ship for the first six weeks of the voyage. The ship didn't have an assigned place for me to work, so before departing from port, I hauled a small desk and folding chair aboard, found an empty mop closet, and set up shop. I was very proud of my tiny domain. However, I noticed my experienced running mate didn't have an office; he seemed busy walking around all of the time. I asked him how he could possibly minister without an office. He shifted his eyebrow, stared at me with incredulity, then pointed his index finger to the raised heel of his shoe, admonishing me, "My office is size 13." He didn't need a place for people to come to him. He saw his calling as going to people, wherever they are, whatever condition they may be found, whatever circumstance they may be facing.
>
> —*Military Chaplain*

The concern about where worship will be held doesn't have the same priority it does in a local church. Some chaplains call incarnational ministry simply ministry by walking around (MBWA)—they want to be among those they serve and meet people where they are at. Chaplains dedicate time on their calendar several times a week to MBWA. They physically move toward where people work. The acronym MBWA prompts them to be away from their office and the distractions of e-mail, research, and projects in order to engage people.

Incarnational Ministry Is Not Event Centered

Every Sunday morning, churches all around the planet hold an event where people gather, music glorifies, the Word is proclaimed, communion is served, and the benediction is announced. Then the gathered scatter until the next Sunday. Pastors often don't connect with members of their congregation during the week. Members may connect with their smaller community group between weekends, but they lack familiarity with others in the broader worship gathering. People don't know other people's names. As a result, many churches drown in a pervasive pool of niceness. Brief greetings are circular. "I'm fine. How are you?" is rebounded with, "I'm good. How are you?" This is repeated before the service, during the greeting or passing of the peace, and following the service. Relationships are stunted beyond a smile and a handshake because conversations are trapped in a culture of niceness.

Worship led by chaplains—whether their worship tradition uses soundboards, slides, and theater lighting or prayer books, hymnals, and candles—is very different. Worship is not based on fixed times for services. It is flexible because chaplains leverage the organizational schedule to allow as many people as possible to gather. If employees are working in shifts, the service may be at midnight. If students are not on campus during weekends, midweek worship becomes a priority.

Chaplains lead worship for the same people they serve alongside the entire week. Incarnational ministry is not event centered because it prioritizes the gathering of people regardless of a schedule. It is more about a gathered people and less about a gathering place. There are no pews at a rodeo or a racetrack, or in a classroom, foxhole, prison cell, cancer ward, or locker room. Yet these locations do not distract the chaplain from bringing a community of Christians into an awareness of God's presence no matter the hour of worship.

Those considering chaplaincy will be challenged to find a creative space and time to worship. They will be free to experiment and innovate. Wherever their location, whatever their accessories, and whenever their service, the worship event isn't the culmination of the week. It marks the start of the week. And after the chapel service, everyone stays around. Whether a hospital or prison or ship, there simply isn't anywhere else to go.

Bounded Sets and Centered Sets

The late missiological anthropologist Paul Hiebert provides a useful model for understanding chaplaincy. His seminal work, "Conversion, Culture and Cognitive Categories,"[4] explores differences between bounded sets and centered sets. A *set* refers to a group of objects belonging together because they share similarities that, when combined, make them distinct.

Most sets are *bounded sets*, because their focus is on the boundary. If your twenty-first birthday is tomorrow, then you are within a distinct set of people under twenty-one. If your birthday is today, then you are no longer in the set. Hiebert describes four parts of a bounded set: it has definitive characteristics, a clear boundary, uniformity, and a static state. An organizational example of a bounded set is the military. There are *definitive characteristics* shared by the Army, Navy, Marine Corps, and Air Force. There is a *clear boundary* someone must cross to get inside, by way of an oath of enlistment followed by boot camp. There is *uniformity* within the bounded set characterized by haircuts, uniforms, and saluting. The bounded set is also *static*—you are in the military whether you serve as a recruit or a master sergeant or a general, and you remain a sailor whether you are in combat or in port.

In a *centered set*, the focus is not a boundary but a central goal. For example, in a set of people committed to losing weight, there is no boundary defining a specific number of pounds. Rather, the central goal is to lose weight. All those who are dieting and exercising are moving in a direction toward the goal. "Direction" and "movement" are terms used when talking about the center set. This set is made up of all objects facing and moving toward the center. Some objects may be far from the center, but they are dynamically moving toward the center. On the other hand, some objects may be near the center but are moving away from it, so they are not maintaining their part in the set. The boundary remains as long as the focus on the center is maintained.

Christianity as a Bounded Set

Christianity is easily understood as a bounded set. Since congregations can't truly know the minds of others, churches choose *definitive charac-*

teristics that are witnessed and heard, such as personal testimonials and professions of orthodoxy. Additional definitive characteristics focus on ecclesiastical doctrines such as soteriology and eschatology. Theology is taught based on these doctrines. There is an expectation that members sustain right practices and maintain certain behaviors, whether it be daily devotions, dietary restrictions, or modest attire.

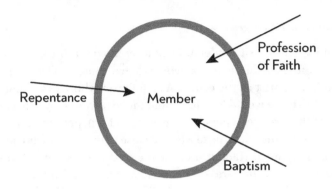

Figure 4. Christianity as a Bounded Set

There are also *clear boundaries* between a "Christian" and a "non-Christian." There is no space in between. Sustaining the boundary is critical to maintaining the category, because clear boundaries serve to identify who is a Christian. A clear understanding of the boundary supports communicating the message of how a person becomes a Christian. Local churches and larger denominations organize themselves around people who share the same beliefs and values. Those who disagree with the boundary requirements remain outside.

Objects within the set are *uniform*. We would view all Christians as essentially the same. There are mature Christians and young converts, but all are Christian. Christianity is not limited to one language or culture.

Bounded sets are *static*: most churches stress evangelism as the major task of the church—getting people inside the set. Moreover, most evangelical churches see conversion as the capstone event where an outsider crosses the boundary from "non-Christian" to "Christian." Yet once a person becomes a Christian, he is 100 percent Christian. There is effectively nothing more to acquire, because it is the sacrifice of Jesus, and not human merit, that guarantees salvation. The new follower of Jesus will be expected to grow spiritually, but this is not essential to the category of becoming a Christian.

Seminaries typically teach courses that prepare students for church ministry within a bounded set. This makes sense because neighborhood churches are organized along that pattern. Pastors inside the local church generally focus on the value of maintaining a healthy boundary.

Christianity as a Centered Set

Christianity is also easily understood as a centered set. The key is defining the *center* and the relationship of people to that center. A Christian would focus on Jesus Christ as the center. As a follower who seeks to know and grow in Christ, she would face Jesus and move toward him. The closer to the center, the stronger a person is growing in faith, practice, and knowledge of Jesus. Yet there are those who are close to the center who no longer face Jesus. They are distracted and, like the seed sown among thorns, they hear the word, "but the cares of the world and the deceitfulness of riches choke the word, and it proves unfruitful" (Matt. 13:22). The distracted no longer face Jesus, nor did the Pharisees whom Jesus rebuked because they "outwardly appear righteous to others" (Matt. 23:28).

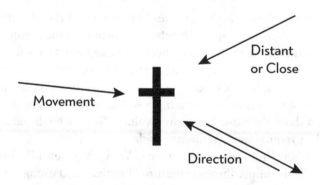

Figure 5. Christianity as a Centered Set

Then there are people at a distance who know little about Jesus, yet they believe he is their Lord and are moving toward him. No one could be more spiritually distant from Jesus than the thief on the cross. Yet he turned toward Jesus in his remaining minutes and said, "Jesus, remember me when you come into your kingdom" (Luke 23:42). Some will be closer to Christ in their knowledge and maturity. Others have little knowledge but desire to deeply grow. All are Christian.

For centered-set Christianity, conversion is the beginning and occurs when a person turns around to face Jesus. We turn from our worship of celebrities, possessions, fashion, money, and status by "looking to Jesus, the founder and perfecter of our faith" (Heb. 12:2). A God-honoring change occurs as the old center is abandoned and Jesus establishes the new core. In the centered-set model, *movement* and maturity of faith are as valued as *direction*. Having turned around, one continues to move toward the center.

The centered set does not remain static. Conversion is the initial place at which a person turns toward Jesus and begins a new journey. The fragile follower is as much a part of the centered set as the seasoned chaplain who shares the gospel. The fact that a chaplain has a theological degree is irrelevant to defining the set. The key is that they are both moving toward the center. They both grow in their love and knowledge of Jesus. Centered-set Christianity is characterized by an active, dynamic relationship with Jesus. As Hiebert writes, "Every decision throughout life moves us toward Christ or slows us down."[5] In this model, the direction we face is more valuable than the distance from the center. We strive to continually face Jesus and move toward him.

Both bounded and centered sets are necessary. Salvation and evangelism are core values within a bounded set. A person is either in Christ or not in Christ. Chaplaincy, however, most reflects ministry in the centered set. If chaplains take a bounded-set position, who qualifies to be included in the worship service or Bible study? Where precisely is the boundary? Who is "in" and who is "out"? How much must a person know of doctrine and the Bible before that person is a Christian? What difference in lifestyle proves a change of heart? At what point does conversion take place? These are tough questions typically addressed by the local church. Yet from a centered-set perspective, there is no fence of theological orthodoxy or denominational superiority. In some ways, this is similar to the early church. In Acts we see the "fence" of Jewish orthodoxy, particularly circumcision and dietary laws, no longer remaining a barrier for entrance into the Christian community.[6]

Christian chaplains model the incarnational presence of Jesus Christ outside the local church. Like Jesus, they are as much at home with the nonreligious and outcasts as they are with those of their own background and social standing. Jesus's friendship was accessible to those shunned by the religious. Chaplains working for secular organizations are deeply invested in ministry converging at the centered set. The traditional denominational distinctions that identify a bounded set are de-emphasized in order to laser-focus on the center. Since every decision moves us toward Christ or slows us down, chaplains constantly shepherd their community to focus on and face Jesus, who is at the center.

A few years ago, I had the opportunity to visit Alice Springs, Australia. Locals told me, "You really can't say you've visited the outback unless you visit Alice Springs." There were seemingly endless miles of cattle ranches with no sign of fences. Instead of building fences around the perimeter, the local ranchers dig wells in the center of their property. There is no need for a fence if cattle are motivated to stay within range of their source of life. Chaplains, like outback ranchers, are called to dig wells. People who are thirsty will come to drink. The focus is on digging deeper wells rather than on building higher fences.

—*Military Chaplain*

2.3 Tribes and the Context of Ministry for Chaplains

For chaplains, our place of employment is the location of our tribe. Birds flock, fish school, cattle herd, and people tend to "tribe." Author Seth Godin writes, "A tribe is a group of people connected to one another, connected to a leader, and connected to an idea. For millions of years, human beings have been part of one tribe or another."[7] Tribes share common interests and a high degree of cultural competence. Chaplains serve as spiritual and cultural translators within these tribes. They contextualize ministry within their tribe and translate moral language to everyday life. The opportunities for influence continue to expand. In the United States, the amount of time chaplains have to connect with fellow workers is growing: in 2018, "Americans of prime working age now work 7.8 percent more hours than they did four decades ago."[8] Gallup reports indicate that the average full-time worker in the United States works forty-seven hours a week, which is one of the highest figures in the world.[9] Opportunities for chaplains grow in the soil of longer contact hours with employees and others who benefit from the chaplain's presence.

The Navy assigned me to serve as chaplain on a ship towering twenty stories above the waterline with a 4.5-acre flight deck. The crew, including the air wing, added up to 5,680 people. This meant the population density on the ship was 1,262 persons per acre. For comparison, according to the US Census Bureau, Manhattan has one-tenth the population density at 112.5 persons per acre (https://www.census.gov/quickfacts/NY). When I arrived at the aircraft carrier *Harry S. Truman*, the crew presented me my uniform name tag. In a grand ceremony, they gave me the customized ship's name tag with my name engraved in it. Let me provide a brief background: In President Truman's 1948 reelection campaign, he visited a West Coast Navy town where an enthusiastic Truman supporter, probably a sailor, shouted, "Give 'em hell, Harry!" That phrase become a lifelong slogan for Truman supporters. And it became part of the official aircraft carrier battle flag, which had crossed cannons and white letters saying Give 'em hell! The battle flag was also engraved on the name tag. So my name tag said in two lines: "Give 'em hell, Chaplain Baker." It suddenly occurred to the crew that my new name tag might send a confusing message. They asked attendees to reconvene in a half hour. Thirty minutes later, with grins of affirmation, they presented a revised name tag, which read, "Give 'em heaven, Chaplain Baker." There is often a degree of cultural confusion when chaplains join a tribe.

—Military Chaplain

Chaplains who are culturally competent typically carry a vision for transformation. They value the narrative of 1 Chronicles 12, where a group of warriors volunteer to join David at Hebron. These were leaders in their community "who understood the times and knew what Israel should do." They were observers of culture and studied the world around them. They could exegete their culture and communicate thoughtful ways to proceed. Chaplains similarly nurture a vision for movement and transformation. While others focus on the mission, chaplains daily focus on the people who fulfill the mission.

As an example, in the early 1980s Rick Warren began what would eventually develop into Saddleback Church. He studied the community around him and developed "Saddleback Sam," a representation of the neighborhood tribe surrounding his fledgling church. Saddleback Sam is a well-educated, young, urban professional, interested in health and fitness, overextended in time and money, and skeptical about organized religion.[10] Warren believed that understanding the needs and the desires of an entire tribe of Saddleback Sams was pivotal for church growth and reaching unchurched people in his community. The results speak for themselves. In August 2018 Saddleback Church became the first church in US history to baptize fifty thousand people. Rick Warren understood the value of tribes and the context of ministry for Saddleback Church.

What Warren did for the local church, chaplains do every day. Instead of studying people in the village surrounding their church, chaplains research and contextualize ministry within the organization they serve. Chaplains comprehend the value of investing their ministry competencies at all levels of their organization, whether a brand-new employee or the CEO.

> During my chaplain ministry to the Marine Corps, I was invited by Wycliffe Bible Translators to present a message to a group of linguistic specialists on furlough at their national office. I was intimidated by the invitation. What could I possibly say to missionaries who spent their lives translating the Bible in native languages such as the Amuesha language of Peru, Hanga language of Ghana, and Cotabato Manobo of the Philippines? In my camouflaged field uniform and laced combat boots, I walked to the front of the room and said, "I live with a tribe. And in our tribe, everyone wears the same native clothing. We eat shared food, called Meal, Ready to Eat (MRE). We sleep in common shelters, called tents. We're a nomadic tribe traveling worldwide over land and sea. We speak a unique language using vocabulary such as 'starboard' and 'port,' 'bow' and 'stern.' All of us honor the chief of our tribe and greet him with a special sign called a salute. My unique role in that tribe is chaplain. Some in the tribe see me as their 'lucky charm.' Others view me as a 'medicine man' possessing special powers. There are those who view me as a threat to their lifestyle. Many see me as a person bearing the presence of Jesus as I live among them."
>
> —*Military Chaplain*

One unique aspect of a tribe is its natural inclination toward competition. A tribe will seek its own competitor.[11] Organizations frequently compare their value against peer organizations. In technology, Apple's voice assistant Siri competes against Amazon's Alexa. In government, the United States and the Soviet Union were in a space race to the moon. In college football, the two rival teams of Army and Navy first kicked off in 1890. In the local church, competitors tend to be other neighborhood churches. Transfer growth due to bigger buildings, greater staffing, broader programming, and better preaching creates competition among local churches.

Chaplains have an advantage over local church pastors. By its nature, chaplain ministry does not compete with local churches. Instead, chaplains embrace local congregations because people within their organization attend surrounding churches. Since chaplaincy is neither event centered nor building centered, chaplains avoid pressure to enter a cycle of competition with local congregations. Wherever rivalry and territorialism are minimized, chaplains and other clergy can focus on being what C. S. Lewis describes as "particular people within the whole church who have been specially trained and set aside to look after what concerns us as creatures who are going to live forever."[12] There are relationships formed with chaplains that will not occur in other contexts.

> "Chaplain, I will retire after twenty years next month; will you pray at my retirement ceremony?" I knew this sailor and how devoted he was to his faith. In fact, he would soon work at a college supported by his faith group. The school was Bob Jones University. His denomination is critical of my own faith group as a Roman Catholic. I told the sailor, "I do not wish to cause any difficulties for you or your guests due to my denomination and can assign one of the other chaplains to cover the ceremony." He exuberantly replied, "You are my chaplain; I want you to be at my retirement." All went well the day of the ceremony.
>
> —*Military Chaplain*

2.4 Institutional Duality of Chaplaincy

The origin of our modern word "chaplain" developed in a military context. It derived from the fourth-century account of Saint Martin of Tours. Martin was a Roman soldier assigned to serve in France during winter. As the story goes, while on his horse riding through the town gate of Tours, he met a suffering beggar freezing in the cold. Young and compassionate Martin grabbed his sword and slashed his red cape in half. He handed the shivering beggar half of the garment. Soon thereafter Martin had a vision in which Christ was wearing the half cloak he gave away. Martin was then baptized a Christian and departed the Roman army to devote his life to the church.

During the Middle Ages, a supposed relic of Saint Martin's cloak was carried into battle alongside soldiers. This precious half of the mantle, called the *cappella*, was kept by a custodial priest called the *cappellano*, who retained the relic in a tent called the *capelle*. This repository for the cloak anglicized to "chapel," a place of worship. Eventually all clergy who served in the military were called "chaplains."[13] Whether or not this story is entirely accurate, the functions of chaplaincy remain central to the actions of this former soldier. Saint Martin's story provides a clue to the institutional duality of chaplains. The *cappellani* were members of one institution, the church, serving in another institution, the king's army. Chaplains today retain this unique duality.

Chaplains are chartered by their institution to care for its people. It's been said that a military chaplain has "one foot in heaven and the other in a combat boot." A similar analogy could be made for all organizations and settings typically served by chaplains. A chaplain is not simply affiliated with, but is fully a member of, two major social institutions. Though the environment of the church is left behind, full clergy status is retained. The authority of the bishop, or presbytery, or council, or church board remains in effect. Contingent on their availability, chaplains continue to attend periodic meetings, conferences, synods, or retreats sponsored by their denomination. Most faith groups require regular communication with their chaplains and set standards for sustaining ecclesiastical endorsement. Yet at the same time chaplains are full members of their employing organization. Chaplains receive similar benefits, obey the same regulations, wear the same institutional clothing, and are on the same pay scale as others within the company. Continuing education, job assignments, salary, vacation, and promotions are under institutional control, not the control of the faith group. Chaplains continue to fully participate in both institutions simultaneously.

Institutional duality inherently brings role conflict. The existence of conflict shouldn't be surprising—surprising would be an absence of conflict. If a chaplain doesn't feel tension between his clergy role and institutional role, then he has slipped too far to one side. Chaplains learn to not only live with the tension but also embrace it as a healthy sign. Tension is not resolvable. If you do slide, shift toward your role of clergy. As a Christian, Jesus is your ultimate source, and you were ordained before you were appointed as a chaplain. Chaplaincy is a profession that deliberately makes role conflict a way of life. The relevant question is not whether tension exists but how useful the tension might be for providing ministry.

Historical Development of Institutional Duality

Institutional duality is not a new concept to chaplaincy. Archival documents pertaining to the military chaplaincy testify to an enduring tension between church and state. As early as 1774, the Continental Army grew out of local and state militia. In a diary written by President Stiles of Yale, "Eighty-three armed men of East Guilford marched off with Mr. Todd, their pastor."[14]

During the American Revolution, chaplains occasionally portrayed a confusing role of clergy and warrior. Some may have slipped too far to one side: "John Martin, after praying with the soldiers at Bunker Hill, seized a musket and fought gallantly to the close of the battle."[15] And again: "Nathaniel Bartlett of Reading, chaplain awhile to Putnam, was accustomed to make his parochial visits with a musket on his shoulder, to protect himself from the Tories who had sworn to hang him."[16] US military service regulations now classify chaplains as noncombatants and prohibit them from bearing arms.[17] The government, not the church, resolved the tension between the chaplain's clergy role and institutional responsibilities. Those supervising the armed forces declared that chaplains were too valuable to carry arms or use weapons. Chaplains could not conduct activities that compromised their noncombatant status. The various military services now assign an enlisted religious specialist to protect chaplains.

The fledgling government prioritized the value of chaplains and their specific role within the military. In November 1775, Navy regulations placed a high priority on the provision of religious ministry. The value of chaplaincy was esteemed enough to be the second of forty-four original Navy regulations: "The commanders of the ships of the thirteen United Colonies are to take care that divine service be performed twice a day on board and a sermon preached on Sunday, unless bad weather or other extraordinary accidents prevent."[18]

The dual nature of the chaplain's role and tension between church and institution continued. It was apparent to the military that some applicants for chaplaincy lacked ability to perform their expected duties. Without a minimum standard of ecclesiastical qualifications, the gate for commission was too wide. In response, general regulations issued by the Navy in 1841 required, for the first time, that any person appointed a chaplain in the Navy "be a regularly ordained or licensed clergyman, of unimpeached moral character."[19] Up to that time there was no requirement for ordination. Although a later ruling by the attorney general determined that the Navy did not have the authority to issue such regulations, the dual nature of chaplaincy remains to this day. Currently the federal government requires faith groups to verify, in writing, that the potential chaplain is "credentialed and qualified for an appointment within the military chaplaincy."[20]

Opportunities and Challenges of Institutional Duality

What does it mean to hold membership in two major social institutions? Benefits of this dual relationship include unparalleled opportunities to relate as an insider. Chaplains retain frequent and positive ministerial contact not only with members but with the institution itself. Challenges and risks are unavoidable.

Within the military, chaplains risk conflating their love of God with their service to nation. Some faith groups challenge the propriety of clergy wearing uniforms, holding officer rank, and saluting the flag. There remains the risk of chaplains subordinating faith-group expectations to military goals. Yet this is part of a larger national conversation. The conversation of institutional duality expands to the relationship between church and state. What is the place of religion in American public life? Within the United States, the national motto, In God We Trust, is reflected on currency and reinforced by language found in the Pledge of Allegiance, "one nation under God." The inclusion of God's name continues to be challenged, yet it reflects the dual and often ambiguous relationship between the secular and the sacred. It truly describes a chaplain fulfilling sacred responsibilities within a secular institution.

From the Navy's perspective, I see the need for chaplains who can connect with sailors and marines quickly, especially at the rate that folks turn over and the fact that a chaplain's ministry depends heavily on one's ability to develop meaningful relationships. From the perspective of evangelical Christianity, I see the need for chaplains that are not only committed to being on-mission for Jesus, but who also know how to maneuver ministry in a pluralistic environment without forcing their faith on those who don't want to hear it, but still ready to share it for those who do. It truly is a ministry of presence, and I've seen that in my own experience. Nineteen years of service in the Navy has taught me more than I can say about how to integrate faith and work without disrespecting the different positions of others.

—*Military Chaplain*

2.5 Ecclesiastical Environment in the Institution

If there is a designated chapel at your workplace, it is likely sponsored by the organization you are serving. Colleges, hospitals, prisons, VA medical centers, continuing-care retirement communities, camps, and military bases frequently have fully functioning chapels. Other locations, such as airport terminals, stadiums, industrial complexes, precincts,[21] and other workplaces, often designate a prayer or meditation room.

Freestanding chapels—the type frequently found on college campuses and military installations—often retain their unique faith identifiers, such as a cross or stained glass. For example, the exterior façade of Stanford University's campus chapel has a massive mosaic depicting Jesus delivering the Sermon on the Mount. This public building was completed in 1903.[22] Newer chapels are frequently designed with no permanent fixtures of religious symbolism. Since multiple faiths use the chapel, each one brings its own portable unique identifiers. As an example, the altar cross may have a crucifix on one side for Catholic Mass; turn it around, and there is an empty cross that is utilized for Protestant worship.

Chapel ministry—focused on providing services based on one's own theological training and faith-group practice—brings a tremendous amount of satisfaction and reward. Diverse Christian chaplains bring distinct worship styles. You may discover yourself working alongside other Christian chaplains who are far afield of your theological training or your typical expression of worship. As a chaplain, how will you publicize your worship services? Since you are providing ministry according to your faith background, will it align with others alongside you in the chancel? Will it be clear to potential attendees what to expect at a service? How will you ensure "truth in advertising" for your programming? How will you remain adaptable to the environment and unique culture of your organization?

> While serving as a chaplain to marines in combat, I had the opportunity to officiate a Christmas Eve service in a large tent with two hundred marines. It was a common tradition in my faith group to close worship by singing "Silent Night" by candlelight. Yet flames were prohibited because it was hazardous to simultaneously light two hundred candles inside a canvas tent. Instead, we found plastic glow sticks. It had a similar effect, although we traded the warm yellow flame for the icy green glow. This event required some flexibility and imagination, and I believe it remains unique among candlelight services.
>
> —*Military Chaplain*

On rare occasions, you might be asked to conduct or participate in a worship activity conflicting with your religious convictions. These requests most often come from someone within your organization hoping to benefit from your availability or expertise. The invitations are not meant to be problematic, yet their aspirations are not aligned with your faith group's theology and practice. For example, a couple might request that you baptize their infant. However, your faith group does not practice paedobaptism. Perhaps your supervisor, a chaplain not of your faith group, invites you to participate in communion. But you only serve communion using grape juice and she only uses wine. Before you decline a request like this, you first need to know whether or not the invitation violates your faith group's requirements.

At times your personal convictions and your faith group's expectations may not be aligned. You may receive a request that conflicts with your conscience, but your church either holds a position different from yours or does not have a position. There may be occasions when you are not aligned with both your church and your institution. This is a precarious position. When chaplains face a challenging request to perform or provide religious ministry that is contrary to their conscience, they should research their faith group's requirements, regulations, or convictions before declining the request. They need to know whether their faith group historically and currently sees this as a violation. Chaplains cannot misrepresent their faith group without the risk of their endorsing agent withdrawing the ecclesiastical endorsement.

Sermon

For many Protestant chaplains, the sermon forms the centerpiece of worship. Music, prayer, liturgy, and communion are often shaped by the reading and proclamation of the Word. However, this is not a unanimous view. When you join a group of Protestant chaplains who share many theological values yet represent a variety of denominations, it would be wise to meet together prior to the worship service and discuss the following topics:

- What is the most important part of your worship service?
- What is the typical basis for preaching? Is it topical, expository, or the lectionary?
- What is the pulpit rotation and what faith groups will be represented?
- How much time does the institution allocate for sermon preparation?
- What is the expected duration of the sermon? Is it shorter on communion Sundays?
- Are there terms or phrases within our institution that help contextualize the sermon?

- Are there terms or phrases to avoid (e.g., favorably referring to a college sports rival may trigger a negative reaction)?
- Are there preaching topics to intentionally avoid or deliberately address?
- What do we wear for worship (e.g., alb, robe, gown, dress, stole, suit, uniform)?

Some chaplains prefer to speak from prepared scripted sermons. Others are adept at memorizing or offering extemporaneous messages. You may need to adapt your style or empower others to preach.

Chaplains experienced with call-and-response preaching frequently lead gospel services. I am neither gifted nor trained to communicate in this style. The affirming "Amen!" comments by the congregation cause me to lose my place with scripted notes. After completing my second service, an attendee offered these helpful yet ego-busting words, "Chaplain, we don't trust anyone who needs notes to preach." I realized he was right. Since I was the only chaplain, I sought and appointed lay leaders experienced at preaching without notes. My new role at the service was to sit on the dais and offer the pastoral prayer as a participating member of the worship team.

—Correctional/Prison Chaplain

Baptism

Jesus entrusted two specific worship elements to the church: baptism and the Lord's Supper. Baptism and communion remain opportunities for unity as well as potential perils of division. Different faith groups use different terms for these elements—they are "rites," "sacraments," "ordinances," or "practices." Baptism is a rite of Christian initiation in many denominations. Protestant chaplains who integrate baptism into the worship service should clearly understand the theology and practice of baptism according to their faith group. Here are some questions to consider:

- Does your faith group have a mandated liturgy for baptism?
- Do you baptize babies and confessing believers?
- Are you limited to immersion or sprinkling or pouring?
- Is it part of a public worship service, or will you officiate a private baptism?
- Will you rebaptize someone?

- If you immerse, what accommodations are made for those in prison, in hospital, or on ship?
- Is there a certificate or other documentation you provide?
- Where do you record the baptism for your own records?

As our Navy ship steamed various oceans, I collected water samples from the Seven Seas and combined them together in a gallon jug. For baptisms, as I read portions of Psalm 107, I would deliberately use some of that water as a contextually appropriate theme for sailors who go "down to the sea in ships, doing business on the great waters." Every ship has a big ship's bell used for ringing in fog. Often, the crew manufactures a portable metal brace to support the inverted brass bell. Sailors polish the bell, turn it upside down, add water, and the bell turns into a temporary baptismal font. Following a bell baptism, sailors engrave the name of the baptized person inside of the shell. If you visit a nautical museum and see a ship's bell, look inside to find engraved names of those who received a bell baptism.

—*Military Chaplain*

Lord's Supper

Another element of Christian worship creating a powerful sense of unity is communion. Yet a diversity of faith groups imbue this event with their unique theological underpinnings and ecclesiological traditions. Unless they are standardized, this wide range of communion practices may confuse chapel worshipers. If they experience inconsistencies, it could be detrimental to worship. Does the balance lean toward chapel attendees or offset toward maintaining the chaplain's church tradition? Prior to the service, chaplains will dialogue with one another: "This is what I can do. That is what I can't do. I'd like to try some new things. I would like to see other expressions of worship and participate in them without violating my ordination vows." Questions that chaplains might discuss together include:

- Do you call it communion, the Lord's Supper, Eucharist, or Mass?
- Is it a rite, sacrament, ordinance, practice, or memorial?
- What words do you say?
- What is the frequency of communion: weekly, monthly, quarterly?

- Do you use wine, grape juice, or both?
- Do you serve a loaf, wafer, or unleavened bread?
- Do worshipers come forward or stay in the pew to receive?
- Do worshipers drink from a common cup or distribute individual small cups?
- Do worshipers dip their bread into the cup by intinction?
- Do chaplains distribute the elements among themselves first[23] or last?[24]
- Is communion received by all simultaneously with small cups?
- What do you do with the residual bread and liquid?

One frequent concern is whether your faith group practices an "open" or "closed" communion table. An open table typically invites anyone who professes faith in Jesus Christ and is baptized. A closed table is typically restricted for those within the denomination of the chaplain. In a chapel service co-officiated by chaplains endorsed by the Lutheran Church–Missouri Synod (LCMS) and United Methodist denominations, the two could not participate in communion together. The LCMS endorses the doctrine of closed communion. This church policy requires the sharing of the Eucharist only with those who are baptized and confirmed members of the LCMS.[25] United Methodists practice an open table where "There are no conditions for church membership or completion of a class required."[26] Therefore, the two chaplains could share the entire service together with the exception of communion. Who will then officiate communion? Will there even be communion? If no communion, will the chapel community feel penalized?

Obviously, baptism and communion practices are simpler if you are the sole chaplain officiating the service. When you regularly conduct baptisms and facilitate communion, you may want to share with chapel worshipers why your activities may look different from their home church experience. You are in a unique position to teach that there are many Christian expressions of both baptism and communion.

Weddings

Some chaplaincies tend toward frequent weddings due to the age of their constituents. College campus chaplaincy and military chaplaincy serve a population of young adults. Chaplains serving in those contexts can expect frequent requests for premarital counseling. The first appointment frequently concludes with the question, "Chaplain, will you officiate our wedding?"

Before you answer, you need to investigate whether you can legally perform wedding ceremonies. Each state has its own regulations. There may be a requirement to register, pay fees, and submit documentation from your faith group certifying that you are ordained or licensed. Policy is determined by the location of the wedding.

> When I perform weddings in Hawaii, the registration process is different from weddings I officiate in San Diego or Seattle. Marriage officiant requirements are different state to state because, as a celebrant, I perform both a religious service and legal ceremony.
>
> —*Cruise Ship Chaplain*

Beyond a chaplain's legal responsibilities to the state, there are expectations from the chaplain's faith group that are theological and ecclesial in nature. Chaplains may be required to use a liturgy approved by their faith group. Some denominations require weddings to be inside a church building. Marriage for Roman Catholics is a sacrament and therefore officiated only by Roman Catholic priests. The following are suggested questions for prospective and current chaplains to discuss with their ecclesiastical endorsers:

- Can I perform weddings between non-Christians?
- Can I perform weddings between a baptized believer and a non-Christian?
- Can I perform weddings between people from two different faith groups, such as the Latter-day Saints and Judaism?
- Will I perform weddings for couples currently living together?
- Will I officiate a same-sex wedding?[27]
- What does your faith group allow regarding same-sex marriage?

These are challenging questions that are central to ministry as a chaplain. It would be rare to find denominational policy providing instantaneous answers to these questions. Due to the independent nature of chaplaincy, it is important for the chaplain to frequently communicate with the ecclesiastical endorser representing the chaplain's faith group. The chaplain may not have the discretionary time to research some issues. The ecclesiastical endorser can streamline the process by providing assistance.

In my practice of chaplaincy, I attempt to maintain a position that is theologically conservative and pastorally compassionate. At times the balance is difficult to preserve. For example, I perform weddings for students at my college who ask me to officiate. I inform them that I perform Christian wedding services. If that meets their expectations, then I am available. I require premarital counseling and remain a certified facilitator of the Prepare/Enrich assessment. This assessment allows me to use our premarital appointment times to focus not only on their wedding but, more significantly, their marriage. Together, we work toward gaining personalized insights into relationship dynamics, commitment levels, personality, spiritual beliefs, and family systems.

—*College Chaplain*

Funerals

Do not be surprised if the first service you are invited to officiate as a chaplain is a funeral or memorial service. Chaplains are most frequently asked to conduct funerals by families with no church affiliation. Obviously, a family connected with a local church would coordinate the funeral with the church staff. The frequency of funerals is presumably higher in hospice, hospital, VA, first-responder, and military chaplaincy because the organizational population has an elevated mortality risk due to health concerns or the potential of violence.

Funerals and memorial services hold much in common. They are religious ceremonies attended by people who share a common loss. The service supports the grieving family by gathering together caring friends, coworkers, and neighbors. This celebration of cherished memories helps the bereaved family and grieving community to publicly acknowledge the death of one of their own. If a chaplain officiates a funeral or memorial service, religious elements will typically include Scripture readings, prayers, a eulogy by friends or family, a brief message by the chaplain, and hymns. The order of service for a funeral or memorial service will follow the chaplain's faith tradition. As an example, a Protestant chaplain cannot preside over a Roman Catholic Mass.

A funeral service is held to memorialize a deceased person with the body present. A memorial service is held to memorialize a deceased person with the body not present. If a burial occurs prior to the service, it is considered a memorial service. Families may choose to have a funeral followed later by a memorial service. They may prefer to hold a private funeral and a public memorial service. They may decide to hold only one. While a memorial service does not include a casket, it may display an urn holding ashes. Both services typically reflect elements of the decedent's religious tradition as much as the chaplain can accommodate. For example, if the decedent regularly used the Lord's Prayer as part of worship yet the chaplain's liturgy does not include it, then the chaplain might consider including it in the funeral or memorial service.

At a funeral, the survivors and next of kin are the chaplain's focal point. A memorial service typically expands attendance to include the decedent's fellow employees. Frequently, the decedent's employing organization is involved in the memorial service. This is especially true in law-enforcement, firefighting, disaster-relief, first-responder, and military chaplaincies. Often the memorial service will be held at the location of the decedent's employment.

Since a memorial service occurs after the remains have been cared for, there is more time for planning. As popularity of cremation grows, families may ask the chaplain to plan a more engaging and personalized memorial service or celebration of life. The employing organization, in consultation with the decedent's family, can purposely prepare the ceremony and decide how to appropriately respect the deceased.

Supervisors may expect everyone in the organization to attend a memorial service, no matter their individual faith. Memorial services thus tend to be public observances. Therefore, the chaplain's brief message can be nuanced to recognize the individual as well as create space for fellow employees to mourn. The chaplain might connect the organization's commitment to all people either in the chaplain's welcome or brief message. Further, Christian chaplains are appropriate to share their theology and hope in the resurrection, while simultaneously remaining aware that some attendees may not be there by choice.

Here are some questions to discuss with your ecclesiastical endorser as well as your organizational leadership:

- How do I officiate a funeral versus a memorial service?
- If invited, how do I participate in a memorial service for a deceased Roman Catholic or Muslim?
- How do I officiate a nondenominational memorial service?

- How do I officiate a nonreligious memorial service?
- How do I conduct a funeral for a suicide victim?
- How do I officiate a memorial service for a child?
- How do I prepare for a funeral of a slain police officer or fallen soldier?

Summary

The ecclesiastical environment within an institution is important to assess and discern. Chaplains should do this well before they fill a position. It begins by developing a pastoral identity within the context of one's faith group. As the chaplain starts ministering to the broader organizational community, it is invaluable to stay connected with one's faith group. The ecclesiastical endorser will bring support to help maintain chaplain integrity and spiritual health. As a chaplain, if your denomination or church is not savvy about chaplaincy, you are in an excellent position to teach it about your unique ministry.

The apostle Paul admonishes us to know the difference between simply *trying* to minister and *training* for ministry. Training is the key, "For while bodily training is of some value, godliness is of value in every way, as it holds promise for the present life and also for the life to come" (1 Tim. 4:8). As you train, consider those within your faith tradition and also those in the Bible who form your core pastoral identity. The character you develop will propel you or neutralize you. It will help you define your limits. One idea is to imitate those you respect most. Many who enter the pastoral ministry discover an unhealthy need for constant affirmation and struggle with insecurity. They relate on a personal level with these words from Gordon MacDonald: "I came into the ministry as an insecure person, specifically needing affirmation. I needed for people to like me, and I equated applause with affirmation. I've had to transition from being a driven person to being a called person."[28]

I recently attended a worship service at a chapel led by chaplains endorsed by the Presbyterian, Baptist, and Seventh Day Adventist faith groups. Despite faith group differences, the three chaplains were clearly aligned and focused on proclaiming Jesus. Each one participated throughout the service and alternated through the welcome, prayers, preaching, and liturgy. Their distinctives were not diluted. Their training for chaplaincy allowed them to serve the majority of attendees who were not Presbyterian, Baptist, and Seventh Day Adventist. Barriers to community inhibit the Holy Spirit (see 1 Thess. 5:19), and as Paul challenged the church at Ephesus, "[Be] eager to maintain the unity of the Spirit in the bond of peace" (Eph. 4:3). If Christian chaplains, and their respective faith groups, are to proclaim Jesus by announcing his kingdom, then they follow their Savior and Lord by emulating his respect toward those he served.

—Ecclesiastical Endorser of Chaplains

The offer to co-officiate a chapel service is invitational and not impositional. There may never be another opportunity to partner with clergy from other faith groups in the same manner as found in a chapel. However, chaplains can be selective about co-officiating chapel services with colleagues who have theological beliefs counter to the chaplain's denominational ecclesiology. It is the chaplain's prerogative to decline co-officiating a chapel service with other chaplains because of individual conscience or denominational prohibitions. The decision not to participate with other chaplains in a chapel service should be preceded by a conversation with the chaplain's ecclesiastical endorser. Chaplains would be wise to contact their endorser or faith group representative early in this decision process. Denominational policy or practice should remain core to their decision. It is the faith group requirement in concert with the chaplain's conscience that justifies the decision.

To summarize, chaplains serve in a context where they cannot be selective about who attends their worship services. They frequently minister in a multistaff context alongside other chaplains who represent a variety of denominations and ecclesial traditions. If a chaplain is asked to participate in a worship event that he believes is beyond his denominational parameters, then the chaplain should immediately contact his endorsing agent. If the endorser prohibits participation, then a referral is made to another chaplain who might conduct such services. There is no reprisal if the chaplain cannot participate. In this way, chaplains remain faithful to their denominational practices and beliefs while also respecting chaplains of other faith groups.

Discussion Questions

1. In what ways can you invest in understanding, rehearsing, and practicing your own faith-specific delivery of ministry?
2. What activities, liturgy, attire, and displayed items (e.g., chalice, candles, cross, Bible) does your faith community identify as essential and required when conducting a worship service?

3. How does your pastoral identity influence your chaplain ministry?
4. Why is your relationship with your ecclesiastical endorser or supervisor of chaplain ministries important?
5. How would you define incarnational ministry?
6. In what way does your faith group identify itself as a bounded set?
7. How does a chaplain understand Christianity as a centered set?
8. How would you translate a worship service into your tribe's language? Could you do it for a completely different tribe? Consider the many organizational tribes that chaplains serve: hospital, hospice, military, correctional, corporate, college, first responder, sports team, etc.
9. Why is awareness of institutional duality important for a chaplain?

CHAPTER 3

The Chaplain as Facilitator

> I don't want my faith to change you. I want your faith to change you.
>
> —*Rabbi Chaplain*

3.1 Definition of Facilitate and Facilitation

Many organizations recognize the benefit of chaplains because they realize that faith is integral to a person's identity. Chaplains bring great value to organizations when employees and other beneficiaries have confidence that their diverse religious needs are respected. Singularly unique to the ministry of chaplaincy are religious support and assistance given to others not sharing the same theology or faith expressions as the chaplain. This capability is called *facilitation.*

Chaplains are expected to arrive at their institution having expertise in providing ministry to those sharing their faith. Organizations then expect their chaplains to grow competencies in facilitating faith-based support of individuals and groups not their own. Chaplains practice facilitation when they ensure that religious requirements are met for those who can't identify with their beliefs or practices. The growing diversity of religious expression in the United States impacts chaplains far more than parish clergy, since few Baptist church pastors are responsible for ensuring that neighborhood Christian Scientists, Jehovah's Witnesses, Roman Catholics, and Lutherans have a place to gather and have a qualified worship leader, let alone non-Christian-based traditions. Unlike the parish minister, chaplains develop strong competencies in facilitating the spiritual care, religious requirements, and faith expressions of others within their institutions.

Religious diversity continues to blossom. The first two centuries of American national life were marked by a narrow denominational pluralism within a Judeo-Christian society. In 1914 the Federal Council of Churches (FCC) established the Washington Committee on Army and Navy Chaplains. It consisted of two Episcopalians, two Methodists, and two Presbyterians.[1] Four years later, it expanded membership to reflect the thirty-two denominations belonging to the FCC.[2] Faith group representation in the United States continues to flourish. As of this writing, the federal credentialing board[3] for the Department of Defense identifies 221 faith groups, including Protestant, Roman Catholic, Eastern Orthodox, Buddhist, Islamic, Hindu, and earth-based faiths, such as heathens and Asatru.[4]

The previous chapter discussed the first functional capability of providing ministry for those aligned with a chaplain's faith group. This second capability of facilitating ministry meets the expectations of those having different religious requirements. Many employees or other beneficiaries cannot embrace their chaplain's faith group's *orthodoxy* (authorized doctrine) or *orthopraxy* (authorized practices), and a chaplain's faith group and conscience often conflict with other doctrines or religious practices. What appears as an impasse is actually an opportunity for the chaplain to champion the religious practices of others, despite the chaplain's inability to actually perform their religious functions due to doctrinal differences. When chaplains accept this opportunity, they increase their value to the institution and fulfill institutional expectations for chaplaincy.

Working with people in institutions such as a prison, a college, the military, or a hospital requires chaplains to appreciate and understand the religious traditions and faith-specific requirements reflected throughout this diverse population. Often chaplains will identify religious needs through an assessment tool. Chaplains will send a survey to employees and others within the institution requesting them to identify their faith requirements. When chaplains cannot directly provide for these groups or individuals, they coordinate the individual and collective religious requirements of others. By developing cooperative relationships and partnerships with local religious leaders who can serve members of the institution reflecting a different faith background, chaplains are able to facilitate individual religious requirements. Chaplains are expected to schedule, coordinate, budget, and contract with local religious leaders when there are members within the institution requesting specific religious requirements unavailable elsewhere.

Chaplains frequently develop robust lay leader programs within their organization and ensure that these volunteer lay leaders are trained and approved by the particular faith group they represent. For example, a Latter-day Saints lay leader cannot be from the Reorganized Church of Latter-day Saints (Community of Christ), because their theologies are not aligned. A chaplain learns that there is a difference between the two, even if the chaplain does not understand the nuances separating their particular theological tenets. Prior to training and certifying lay leaders within their organization, chaplains require specific faith group documentation indicating that the potential lay leader is in good standing and has permission to represent the faith group.

Chaplains succeed in facilitation when they publicize various religious opportunities and activities of all faiths throughout their organization. The chaplain ensures that these religious activities are accessible to any employee. Religious services should be publicly open to anyone within the institution. It is neither good policy nor good practice for the chaplain to restrict attendance only to those practicing that faith, recognizing that some faiths limit participation within the service to adherents. As an example, non-Catholics are welcome to attend Mass as long as they do not receive communion.

This inclusiveness of faith diversity assures institutional impartiality. Impartiality also means the organization will not promote some services while excluding others. Institutions seeking to promote a culture of diversity, tolerance, and excellence will do so by diligently supporting religious practices unless there is a compelling reason inhibiting that goal: "The Free Exercise Clause protects citizens' right to practice their religion as they please, so long as the practice does not run afoul of a 'public morals' or a 'compelling' governmental interest. For instance, in *Prince v. Massachusetts* ... the Supreme Court held that a state could force the inoculation of children whose parents would not allow such action for religious reasons. The Court held that the state had an overriding interest in protecting public health and safety."[5] Organizations strive to foster mutual respect for the diversity of religious expression.

Religious Observances

Religious observances include worship services and other rituals required of a particular faith that comport with doctrinal requirements for holy days and days of religious obligation. As chaplains gain knowledge of the diversity of faiths within the population they serve, they can better understand the different types of faith expressions and expectations people have regarding religious observances. These expectations include the anticipated size of group participation at worship services, specific doctrinal requirements, and unique faith group observances for holy days and seasons. Chaplains then communicate these expectations to the institution and recommend how the organization can best support diverse faith groups through human resources, funding, scheduling, and space allocation for gatherings.

New chaplains should attend all scheduled worship services held at their institution soon after arrival, including those of faiths not their own. It is valuable for chaplains to witness the variety of worship services within the context of their organization.

> Soon after arriving, I attended Roman Catholic worship services to see how the chaplain priest delivered Mass. To my surprise, at the end of each liturgical prayer, instead of saying "Amen" the entire congregation of uniformed marines shouted "Ooh-rah!" At the sound of this Marine Corps battle cry, I nearly fell off my kneeler. The priest loved it. The marines loved it. Yet the priest's bishop didn't love it. The priest, officiating Mass, had to realign his liturgy to conform to his faith group. "Amen" once again replaced "Ooh-rah!" It wasn't nearly as fun to listen to their Mass. However, it aligned with the liturgy of the word approved by the United States Conference of Catholic Bishops. Issues like this do not usually appear in a local church. A chaplain, no matter what faith, must clearly understand, align, and practice in the manner of their faith group.
>
> —*Military Chaplain*

The US military granted several of its members permission to participate in the hajj, an annual pilgrimage to Mecca, Saudi Arabia. Major William Trimble, executive officer of a battalion and a practicing Muslim, represented the Department of Defense on invitational orders during the hajj: "While attending Islamic Services at the Ramstein (Germany) Air Base South Chapel, Trimble learned through the chaplain of a program that was selecting members of the military to represent the Department of Defense on an invitation from the Saudi Minister of Defense and Aviation to participate in Hajj."[6] The chaplain was essential in facilitating the major's faith group requirements.

Where do you find ashes for Ash Wednesday in the desert during combat operations in the Middle East? Many marines expected to receive ashes on their forehead as a sign of repentance marking the start of the Lenten season. My faith group does not have a requirement to hold an Ash Wednesday service nor does it prohibit conducting a service. As the only chaplain, I decided to announce a worship service. Preparing for the service, I realized we did not bring any ashes. Traditionally, ashes for distribution are from burning Palm Sunday fronds of the preceding year. This was not possible. The solution started with a hike in the desert to a nearby oasis, foraging for fallen palms, then returning to camp and burning the fronds into ash.

—Military Chaplain

Facilitation of an employee's religious practices may be constrained by context and availability. Whereas it would be easier for the chaplain to procure ashes in the United States, preparing for Ash Wednesday brought its own challenges (see the preceding story). This is where creativity, perseverance, and grit[7] combine. Chaplains continually anticipate upcoming religious observances in order to meet the needs of those they serve. The most successful chaplains are those who are committed to "get the job done" when it comes to facilitation.

Dietary Observances

Religious dietary observances include traditional or doctrinal requirements on types of food or the means of food preparation. To the extent that health and safety are not compromised, chaplains encourage organizations to provide or authorize individuals to prepare supplemental food in order to meet religious dietary observances. Chaplains are proactive in ensuring the availability of halal and kosher and kosher-for-Passover Seder meals appropriate to the observance. Chaplains should familiarize themselves with the dietary observances of various faith groups. Here are some of these:

Religion	Dietary Observances and Sensitivities
Baha'i	The majority of Baha'is avoid drinking alcohol.
Buddhism	Buddhists do not eat meat, fish, or eggs and avoid drinking alcohol.
Christianity	Some Christians avoid drinking alcohol. Some prefer not to eat meat on Fridays. Seventh-day Adventists observe a well-balanced vegetarian diet.[8]

Hinduism	Hindus' diets are mostly vegetarian, supplemented by seafood, chicken, and eggs. They abstain from eating beef and pork.
Islam	Muslims eat only halal meat. Pork and any other food derived from the pig is forbidden, as is alcohol.
Judaism	Jews cannot eat pork or shellfish. They cannot eat meat that is not kosher. They cannot mix dairy and meat products.
Rastafarianism	Most Rastafarians are vegetarian.
Sikhism	Most Sikhs are vegetarian.

Religious Apparel

Religious apparel is defined as articles of clothing required by doctrine or worn in traditional observance of the religious faith practiced by people within the organization. Many employers, such as hospitals, prisons, police and fire departments, and the armed forces, have apparel standards that require employees to wear institutional clothing. Other organizations may expect their members to wear apparel that is neat and conservative, such as campus faculty, hospice, or continuing-care retirement community employees. From whom will members of an organization seek permission to wear a visible clothing accessory identifying their faith? What criteria are used to support religious accommodation? On behalf of the employer, the chaplain will often be asked to prepare guidelines indicating when and where the apparel can be worn. Is it reasonable for the organization to define what is neat, discreet, and conservative? Would an employer allow someone to wear a necklace with a visible cross yet prohibit another employee from wearing a necklace with a pentagram pendent?

Chaplains usually wear religious apparel required by their faith group when conducting public worship services and performing religious rites or rituals distinct to their religion. Rabbi chaplains wear a yarmulke at Jewish services. Roman Catholic priests typically wear a chasuble, alb, and cincture at Mass. There are circumstances when a chaplain would not be expected to wear vestments. For example, if the religious service is outside and the wind is strong, it may not be reasonable to wear vestments. Additionally, if the mode of transportation to the location of worship requires a chaplain to restrict items, the chaplain may limit clergy attire to essentials.

Every Sunday a helicopter carried me to each of our six ships steaming together in the ocean. The fastest way to move from one ship to another is
by one shared helicopter carried on the largest ship. The other ships don't
have landing space. The process started by hovering fifty feet over a ship,
kneeling on the cargo deck, tethering to a line, and leaning backward out
of the open side door. The helicopter hoist would take the slack out of my
rope as I slowly lowered to the ship deck. An hour later, the helicopter would
again hover above the ship, drop the cable, and slowly reel me up. We would
whisk away to another of the six vessels where the process repeated. Over
my shoulder slung a green chaplain's kit with worship and communion sup-
plies: a chalice, a paten, and a stole. No other vestments were allowed due
to their bulkiness.

—*Military Chaplain*

Hair, Grooming, and Appearance Standards

Hair and grooming standards expected from employees and others
served by the institution, such as the incarcerated, occasionally conflict
with individual religious requirements. For example, some faith groups
require beards. However, the military is concerned that beards create
a potential safety risk. Facial hair cannot ensure an effective seal when
wearing a protective gas mask. Currently, very few members of the armed
forces have beards: "There are a small number of soldiers, out of 1.1 million, who do have beards because they have an approved religious accommodation, but with the understanding that they may have to shave
them if a chemical attack is imminent and their commander orders it."[9]
The Army is granting waivers on a limited basis for beards, thereby allowing several Sikhs, Muslims, and a Hasidic Jewish rabbi to join their
ranks. When the Army acquiesced to authorizing beards for religious
soldiers in early 2017, the move was a response to years of religious accommodation requests, as well as a lawsuit from Sikh soldiers seeking
to serve in the military while adhering to the tenets of their faith. In May
2019, fourteen Sikh high schoolers received waivers to enter the Army
with beards and turbans.[10]

If an organization sets a hair and grooming policy precedent, then the
accommodation applies to all faith groups. The Army directive authorizing
beards was not limited to widely recognized religions.[11] A soldier adhering to and practicing Norse paganism requested an accommodation for
his beard. The Army accepted a request to add this religion to its list of
faith codes, and, per a 2013 ruling, the Hammer of Thor was authorized for
placement on military cemetery headstones.

Boundaries of religious accommodation continue to expand, and also gain greater clarity. In 2019, an Army soldier applied for a beard exemption as part of his devotion to the Church of the Flying Spaghetti Monster—a faith also known as "Pastafarianism." He wrote to the Army, "This request is based on my deeply and sincerely held belief in the Pastafarian faith. It is my personally held belief that growing a beard will bring me closer to my God and bring me into his favor." An Army spokesperson stated that the military denied his request: "While we cannot speak to the specifics of any particular case, religious accommodation can be disapproved if it is determined that the request is not based on a sincerely held religious belief or if the accommodation would create a specific hazard that cannot be reasonably mitigated."[12]

Hair and grooming standards are not the only subject of accommodation requests. Organizations also find religious implications in appearance standards of employees and others served by the institution. As an example, there is an increase in tattoo and piercing policies. Tattoos that are religious would typically be allowed. Offensive tattoos advocating religious discrimination or intolerance would likely be prohibited. It is more common to find organizations resolving these issues through policy. Employees who face the public or serve external customers may have a standardized dress policy requiring apparel to include long sleeves and shirt collars. While long sleeves might obscure arm tattoos, the policy might reasonably reflect the expectations of the employer while not restricting employee individual expression when not at work.

Religious Medical Practices

There exist doctrinal or traditional objections to receiving immunizations and transfusions, and to providing DNA specimen samples. Campus chaplains occasionally receive faith-based requests for immunization exemption from incoming freshmen. Military chaplains supporting recruit training also coordinate with medical staff when immunization waiver requests are received. Chaplains in health services as well as first-responder chaplains who serve police and fire units will sporadically be involved in religious medical practice issues.

As an example, in 2019 a measles outbreak in New York City led to a public health emergency with mandatory vaccinations. The outbreak was concentrated in Brooklyn among Orthodox Jewish communities. Many rabbis and other religious leaders supported the public health decision. Rabbi

Yuval Cherlow, founder and head of the ethics department of the Tzohar Rabbinical Organization in Israel, said, "Most rabbis encourage vaccination based on the Torah commandment to protect one's life."[13] A vaccination order of this magnitude was last seen nearly three decades ago: "The last time city public health officials relied on mandatory vaccinations also involved a religious community, when a far more virulent measles outbreak swept the country in 1991. In Philadelphia, health officials sought a court order to force parents at two congregations to vaccinate their children."[14]

A religious objection to medically treating an employee must be balanced against the medical risk to the member and others within the organization. Could one noninoculated freshman risk the health of other students living in the same dorm? In the military and in police departments, there may be members who would resist receiving a transfusion if they were wounded in the line of duty. Jehovah's Witnesses believe blood transfusions are prohibited based upon certain biblical passages. Christian Science founder Mary Baker Eddy argued in her book *Science and Health* that sickness is an illusion that can be corrected by prayer alone. Christian Science believes members should rely on spirituality instead of medical treatment.

3.2 Religious Accommodation

One reason institutions employ chaplains is to accommodate the religion of people in the institution. The following justifications, while stated individually, are frequently combined to inform an organization's responsiveness in accommodating the religious needs of employees and other beneficiaries.

1.   Institutions provide chaplains to address issues of isolation. In some circumstances, beneficiaries are isolated, and the institution uses chaplains to reach out to those individuals. Chaplains serve those without access to regular ministries and services of their faith. As examples, military service members stationed in a combat zone and prisoners in maximum security continue to have specific religious needs.

A soldier preparing to engage in combat came to me and asked for me to bless his medallion bearing the image of the Virgin Mary. I was both honored and perplexed. My response was, "My faith group does not bless medallions, and Roman Catholic Code of Canon Law requires sacramentals to be blessed by a bishop, priest, or deacon. Since there is no priest or deacon available, would you like me to simply offer prayer for God's protection over you?" The soldier nodded his head. I held the medal and offered prayer. This did not violate my integrity or conscience. Chaplains often have resource-related or context-related constraints on the form of their ministry.

—Military Chaplain

2. Institutions provide chaplains in response to the unique character of organizational activity, such as first responders or the military. Institutions benefit from clergy with expertise in the organization's specific activity. These institutions expect chaplains to serve those who may already have community access to ministries and services of their faith. As an example, off-duty police officers and firefighters could go to their local church and talk to their minister. Yet community clergy cannot respond to them in the same way as someone accustomed to being in that environment. Ministers of their faith likely cannot relate to the trauma experienced by first responders. Community clergy do not serve in the adrenaline-pumping context of an emergency responder cohort.

However, police and fire chaplains, skilled in responding to critical-incident stress, moral injury, and posttraumatic stress, are prepared to support first responders as they cope with frequent trauma. Police and fire chaplains are also uniquely skilled to care for family members of first responders suffering from secondary trauma in the aftermath of critical incidents. Chaplains are there because employees experience problems unique to their employment, and the institution responds by providing this resource to those individuals. Chaplains bring expertise to the organizational context because they understand the unique character of activities within the organization. These activities may include trauma experienced by first responders, violence in the military, or end-of-life decisions in hospital settings.

3. Institutions provide chaplains to communicate the religious needs of individuals back to the institution. The individual reaches out to the institution through the chaplain. Chaplains help the organization know how to best respond to the specific religious needs of individuals. Chaplains are champions for ensuring that employees and other beneficiaries, such as adults with disabilities, patients in hospitals, and students in colleges, have opportunities to observe their faith.

Some institutions employ chaplains for one of these religious accommodation reasons. Others employ them for all these reasons. What holds the three reasons together is the idea that the chaplain helps the institution accommodate the religious needs of those who serve, or are located within, the institution.

The cornerstone of chaplaincy in each of these justifications is responsiveness. Organic to the position of chaplain is an expectation of receptiveness to the spiritual needs of those the chaplain is employed to serve. The context of ministry is, in part, driven by the needs and faith commitments of individuals inside the institution. A chaplain's obligation to responsiveness includes advocacy for people who have religious needs, especially for those in remote institutions. Additionally, the chaplain acknowledges and is interested in supporting those representing nonmajority faith groups who have unique religious requirements. Chaplains respond to them by advocating ways to accommodate their specific religious needs consistent with policy or law. As a responder, the chaplain is not setting the agenda for every encounter and instead is focused on being open and listening. Chaplains are communicators who continually articulate the institution's desire to respond to religious requests.

A chaplain in a corporation may be involved with the human resource department in deciding means of accommodation. In the government context, it is important for chaplains serving in corrections or the military to be involved in the development of both accommodation policy and accommodation practice. While chaplains certainly won't have the last word, they are involved in an advisory capacity by helping their institution think through accommodations.

> As a corporate chaplain, I work with the team member and walk with them through the HR process of getting an accommodation so they can celebrate the holy day of their choice. I make a point in orientation of recognizing that not all team members have the same holidays or holy days that are recognized on a typical work calendar. I invite them to share with me their needs according to their faith requirements. It is important for their religious needs to be met.
>
> —*Workplace, Industrial, and*
> *Corporate Chaplain*

Most employers seek ways to reasonably accommodate an employee's religious beliefs or practices. The chaplain is frequently called upon to assess the accommodation request and recommend a reasonable solution. Most requests can be met by making adjustments that will allow employees to maintain the integrity of their religious practices without unduly burdening the employer. The most common accommodations include a more flexible work schedule, work-shift substitutions, modifications to workplace policies, approval of apparel modifications, and support for dietary requirements. For example, a chaplain would likely want to support a reasonable request by practicing Jewish employees for a separate refrigerator in the employee lounge to maintain dietary observances. Employees occasionally ask chaplains to advocate for variance in dress and grooming standards in support of religious accommodation. These requests might include permission to wear religious head coverings, such as a Jewish yarmulke or a Muslim headscarf. They could also include hairstyles such as Rastafarian dreadlocks or a Sikh's uncut hair and beard. The chaplain should help the institution be creative in finding ways to accommodate such requests if at all possible.

Employees typically initiate a request for religious accommodations based on their worship practice, religious calendar, unique attire, or grooming requirements. It is the responsibility of the employee to articulate the religious requirement as the basis for the accommodation request. The chaplain is typically coordinating a creative discussion between the member and the management.

Determination of reasonable accommodations is not focused on a particular faith group's *orthodoxy* (authorized doctrine) but on its *orthopraxy* (authorized practices). Yet religious practices are not restricted to doctrinal rituals. As an example, Roman Catholic beneficiaries might say it is really important for them to have a lighted candle when reciting evening prayers. After some research, the chaplain learns that Roman Catholic doctrine does not require the presence of a candle while saying evening prayer. The chaplain, on behalf of the organization, evaluates this sincerely expressed request by adherents even though it is not backed up by doctrine. As a chaplain, you would advocate approving this request because it is sincere, even though it isn't required as part of the Roman Catholic ritual. Your responsiveness supports the individual practice of faith.

It is not uncommon for organizational policy to restrict the practice of a religion if there is a perceived risk of undue hardship or safety. Safety concerns are legitimate because they impact other employees and beneficiaries of the institution. As an example, a request may be approved for lighting candles at a worship service held in an industrial site if a fire extinguisher is in the same room. Yet a request for burning candles may be denied at a hospital due to a potential safety hazard imposed by nearby oxygen tanks providing patient support.

Employers occasionally take some risk for the benefit of those requiring religious accommodation. A particularly vivid example of this is the authorized use of religiously justified psychoactive hallucinogens to support the faith needs of adherents. These drugs are illegal in most situations in part because they decrease workplace safety and detract from workplace efficiency, effectiveness, and mission. Yet in the US military, sacramental use of peyote by Native American service members is conditionally authorized. Peyote contains the psychedelic drug mescaline. The Office of the Secretary of Defense published a memorandum to the military imposing limitations on its possession and use, "for bona fide traditional religious ceremonial purposes."[15]

Most requests for religious accommodation can be resolved at a low level. As chaplains listen to both the employee and the employer, they seek to find reasonable solutions that can be supported by both parties. Chaplains strive to educate organizational leaders on the benefits of, and requirements for, religious accommodation.

When I served as chaplain aboard an aircraft carrier, I received an accommodation request from a small group of Wiccan sailors who sought permission to meet together as a recognized group sharing common beliefs. I then met with the most senior person on the ship, the commanding officer, and said, "Sir, this group called Wiccans would like to meet and I support their request." He said, "We will have no Wiccans on this ship, they will never meet, and you are dismissed." When the commanding officer dismisses you, you go. However, whereas he thought it was our final meeting on the topic, I hoped it was our first. I prepared my arguments and returned to him, "My goal, as your chaplain, is to keep you off the front page of the *Washington Post*. Christians, Jews, and Muslims already meet on your ship. It's legitimate for any other faith group sharing common beliefs to meet as well. The question isn't about whether they can meet but how they can practice their beliefs in a standardized and safe way. This is my recommendation: All worship services are public, anyone can attend. All worship gatherings can have two candles burning, whether they actually want two or fifty. Also, any burning candles require a fire extinguisher in their proximity. Worship services will not include anything sharp, so there will be no knives or needles or swords. All worship services can include vestments. You can always add attire, but no one can take off their clothes. All worship services will be advertised in the same way, using the same format. No one group will receive any particular favor over another one." The commanding officer said that made sense to him. I then met with the Wiccan group. They were very excited the ship would legitimize them by purchasing texts and providing a place for their meeting. They met for an hour on Saturday mornings in a space provided by the chaplains. Because all worship was open to the public, one of our chaplains attended as an observer.

—Military Chaplain

3.3 Constitutional Foundation for Governmental Chaplaincy

Even though the First Amendment's establishment clause bars the government from creating a religion, the government is nonetheless permitted to employ chaplains in order to serve authorized persons in specific contexts.[16] The two most prominent contexts are the military and correctional institutions. In both of these settings, individuals are likely to be isolated from clergy representing their faith communities and thus unable to engage in religious activities. Although perhaps not required to do so by the free exercise clause, the government nevertheless has legitimate interest in protecting the religious liberty of those under its jurisdiction. An important way the government accommodates these individuals is through chaplaincy. Chaplains are at the forefront of advocating religious liberty for staff, employees, patients, prisoners, and other beneficiaries in the organization.

As a prison chaplain, I play a vital role in providing the free exercise of religion. Inmates do not have the option to go to down the street to visit another church, so it's important that the chaplain keep this in mind when planning services and when trying to recruit volunteers for other faith groups.

—Correctional/Prison Chaplain

There are publicly funded and volunteer positions for clergy to minister within governmental organizations such as the prison system, the military, the FBI,[17] the Secret Service, police and fire departments, Veterans Affairs, public hospitals, and the US Public Health Service.[18] Justification for these chaplaincies is found in various statutes and regulations. These rules permit chaplains to serve in public institutions while being supervised by the government. The following criteria keep religious accommodation requirements consistent with the establishment clause.

Criterion 1: Government-Imposed Burdens

Accommodation must respond to a government-imposed burden on religion. If there's no real burden, then the government is plainly providing a benefit. As an example, the government provides an exemption to religious employers from Title VII restrictions on religious discrimination in hiring. This is because religious employers have legitimate reasons for wanting to hire employees of a particular faith. The exemption alleviated the government-imposed burden.

What is the burden on a first responder? Why do you need a chaplain in a firehouse or police station? Why can't first responders go to their parish priest, rabbi, or minister? The answer is similar to that given for military chaplains. A crucial and valued aspect of chaplaincy is having someone with the experience of trauma, of being in situations of real crisis, of knowing what it's like to lose somebody on your interior fire attack crew or to have witnessed a police shooting. First-responder and public-safety chaplains can care in a way that has credibility because of their experience built up over time. They form personal relationships. They have access to secure areas due to special clearances.

Another government-imposed burden found in the military, in hospitals, and in prisons is isolation. Typically, people can't leave the military base, walk off the boat, rise from their hospital bed, or exit their cell in order to attend worship services. Comprehensive systems exist to encompass the member's life that include the member's work, food, clothing, recreation, education, family, and health care. Excluding religion from this all-inclusive system would itself be a hardship. These people legitimately need access to a chaplain.

Criterion 2: Responsiveness

Chaplains pay attention to the needs of others. Chaplains learn about the religious needs of those within the institution and then respond by facilitating voluntary religious opportunities that are privately chosen and not predetermined by the organization. Chaplains create and curate opportunities that fulfill various expressions of faith. Responsiveness means that the institution, whether a correctional facility, VA hospital, or military base, does not have a particular positive or negative religious bias of its own. Being responsive means supporting members within the institution because some within the institution believe that religious life is important to their well-being. The government's commitment to responsiveness is to a beneficiary's specific religious need that has been burdened by the government.

It is significant, however, that the response be proportionate to the burden it is designed to address. The ministry and services provided are proportional to the need. As an example, the formation of chaplaincy for an IRS field office might not warrant the employment of a designated government chaplain because the employees are unlikely to have any religious burden that the government needs to meet.

Criterion 3: Religion Neutral

Accommodation must be religion neutral, that is, available to all faiths. If the government pays chaplain salaries and provides worship spaces, the benefit must be available to all who want it. The government has a duty to not be selective. This is a critical part of understanding the role of chaplaincy. Sometimes a chaplain is able to provide what a person needs. Other times a chaplain connects a person with resources to make sure the person has access to the required spiritual care. It would be improper for one faith group to get significant access and benefits because the organization's executive specifically identifies with that faith group, while another faith group, with more worshipers, receives fewer resources. In order for the organization to not favor one religion over another and remain religiously neutral, it could implement a policy allowing an employee to receive time off for two religious holy days per year, whether Christmas and Easter, Yom Kippur and Rosh Hashanah, Eid al-Fitr and Eid al-Adha, or another two religious days of the employee's choosing. Because resources are finite, there needs to be an identified connection between various faith group requirements and an organization's religiously neutral distribution of resources.

Criterion 4: No Hardship Imposed on Third Parties

Religious accommodation must not impose unreasonable burdens on nonpracticing employees. Will governmental accommodation for a few impose undue costs upon others? Does this collateral burden upon others demonstrate favoritism toward a few? If the government has a limited amount of discretionary dollars supporting military members, then is the allocation best spent for butter, bullets, or Bibles? Questions the chaplain should ask about accommodation include: What is the actual requirement? When is the resource required? Can it be done in a different way? For example, can a sailor's cap serve as a yarmulke for a Jewish sailor? Finally, is it a requirement or just a "nice to have" tradition, such as a Christmas tree?

As a chaplain serving four thousand marines in the Middle East, I prepared to baptize eight marines in the arid desert following Sunday chapel service. Locating a large collapsible rubber water tank, I requested that it be placed next to the chapel tent. I asked a marine who managed the regimental drinking water if he could provide water for the portable rubber tank. The resourceful marine brought the water trailer over to the chapel and completely drained all five thousand gallons of regimental drinking water. Fellow marines not attending the chapel were not impressed. They were forced to bear the brunt of the religious accommodation request by sacrificing their supply of drinking water. The colonel called me, not the well-intentioned marine, into his tent and appropriately gave me a verbal lashing for my poor judgment.

—*Military Chaplain*

The Chaplain's Creative Tension

Chaplaincy creates additional tension because the chaplain must consider not only requirements projected by the faith group but also expectations of the hiring organization, which tends to function in a pluralistic environment. An endorsing organization is critically important to governmental chaplaincy because the government can't determine whether someone is authorized to serve as a minister. Therefore, chaplains receive their credentials from distinctive faith communities. Yet they soon become employees of a different organization. The terms of their employment are going to depend on the circumstances of the hiring organization. This creates a tension because the employer may expect the chaplain to perform activities that the authorizing faith community would not want. How do you resolve the tension between the two? It may not be easily resolved.

The chaplain is typically not an employee of the faith community that ordained him. Yet the religious group continues to hold authority over his ecclesial status as a minister. As a result, the ecclesial power creates tension to some degree. Yet it also reflects the reality of one who is a minister of a particular religious organization working within a very different institution. Chaplains learn to negotiate the tension between the faith community that sent them and the employing institution that hired them.

Regarding participation in communion, my denominational policy states, "Local boards of elders have been given the responsibility to decide at what age and under what circumstances young children may be served." However, as a chaplain serving an institution, I do not have the benefit of a board of elders. Therefore, I have greater discretion as to the age of participation in the Lord's Supper.

—Hospice Chaplain

3.4 Cooperative Pluralism and Practice of Access

If the institution is large, it likely will employ multiple chaplains. Additionally, if the organizational mission requires it to quickly expand in response to a natural disaster, civil emergency, or military engagement, it will likely have a greater need for chaplains for the duration of this specific period. The surge of available chaplains increases institutional capacity to provide pastoral care and ensures that those within the institution have greater access to religious ministry and programs.

Most organizations seek faith-group diversity in their chaplaincy program in order to better serve the broad spectrum of religious needs represented throughout their workforce. The benefit of having chaplains endorsed from a variety of faith groups is a wider breadth of ministry, rites, sacraments, ordinances, and liturgies across the organization.

As the institution gains greater capacity by intentionally hiring a religiously diverse chaplaincy, the commensurate risk of chaplains not being cooperative with one another grows as well. The very benefit to the institution of having a diverse distribution of chaplains often brings its own tension. Chaplains frequently have biases against other chaplains due to differences in their respective faith-group theology. To mitigate this issue, chaplains must embrace the challenge of establishing and maintaining cooperative pluralism within the organization.

"Cooperative pluralism" is a term for the practice of sustaining acceptable and supportable coexistence between adherents of different religions or faith groups. This idea does not characterize local churches. A pastor may attend a local clergy association or occasionally participate in a civic religious service alongside other community religious leaders, but chaplains regularly practice ministry flanked by colleagues not from their faith group. As an extraordinary and heroic example, four US military chaplains gave their lives to save others when the troop ship *Dorchester* was torpedoed by a German submarine on February 3, 1943. As chaos and confusion reigned, the chaplains helped others into lifeboats, gave their own life jackets to those who had none, joined arms, said prayers, and sang hymns as they disappeared with the ship. "The altruistic action of the four chaplains constitutes one of the purest spiritual and ethical acts a person can make. When giving their life jackets, Rabbi Goode did not call out for a Jew; Father Washington did not call out for a Catholic; nor did the Reverends Fox and Poling call out for a Protestant. They simply gave their life jackets to the next man in line."[19]

Cooperative pluralism is exemplified when chaplains representing various faith groups serve selflessly alongside one another. This partnership is both rare and precious. If not practiced, it can bring tension and fracture relationships. Not all clergy feel called, prepared, or confident to serve alongside others who are outside of their faith community. Cooperative pluralism is the framework behind facilitation. It includes the practice of mutual respect for people of other faiths, shared responsibility to connect with others, and amicable coexistence between adherents of different religions. Cooperative pluralism is to be inclusive without compromising your faith. This principle is often called *cooperation without compromise*.

> "Chaplain, will you offer the prayers at my retirement ceremony?" I replied it would be a great honor. The medical doctor retired with many years of service at the rank of captain. It is normal for a chaplain to assist at a retirement ceremony. I previously retired, so I was even more grateful to support this former shipmate. My ministry also changed, and I now served as a Roman Catholic bishop. I prayed at the ceremony. The doctor quipped in his closing comments, "Only in America can a Jewish kid from Queens, New York, become a Navy doctor and captain, then have a Catholic bishop pray at his retirement."
>
> —*Former Military Chaplain*

Chaplains are entrusted to cooperate without compromise. The chaplain of the Senate, a previous military chaplain, notes, "Military service provides a model of pluralism, a model for pluralistic ministry. The civilian sector would learn an awful lot from the *cooperation without compromise* model, which is the motto of so many of the chaplains in the service."[20] There is no place in chaplaincy for the turmoil that exists in many faith groups, which polarize and splinter over seemingly irresolvable theological and social issues. Chaplains are called to be ecumenical leaders among people of all faith groups, promoting unity and cooperation in their ministry.

Cooperative pluralism allows the chaplain to be present in the lives of others through personal character, integrity, compassion, values, and example. It leads to invitations for the chaplain to discuss faith. It results in multiple conversations that bring healing and hope through a variety of activities. At the same time, cooperative pluralism does not support proselytizing. One federal agency defines proselytizing as using "any form of coercion, real or implied, to compel or unduly persuade inmates to attend services, programs or special activities in the Chapel or to make inmates follow a particular religion because its value is seen as significantly greater, more important and more rewarding than the faith commitment, or lack thereof, currently held by them."[21]

Some clergy avoid entering chaplaincy because they seek a ministerial position that allows direct proselytizing. Yet chaplains exchange proselytizing for an opportunity to establish a foundation of trust with others. The value of a trusted relationship becomes clear. A chaplain is not likely the first nor last clergy someone will talk with. As Paul writes, "I planted, Apollos watered, but God gave the growth. . . . For we are God's fellow workers" (1 Cor. 3:6, 9).

As we approached battle, many marines were reflecting on their faith. It started with two marines requesting baptism and soon grew to forty. At one point, twelve came together and requested individual baptism. I listened to their stories about friends, family, and colleagues who had invested in them over the years. A broad assortment of Christians had nurtured them. I was suddenly in a culminating position to recognize the efforts of this link in their chain of faith. One of my most significant ministry moments was baptizing them in the shallow shore water of the Persian Gulf. Few Christians have been baptized in those waters since the seventh century when Islam swept the Arabian region. It is common for some chaplains to be sowing the foundations of faith while other chaplains experience a harvesting.

—Military Chaplain

Tension and Balance

Chaplains minister in tension while sustaining a balance. There is a four-way balance for chaplains: serving God, serving people, serving the institution that employs them, and serving their endorsing faith group. There is a tension between their ecclesial body and the institution that employs them. There is the tension of being a spiritual caregiver to all people while serving as a religious provider to some. Many chaplains ask, "Am I caring for this person because he is a member of the institution, or am I caring for him as a provider of his faith requirements?" There is another tension between being inclusive of all faith traditions and not compromising a chaplain's specific beliefs.

Chaplains sustain acceptable and supportable coexistence between adherents of different religions. It is more than being nonsectarian. It includes proactively engaging ministry with a commitment to teamwork, mutual respect, understanding, and realizing that a narrowly partisan denominational viewpoint will actually bring more harm than benefit to people associated with their chaplain.

FOUR-WAY BALANCE	Serving God	Serving People	Serving the Institution (Employs Chaplain)	Serving the Faith Group (Endorses Chaplain)
Tension 1:			Tension between employer and endorser	
Tension 2:	Tension between role of spiritual facilitator and religious provider			
Tension 3:		Tension between caring for people as members of the institution and caring for people as provider of their faith requirements		
Tension 4:	Tension of not compromising own beliefs ...			... and being inclusive of all faith traditions

Practice of Access

Chaplains are access providers when it comes to the capability of facilitation. However, access is unidirectional. Chaplains advocate for people within the organization to have access to external religious groups. Access by organizational members to religious groups does not mean access of religious groups to members within the organization. Access is not reciprocal. It moves from inside the institution toward the outside community. Chaplains ensure religious access is one-way in order to protect organizational members. As an example, some churches practice what seems a beneficial ministry to local hospitals. On Sunday afternoon, volunteer church members gather as a group in the hospital lobby with the goal of canvassing all patients' rooms. Yet does this respect the patient who seeks privacy? Who will protect that patient from this seemingly well-intentioned group? Is their ministry more about the needs of church members or the needs of patients?

To accommodate requests from outside religious groups seeking access to people within the institution, it is recommended that a chaplain maintain a physical or virtual community bulletin board announcing neighborhood faith group activities. This is a proactive way to sustain rapport with external faith groups while remaining fair to all. It is also respectful in restraining outside religious groups from reaching in without prior permission. Chaplains safeguard their organizations by not permitting access of outside faith groups to their people unless invited.

I served at a military installation where a local church bus would drive onto base each Sunday and stop at the barracks. After the driver pushed the bus horn, a loudspeaker would invite enlisted personnel to jump on the bus for transportation to the church, followed by a free potluck lunch. While I never doubted the good intentions of this ministry, I stopped the bus from driving on base because there were no airmen asking for the bus. The church's "bus ministry to airmen" was an initiative by the church and presumed access of the church bus onto the base. Access always falls one direction: from the airman toward the church or employee toward the religious service.

—*Military Chaplain*

Discussion Questions

1. What is the difference between orthodoxy and orthopraxy?
2. What happens when a chaplain cannot directly provide religious services for another faith group?
3. How does a chaplain develop a robust lay leader program?
4. What religious observances and holy days are essential to your faith group?

5. What are several constraints that might impact a chaplain's facilitation of an employee's religious practices?

6. Where will members within an organization turn when they seek permission to wear a visible clothing accessory identifying their faith?

7. Under what conditions is it reasonable for the organization to define what religious apparel is neat, discreet, and conservative?

8. What would you do as a chaplain if an employer allows someone to wear a necklace with a visible cross yet prohibits another employee from wearing a necklace with a pentagram pendent?

9. You are a campus chaplain and a student comes to you asking that you intercede on his behalf. Due to religious objections, he refuses to receive an immunization and requests that you provide him with a waiver. What will you do?

10. The US Equal Employment Opportunity Commission (EEOC) states: "Unless it would be an undue hardship on the employer's operation of its business, an employer must reasonably accommodate an employee's religious beliefs or practices." What is meant by "undue"? Give an example.

11. What is cooperative pluralism? Why is it typically not practiced in local churches? How does it align with the principle of *cooperation without compromise*?

12. Describe what is meant by tension and balance in chaplaincy ministry.

13. What principle is practiced when a chaplain advocates for people within the organization to have access to external religious groups? Why isn't access reciprocal?

CHAPTER 4

The Chaplain as Caregiver

Tell me how much you know of the sufferings of your
fellow humans, and I will tell you how much you have
loved them.

—*Theologian Helmut Thielicke*

4.1 Definition of Care and Caregiving

Chaplains are uniquely qualified to deliver professional care, pastoral counseling, and coaching to members at every level of their institution. Don't be surprised that most opportunities to care for others reach beyond a faith-specific context. Those who come to chaplains for help do not typically recognize you as their worship leader. They may know you are a religious person, but they will not likely understand or value your faith tradition. They seek you as a professional who cares about people.

Caring for others is the baseline for who we are as chaplains. While employees dedicate their time and energy to advance the mission of the company, they gain assurance that the chaplain's focus is on them. They believe chaplains value their welfare as an end in itself, even above the mission of the organization. When affirming the core responsibility of giving care, a chaplain confidently says, "Everyone else is focused on the mission. I am the one person, chartered by the institution, to care for everyone else while they remain focused on the mission."

Chaplains gravitate toward restoring and sustaining the well-being of others. Seminary education, paired with the chaplain's temperament, reinforces skills and expertise needed to accomplish the important work of genuinely supporting others. A new chaplain will discover opportunities to demonstrate authentic care for someone, and there will be others in the organization who observe the chaplain translating care into concern and active engagement. Pastoral opportunities soon expand as people gain confidence in their chaplain. You will hopefully find great satisfaction knowing that you've become a valued member of the organization when someone offhandedly and unexpectedly introduces you to a new employee as "our" chaplain instead of "the" chaplain.

When I served as chaplain aboard a crowded ship of 420 sailors, my room doubled as a place to live as well as a place to counsel. There was not enough space on the vessel for two locations. My room had a bunk bed, a desk, and two chairs. Upon arrival, I glued a plastic sign to my door that read "Open 24 hours." Anyone, at any time, deserved to have immediate access to his chaplain. What better way to connect with those of "no religious preference" than to identify as perpetually available?

I didn't count the cost of these words hanging on the door. It was during our first overseas port visit that I discovered an unanticipated problem. Immediately after the workday, sailors went "on liberty." Many returned to the ship late in the evening. If they had a few drinks ashore, they were more inclined to swing by my office toward midnight to share their deeper yet somewhat cloudy concerns. After a brief conversation, I would recognize their pattern of chattiness and gently invite them to continue our discussion the next day. They would generally be polite, grateful, and depart. Yet they rarely returned. It occurred to me that inebriation not only served to increase their boldness to talk but also dulled memory of our conversation. I was frustrated by my lack of sleep and their lack of boundaries.

It then occurred to me that it was not their problem but mine. I was the one who wasn't clarifying personal time boundaries and could not continue living the fallacy of perpetual availability. Late evening conversations kept me from being alert during the workday. Realizing this self-inflicted issue, I purchased another sign and glued it on top of the first. Replacing "Open 24 hours," the new sign read "Emergencies anytime. Otherwise, open at 8 a.m." The problem was solved!

—*Military Chaplain*

Proximity and availability are core values for flourishing chaplains. They are ingredients for sustaining the competency of care. The chaplain needs to be close to his people. He must ensure that his schedule allocates specific windows of time, in advance, to intentionally spend with people. He needs to prod himself to follow through with honoring those times, even when energy levels and interests may beg redirection. It is far too easy for chaplains to sequester themselves in their offices with "urgent" needs, such as e-mail and worship preparation. For a chaplain, nothing replaces the important need of merely being present with one's people.

As chaplains are integrated into the fabric of the organization, people seek them more frequently as a source for advice, mentoring, information, coaching, guidance, and support. Chaplains understand the circumstances of others within the organization because they are impacted by the same events. Pastoral care becomes more effective when based on strong relationships developed in the context of shared community life within the institution.

Organizational leaders trust their chaplains to care and counsel others outside of a faith-specific context. They value the chaplain as a "safety valve" for their people. As senior leaders, they will recommend the chaplain to others because they are confident that their chaplain cares for every person. They understand that quality pastoral care rests on a firm foundation of commonly shared experiences, the proximity of the chaplain to the counselee, and the chaplain's commitment to maintain confidentiality. Executives expect their chaplain to continually innovate new and creative ways to be available. As an example, an on-call hospital chaplain could make rounds after midnight to check in with the night-shift staff. The nurses and staff will be grateful to see the chaplain deliberately caring for them at inconvenient and less busy times.

Caring for both religious and nonreligious members is not limited to pastoral counseling. Whereas counseling is frequently focused on problem solving, intervention, and short-term challenges, chaplains also offer preventive training with the hope of avoiding disruptive or self-destructive experiences. In support of this training, chaplains participate in a number of preventive programmatic initiatives. They are expected to research, develop, and teach topics such as suicide prevention, domestic violence, substance abuse, sexual assault, and victimization. Chaplains serving in first-responder or military contexts are knowledgeable of critical-incident and operational-stress issues. Chaplains frequently teach competency development in moral and ethical decision making, resiliency, and conflict resolution.

Chaplains hang out around college students, comfort hospice patient family members, coach incarcerated members, and serve coffee to first responders throughout a community crisis. They offer support, advice, comfort, and referrals when appropriate. Examples of chaplain care include pastoral counseling, modeling communication skills, inspiring hope, confronting fear, addressing end-of-life issues, understanding shame and guilt, and coaching in life skills.

I worked with nearly four hundred employees in the aftermath of their most popular employee collapsing and dying at the office. He was only twenty-four years old and already recognized as the most ambitious and successful sales representative. With the very public and tragic death of their "Player of the Year," the entire organization was traumatized. Efforts to reengage productive work were paralyzed. The open-office collaborative workspace, designed without any walls or cubicle barriers, eerily fell silent. Management offices, with glass walls, sealed their doors in whispered isolation.

As chaplain, my caregiving started by listening to employees and helping them process their grief and shock. For most, this was their closest experience with death. Their mourning was compounded by the young age of the deceased. The care process included distributing a list of available counseling times for one-on-ones. I also met with each department team of twelve to twenty employees at a time, and we walked through common patterns of grief. It was valuable to create space for open conversation. We held a corporate memorial service at the company auditorium. A week later, the funeral was at the deceased family's church. Employees were granted permission to attend his funeral service and burial. The management was highly supportive of these initiatives. They wanted to move through the mourning process and quickly refocus their employees back to the business.

The most challenging experience was gathering colleagues of the deceased into the small conference room where he collapsed. Only those who were in the room with him at the time were invited. Everyone witnessed his death. Several tried unsuccessfully to revive him. One immediately called paramedics. All carried a heavy burden of guilt alongside their grief. As a group they echoed, "We could have done more."

I encouraged them to gather in a circle around the inside wall of the conference room. I invited them to return to the moment when they saw him collapse. We discussed what they would have done differently. Most realized they did all they could. They thanked their colleague who had the presence of mind to call 911. I invited them to share words acknowledging their friendship with the deceased, his attributes, and what they most deeply felt in this moment.

We then, as a group, committed to care for one another as we moved through this process. I suggested they not avoid the conference room in the future. Instead, they could acknowledge their colleague every time they entered in remembrance of his friendship and dedication to their company. I recommended the management consider honoring the deceased by dedicating the room to his memory and adding a plaque recognizing his contribution.

As you look at chaplaincy, please know tragic events like this are not the chaplain's responsibility to solve. They are opportunities to walk alongside people who are digging deeper into their own faith or perhaps thinking faith for their first time. In the process, you move from being a chaplain to becoming *their* chaplain.

—*Corporate Chaplain*

As of the end of the second decade in the twenty-first century, "Christianity has been rapidly declining in the United States while the number of Americans who are religiously unaffiliated is growing. Gallup polls have found a massive, three-decade fall in confidence in 'organized religion' from as high as 66 percent in the mid-1980s to 36 percent in 2019."[1] Simultaneous with this decline, the fastest-growing group of people that chaplains care for is not management or labor, student or faculty, prisoner or guard, officer or enlisted, Gen X or millennial. The fastest-growing group is "no religious preference," or "nones." A Harris poll conducted in 2013 indicated that while a strong majority (74 percent) of adults believe in God, "nearly one-fourth of Americans (23 percent) identified themselves as not at all religious—a figure that has nearly doubled since 2007."[2] In 2013, National Public Radio reported, "One-fifth of Americans are religiously unaffiliated—higher than at any time in recent US history—and those younger than thirty especially seem to be drifting from organized religion."[3] Pew Research Center corroborates this trend in their massive 2014 Religious Landscape Study: "Religious 'nones'—a shorthand we use to refer to people who self-identify as atheists or agnostics, as well as those who say their religion is 'nothing in particular'—now make up roughly 23 percent of the US adult population."[4]

These "nones" are not necessarily atheist or agnostic. Many moved from mainstream religions into New Age movements, where they report being spiritual but not religious.[5] Additionally, the expression "no religious preference" does not necessarily mean no religion at all. In March 2017, the Department of Defense addressed the potential ambiguity by revising their service members' faith and belief categories.[6] The category of "no religious preference" was removed and replaced by specific categories, including "atheist," "agnostic," "no preference," "no religion," and "none provided." Also removed was the category of "Protestant, no denominational preference." Many service members did not identify with the word "Protestant" and previously listed themselves as "no religious preference." One National Guard chaplain commented to me that in his survey, he found a majority of soldiers who had been listed as "no religious preference" (removed as an option) actually wanted to be listed as "Christian, no denominational preference."

When is a "none" also a Baptist? During freshman orientation, my campus chaplain colleagues and I met with 1,300 new students in a large auditorium. Around the room were handmade signs with titles on them such as Roman Catholic, Protestant, Christian Science, Orthodox, Jewish, Muslim, Latter-day Saint, Buddhist, Hindu, and No Religious Preference. At the end of our initial welcome, the freshmen dispersed to their self-identified group in order to meet their faith-specific leader. After several minutes, everyone settled down with their group. Although a Protestant chaplain, I asked to meet with the No Religious Preference group, because when I was in college I most identified with that group. There were just over 100 students in this group. I initially spoke: "Just to confirm you're in the right place, I want to make sure there's not anyone here with religious convictions that aren't obvious through any of these other signs that we see around the room. Are we missing any faith groups?" And one young man timidly raised his hand and said, "Yes." I asked him which one, and he said, "I'm Baptist. I don't see a sign for Baptist." I asked if any other people sitting in this group were Baptist, and about twenty people raised their hands. I said, "You know, it's safe to go to the Protestant group, as Baptists are historically aligned with Protestant theology." They trusted me enough to stand up and walk over to the Protestant group to join many other classmates under the large yet frequently misunderstood Protestant banner. Many Christians no longer identify with the word "Protestant." They rather self-identify as Methodist, Baptist, Pentecostal, charismatic, Church of Christ, Nazarene, Disciples of Christ, evangelical, Brethren, Reformed, independent, fundamental, or simply Christian with no denominational preference. They may resent that their unique group is lumped together under the Protestant umbrella. The term "Christian" may be too wide, while the word "Protestant" may be unfamiliar.

—College Chaplain

Caring for those who self-identify with "no religious preference" is incredibly significant to a chaplain's ministry. They may not adhere to any readily identifiable faith group. They may not define spirituality in religious terms. They may be atheist or agnostic. Nevertheless, chaplains can intentionally communicate these three points to them with confidence, because chaplains understand that human faith transcends the limits of any label.

1. *I am here for you.* Whether they have a need or not for your services as a chaplain, as long as they are part of the organization, you belong to them. You must intentionally communicate that you are approachable and provide them easy access. Even though they may have never talked to a clergyperson before arriving at their new organization, they now have access to a chaplain. The invitation is open-ended as you share the following message through your actions and words: "I am here for you!"

2. *I invite you to explore deeper.* You are a safe person encouraging them to grow deeper in their life's journey. You might say, "I invite you to explore your questions about spiritual growth. I don't need *my* faith to change you. I want *your* faith to change you." You can walk alongside them on their spiritual expedition. You communicate an availability to provide them resources even if you don't agree with the theology or philosophy of the faith they are exploring. You hope and pray that your unequivocal support of their journey will allow opportunities for them to ask you questions about faith because you've created a trusting relationship. If they initiate a question and invite you to respond, you can offer a silent prayer of thanksgiving, then engage them with your own faith-influenced answer.

3. *I invest in you as you prepare for your future.* Chaplains frequently connect with current or future leaders within their organization. Leaders are always looking for ways to better understand people. Leaders would be wise to recognize the significance of religious conviction that is practiced by those they serve. A chaplain might say, "Religion matters to your people and is a motivator for them. If you're a leader in an organization, you may want to learn more about religion, because it's a fact that faith motivates people."

The core capability of caring for others is clearly the domain of chaplain ministry. Plus, as a bonus, your care for others often leads to reciprocation. People tend to care for those who care for them. The mutuality of care rewards a chaplain's sense of purpose and increases a chaplain's sense of belonging to the organization.

I would walk around campus, meet people where they are, and introduce myself as the new chaplain. Somewhere in the conversation, I would invite the person to share with me any faith preferences they might have. When someone mentioned that they best affiliated with the "nones," I would respond that they were receiving a special benefit from me because I was a "nones" chaplain. I would introduce myself to agnostic and atheist students, coaches, and faculty members as well. I assured them that I would be available to them just as much as I would be for anyone else in the organization. I am reminded of Paul, who said, "I have become all things to all people, that by all means I might save some" (1 Cor. 9:22). As their chaplain, you communicate, "I'm investing in you. I have the privilege of caring for you."

—*College Chaplain*

4.2 Pastoral Counseling in Chaplaincy

Giving care is the broadest scope of chaplaincy. Everybody needs and deserves care. When a chaplain extends pastoral counseling by meeting with someone, it doesn't mean the chaplain drives the counseling agenda. Instead, the chaplain listens to understand the counselee's context. In a church setting, most of the people pastors counsel are already attending the church. Many have previously become members, and pastors have established a long, and typically deep, relationship. In chaplaincy, there are many more people seeking counsel who are not Christian. They are looking for short-term resolutions to minor issues that are not specifically faith focused. The dialogue is frequently not anchored in a long-term relationship, and conversations circle around emergent issues that impact work, health, family, and the uncertainty of life. Christian chaplains can provide specific faith-focused counseling, yet they don't presume upon others unless the context is obvious and they are invited to share.

Many organizations look to their chaplain as the pivotal person to deliver unwelcome news. How can a chaplain in receipt of distressing information prepare the hearer? It could start with, "I have some news. It is not good news. I need you to please have a seat before I continue. Your daughter was in an accident. She may not survive." This information brings shock and pain to the recipient. It may be the worst news the person has ever received. Dreadful news brings psychological and spiritual trauma to the recipient. After you deliver the pain, a recipient may avoid you because you remind the person of that pain. The bee that inflicts the sting may not be welcomed back. Your pastoral relationship is compromised. Who is now going to help that person live with the news?

A better idea may be to accompany the person delivering bad news. This allows the chaplain to help the recipient cope and live with the news. For example, in the hospital a doctor delivers the bad news to family. You posture yourself with the suffering, not the doctor. The DNA of the trauma will be on the doctor's face. The spouse is looking at the doctor's eyes when receiving the worst news of his life. You are now in a position to help the family member live with the news. The ability of chaplains to be present with family members changed seismically during the coronavirus pandemic. Visitors were restricted from patient rooms, waiting rooms, and hospital cafeterias. "While exceptions can be granted, many patients are hospitalized without ever having loved ones beside them." Chaplains responded in creative ways as they became intermediaries between patients and families. Laurent LeBien, staff chaplain at East Jefferson General Hospital near New Orleans, "arranges phone calls and FaceTime meetings between patients and their families. He stays in regular contact with their loved ones so that when patients awake, he can offer encouraging updates."[7] Adaptability and compassion remain hallmarks of chaplaincy.

> Dreadful news removes all sense of reality for the person receiving the news. This often moves the recipient into a state of emotional shock. A person may not hear anything else that is said. The chaplain can, and should, practically help the recipient remember what was said. Hold them as they cry (with permission, of course). Help them figure out how to use a phone. Be incarnationally the practical hands and feet of Jesus.
> —*Hospital Chaplain*

Chaplains and pastors have a unique opportunity to offer what no one else can provide. No clinical counselor or therapist has the same freedom to talk about God, faith, grace, love, and hope in the context of counseling. Chaplains understand that what they offer is different from the psychological sciences. They are not to presume they are clinicians, unless they have the requisite degrees and certifications. Chaplains know their limits and make timely referrals to appropriate clinical providers. Minister and professor Craig Barnes speaks for many in the pastoral care field when he writes, in *The Pastor as Minor Poet*, "I'm not a marriage counselor. I respect therapists too much to impersonate one. So I always make a careful referral when speaking to couples in crisis."[8] Although most chaplains are not clinicians, they offer what no secular therapist can: pastoral care and counseling. You can gain clarity on what you have to offer by developing and trusting your pastoral identity. People come to you because you are the chaplain, and most of the time they have little expectation for therapy or long-term counseling.

Pastoral Counseling as a Skilled Helper

The confidence that you are called into this incredible ministry starts with a foundation of faithfulness. A valued way to display this confidence entrusted to you by God, your faith group, and your employer is to communicate attentiveness to all who seek you. Active listening and engagement are foundational in making others feel welcome. A useful and easy-to-remember acronym for communicating effective body language when offering pastoral counseling is SOLER. These nonverbal communication skills were bundled together by Gerard Egan, professor emeritus at Loyola University of Chicago, as part of his "skilled helper" approach to counseling.[9]

S: Sit *squarely* with the person you are with, preferably at a five o'clock position to avoid the possibility of staring. Sitting squarely says, "I'm here with you, I'm available to you. There are no other distractions."

O: Maintain an *open* posture at all times. Avoid crossing your arms or legs because you could appear defensive. Stay in this open position despite a boring conversation or whether it is the fifth pastoral care appointment before lunch. Your posture causes others to feel welcomed and engaged.

L: *Lean* slightly toward the person you are counseling. This says, "I'm with you, I'm interested in you and involved in what you have to say." Leaning back can suggest the opposite. But remember not to lean too far forward, or you may be seen as placing a demand on the counselee. She may find it intimidating.

E: Maintain *eye contact* without staring. Your gaze shows that you are not distracted. It's another way of saying, "I'm interested, I'm with you." Be normal and make sure to blink.

R: *Relax.* It is important to stay calm. If you are restless, it will derail the conversation and distract the counselee. If you relax, this should help the counselee unwind and breathe out stress and anxiety. If the counselee communicates from a foundation of faith, you might begin with an invitation, "Hey, would you like us to start with a brief moment of silence or prayer?"

I received this letter written by a local church pastor: "This wasn't a year I planned on. In late June, my wife was diagnosed with glioblastoma, an aggressive and incurable form of brain cancer. Sadly, the cancer took her life in December. Throughout that six-month journey we saw God's hand at work in many places and people. One of the remarkable aspects of this unwanted pilgrimage were hospital chaplains who cared for us, sat with us, cried with us and walked with us. Other than family, the first person to sit with me was you. You are gifted at being the hands and feet of Jesus to those in need. Further into our journey, God brought other chaplains to us who also cradled our souls and spirits during difficult times. Hospital chaplains are an incredible blessing."

—Hospital Chaplain

Chaplains often work with relatively healthy populations. Armed forces members undergo an extended preenlistment screening. Employees within an institution are hired following a job interview. Faculty members frequently receive additional training regarding indicators of student mental health and wellness. Health-care professionals, first responders, and correctional institution employees have unique professional organizations that commonly address mental health. Yet relatively healthy people also need help. All will have problems. All will face trouble or crisis. All will not be as effective as they want to be. All of them, including their family members and friends, may seek a chaplain.

The three-stage "skilled helper" model, developed by Egan in conjunction with SOLER, works well with a healthy population. It focuses more on prevention than on cure because it encourages people to own and solve their problems. It also helps the chaplain know when it is appropriate to refer. The framework is simple and walks counselees through three stages to help them consider their present state, their preferred state, and the process from the former to the latter.[10]

1. The present: Where are you now?
   - Help the counselee tell his story (open questions, SOLER).
   - Help the counselee break through any blind spots (use reflection).
   - Help the counselee find the right issues to focus on (prioritize and leverage).
2. The preferred: Where do you want to be?
   - Help the counselee imagine specific possibilities (explore his views).
   - Help the counselee discover realistic goals (agenda of choices and changes).
   - Help the counselee find personal incentives (what he gains from commitment).
3. The process: How are you going to get where you want to be?
   - Help the counselee find possible actions (timing and phasing).

- Help the counselee find personal strategies (what will work best).
- Help the counselee identify obstacles (potential advocacy).
- Help connect the faith-filled person to her source of strength, hope, and meaning.

Pastoral Advocacy

Chaplains provide a listening ear and position themselves to be prayer advocates. They encourage others to discover pathways to owning and solving adverse situations. Advocacy is a legitimate function of chaplaincy, and chaplains frequently feel obligated to advocate for others. Pastoral advocacy supports the counselee by building an awareness and understanding of factors within the organizational culture that will help reduce conflict or produce change. In a sense, the chaplain serves as a broker between the institution and the individual. This aligns with the professional competencies expected of a chaplain to "Advocate for the persons in one's care."[11]

As chaplains grow in credibility and gain influence, institutional leaders are able to make better decisions that serve to decrease systemic causes of conflict and promote positive transformation. The determined voice of chaplains can help change lives. They seek to serve people who truly need advocacy. This requires insight. Some counselees can but won't solve their own problems. They want a chaplain to intervene on their behalf because they are impatient or out of manipulation. Yet indiscriminate advocacy will eliminate the chaplain's credibility to influence. The chaplain needs discernment to know whether to advocate or, instead, redirect the counselee toward identifying obstacles and discovering alternative actions and personal strategies. If the chaplain is careless with advocacy, there is a loss of credibility and the chaplain may lose future opportunities of interceding for others. Choose your moments wisely.

There are at least three types of advocacy skills required of chaplains. Seasoned chaplains seek to differentiate between the three and respond in ways that best support the individual and the organization.

1. Institutions need chaplains who can identify unacceptable treatment by leaders, supervisors, and peers. People come to chaplains with legitimate cases of injustice, seeking to gain resolution. They

need someone offering confidentiality. They also understand that the chaplain may have the ability to potentially intercede at multiple levels of the organizational structure. Chaplains who advocate for these people also have a desire to help supervisors recognize the impact of their actions. Chaplains suggest appropriate ways of balancing mission priorities while sustaining a commitment to the well-being of others.

2. Institutions need chaplains who can guide and mentor others toward responsible behavior even when duties are difficult and unpleasant. Some employees and other beneficiaries avoid accountability. They inappropriately associate being held accountable to being a victim. The chaplain can help them recognize that organizational leadership is reasonable when asking them to "pull their weight." Chaplains best help these individuals by listening and gently helping them reframe their circumstance using an alternative perspective. Chaplains can then discuss effective skills to build resilience and endurance.

3. Institutions need chaplains to care for those who find themselves under an unpleasant spotlight as either a troublemaker or an underperformer. These individuals frequently come to the chaplain asking for a bailout. You cannot do what they need to do themselves. Chaplains can coach and care for them while sustaining an unswerving commitment to organizational values. Chaplains can also discuss reasonable expectations for all members to respect and uphold.

Extending Care toward Others

Chaplains care for all people within their organization—there are no exceptions. A rabbi serving as a chaplain once said to me: "Everything you do doesn't begin out of faith, but out of love." Some chaplains might argue that protecting their faith-group doctrine is paramount—as representative clergy, they may sense a preeminent obligation to defend the orthodoxy of their religion. This is shortsighted, however, since chaplains have an equal obligation to minister in the institutions they serve. Balancing the dual obligation of protecting and defending doctrine, which may be of low value in a nonreligious or faith-hostile institutional context, with caring for everyone in the chaplain's domain is challenging.

The defensive posture of chaplains may make them more judgmental and perceived as less open, which prevents them from being fully accessible to their community. Imposing their doctrine on each individual in the institution can have unintended consequences: think of the common caricature of a minister readily practicing theological repair upon people who don't see themselves as broken. Contrast this with chaplains who are fully engaged with a pastoral commitment to others. Regularly stretched beyond the boundary of orthodoxy, these chaplains grasp that God's pronouncement on the tower of Babel resulted in diversity rather than homogeneity. It is in this diverse and sometimes turbulent society that chaplains are called to live.

When someone in their organization claims a different faith or no faith at all, some chaplains may bypass that person. Understanding human nature, this response makes sense as a desire to avoid awkward and confrontational experiences. Just like the nurses, soldiers, athletes, and scholars we serve, we participate by moving toward discomfort and being willing to feel awkward in our efforts to minister. Whenever chaplains feel safe and secure that everyone close to them is in agreement with their doctrine, the credibility of their ministry is at risk. Many don't have "the skills and emotional practice needed to 'lean into discomfort.'"[12] Few things are currently as relevant for moving toward discomfort as when chaplains meet people who embrace a different understanding of human sexuality than their doctrine acknowledges. Yet the gospel narratives show that Jesus did not call spiritual leaders to avoid uncomfortable situations but to foster connections, especially with those who feel excluded and disenfranchised. Chaplains are called to indiscriminately extend themselves toward others. God's desire is for chaplains to meet people on the frontier of their faith, as well as ours. It is God who opens people's hearts and brings us together by divine appointment.

When asked about his connection to campus chaplains, a gay university student said, "I don't want to hear that God loves me despite my sexuality. I want to hear that God loves me for who I am. I look for a chaplain who validates me for my humanness and not as a project." If your doctrine isn't inclusive or affirming of the LGBT+ community, then you will need to remember your dual obligation as chaplain and prevent your doctrine from making your overall ministry in a secular setting ineffective. Consider the tension parents may feel upon discovering something they disapprove about their children that they may eventually accept. Chaplains also have to discover how acceptance may not be the same as approval. Yet there is no excuse for avoidance—the stakes are too high. Only after this self-work is addressed can a chaplain provide resources that support the people chaplains are called to serve.

As we care for people who are transgender, gender-fluid, and nonbinary, it is about educating ourselves as chaplains on terms and pronouns and having a spirit of learning. When I am not sure how to address someone in an encounter, I make sure that I ask the question and become that "safe place" to receive the answer. When I mess up, such as using the wrong name or pronoun with a patient, I apologize. We can't know everything, and our ministry is about remembering that each person is made in the image of God and that we are called to provide care. As chaplains, and especially as chaplain leaders, we should be aware of our biases and be ready to confront our own "stuff" in order to be present with others.

—Hospital Chaplain

Chaplains should consider offering those who identify as LGBT+ the following particular care:

1. *Familiarity*. Know your people and let them know God loves them. Many within the LGBT+ community feel ignored, or even traumatized, by the church and do not sense God's love. How are humans supposed to feel God's love? They are to feel it from the people who claim to follow him and minister on his behalf. Another student offers this advice to chaplains: "Don't spend our time together talking about how I am different. I've a shaky relationship with Christianity already because I've been told that I have not been built right. I've been told I am unlovable. If you spend your entire life hearing you are wrong for not being on the original script of what it means to be human, it tears away your self-worth." Chaplains are called to communicate God's presence and love to all people, especially those who are struggling. Remember this context as you work to make people feel comfortable and affirmed in their intrinsic value as humans and your unconditional love for God's creation. Chaplains communicate familiarity by saying, "I'm sorry you've been hurt. I want to support you."

2. *Resources*. Chaplains are there to communicate that they have the resources available to support spiritual growth for everyone. They offer these resources by building relationships, not by pushing content out of context. If a chaplain hears from someone, "Hey, I want to begin my spiritual journey, but I also would like to reconcile this journey with my sexual preference or gender identity," then it would be unhelpful to respond, "I've never thought of this before. This is new to me and I don't know what to do." Chaplains should inform

themselves of the wide range of resources that are available. While some spiritual and relational resources may be specifically written in support of those within the LGBT+ community, many resources are common for everyone. Chaplains can listen and learn about specific resources from those within the LGBT+ community by occasionally and respectfully attending LGBT+ group meetings within their organization. This demonstrates accessibility as well as openness to discovering new resources that would be most helpful.

3. *Support.* Let people know you are available to talk—and to listen. Don't wait until they've experienced spiritual or emotional trauma. A chaplain's goal is to create an open door by inviting counselees to share the difficulties of life's journey. Many within the LGBT+ community share a desire for support but can't get it: "When I go to my chaplain, I keep my self-identity out of the conversation because I want the chaplain to treat me as normal. I wish I could share deeper but fear the chaplain won't believe I'm normal." How many of us transfer this experience of being judged by church and clergy to how we are judged by God? All humans have deep fears and insecurities, and we are all designed to have our need for acceptance satisfied in an ultimately loving and merciful God. If chaplains can't provide spiritual care for those who have been previously wounded by the church, then who will?

4.3 Eight Quick Counseling Questions

When a prospective counselee comes to a chaplain, the chaplain ensures that the person knows she is talking with a religious professional and not a therapist. Frequently, conversations start with a relational or vocational problem and suddenly go to a deeper place where spiritual and soul-descriptive words are used. The chaplain cannot presume diving deeper into this topic without making sure the counselee is consenting to the conversation. When counseling as a faith group representative, the chaplain would be wise to remember that there is a difference between informed consent and presumed consent. There is a reasonable presumption that the chaplain will not infuse his religion into the conversation unless invited. Inviting the counselee to listen to your theology and receiving her acknowledgment are insufficient. Rather, seek affirmation and not mere acknowledgment from the counselee. The counselee might ask, "Chaplain, how do you see this situation?" The chaplain may respond, "Well, I often look at issues through the lens of my faith. Would that be a beneficial perspective for you?" If the counselee provides an affirmation beyond an unenthusiastic "okay," then the chaplain can share from the heart.

As you care for people through pastoral counseling, counselees will share the experience with their peers. As a result, others will seek you for emotional support, relational reconciliation, and spiritual encouragement. There is an old French proverb: "To heal, sometimes. To remedy, often. To comfort, always." Chaplains typically hold most of their counseling appointments in the context of a private space, like an office, where a third party, such as the office administrator, may observe but not listen to the conversation. This is done to protect both the chaplain and the counselee. To remain above reproach, keep the office door open. Consider playing background music to safeguard privacy while ensuring full transparency. When someone makes an appointment to see you, it might help to have a standardized rubric of questions. Please keep in mind that these eight questions are not necessarily in order, yet they build upon answers to previous questions. Also, every question need not be verbalized. Many counselees answer multiple questions in one answer.[13]

1. *Why are you telling me **this**?*
    Why is it important for you to tell me this information?

2. *Why are you telling this **to me**?*
    Why did you pick me to talk to? Are you telling me this because I'm your chaplain? Are you telling everyone this?

3. *Why are you telling this to me **now**?*
    Why did you pick this time to talk about this? Is there an emergent crisis? For example, in the military chaplaincy, counseling always increases immediately before a required family separation due to deployment. Deployment places tremendous pressure upon relationships and generates a mountain of stress, anxiety, and symptoms of grief. Predeployment decision making is often difficult due to the impending separation. Deeply committed relationships flare up with unexpected conflict due to the instability. Pebbles of concern become boulders of problems.

4. *Now that you've talked with me about this, **what do you need to do**?*
    Empower counselees by placing responsibility back on them.

Some people come to you because you are an authority figure and they want you to tell them what to do. If you recommend the wrong course of action, then you will be blamed. As a pastoral counselor, you need to draw a distinction between being responsible *to* this person and being responsible *for* this person. Chaplains are responsible *to* but not responsible *for* the person. This places physical responsibility and psychological action back upon the counselee and releases you to truly listen and be available. There is a distinction between needing and wanting. If a counselee says to you, "I want you to fix this," your response is, "What do you *need* to do?" You don't ask, "What do you *want* to do?"[14]

A married sailor left the ship, got drunk, and proceeded to engage a prostitute. The next morning, he came to my office with a headache, feeling bad, and confessing his conduct. He asked me to fix the problem by making him feel better. Instead, I ask him, "What do you need to do? There are real consequences for negative behavior, and one consequence is for you to feel the pain of adultery." Unshaven and in tears, he sat in my office with his pain. He shuddered with the stinging and devastating consequences of his decision. Yet he did not try to escape his ache.

—Military Chaplain

Many people are hardwired to seek your counseling because of who you are. Your empathy and care draw them to you. However, you are not expected to carry their burdens. You provide greater benefit to them by walking alongside them. You will learn to balance counseling with other demands placed upon your ministry.

5. *Now that you've talked to me about this, **what do you expect me to do for you?***

This question reestablishes your center of gravity. Whereas the previous question revolves around intended action by the counselee, this question investigates any projected expectations upon you by the counselee—and by you as well. When conducting counseling, many chaplains typically overfocus on problem solving. As you listen to the counselee's concerns, you imagine a matrix of potential solutions, and you become distracted from listening because you're thinking of your response and possible ways of solving the problem. But you are not called to solve the counselee's problem. Instead, you are called to listen, be fully present, and be prayerful. You need to release yourself from expectations. Question 5 actually releases you.

There is risk to the counselor in asking this question. There are many needy people. Opening yourself up by allowing them to project their expectations upon you may be frustrating. But the reward far exceeds any burden. When chaplains ask this question, most people say, "I just want you to listen." Christians and other people of faith may also add, "I want you to pray for me." Their expectations are now meeting yours. Their answer actually decreases your anxiety, because it frees you to talk alongside them while they are actively trying to solve their problem. There will be times when someone has an unrealistic expectation from you. When this occurs, discuss whether the expectation is reasonable and allow the conversation to continue for additional sessions.

6.   *With all of this going on, **how are things with your soul?***
     Whereas the first five questions are available to any secular counselor, social worker, psychologist, or psychiatrist, only the spiritual caregiver asks this question. If your soul is healthy, then your mind, body, and will are in agreement.[15] If your soul is unhealthy, then one or more of these are likely out of alignment. Asking counselees to talk about their souls is an integrative discussion point. People often expect chaplains to ask about their soul, and it may open up a helpful theological discussion. You can shape this question in a variety of ways. With nonreligious counselees, you can substitute "self" for "soul." If they are atheist or agnostic, then you might ask them, "How are things with your heart?" or "How are you doing as an integrated, whole person?" If they attend Christian chapel services, you could ask, "How are you seeing God in this? How is your connection with Jesus impacted by your situation?"

7.   *With all of this going on, **would you like me to pray with you?***
     Because people know you are a pastoral care provider, you can invite them into a source of strength beyond the moment. You can reshape the question as a statement: "I can offer prayer for

you, if you'd like me to." The question is invitational and not impositional. Prayer is not mandatory during the appointment. In fact, it can be seen as dismissive. The chaplain could be tired of hearing about the issue, so the chaplain offers a prayer to conclude a long conversation. Chaplains need to conduct a careful self-assessment in order to best appraise if prayer would be a helpful tool or not. Nevertheless, you will likely be the only person in the organization expected to invite others into prayer.

As a pastoral counselor, you serve as an instrument of God's grace as you listen to people's deepest concerns and lift them up in prayer. The invitation to pray opens a conversation where you ask people to identify specific prayer concerns that relate to their presenting issue. Many people seem eager for prayer, but not all. Before you offer a prayer, you might say, "I offer prayer from my Christian tradition." If there is affirmation beyond acknowledging an okay, then you have permission to proceed. If a counselee doesn't want you to pray in your tradition, you could invite him into a moment of silence before concluding the appointment. Alternatively, some chaplains feel comfortable offering prayer from a variety of faith traditions. They caution not to provide a "one-size-fits-all approach to prayer" and ask the patient, prisoner, or other counselee what concerns warrant prayer.

8. *With all of this going on, **what are you going to do now?***
   This question migrates question 4's *What do you need to do?* into action. Whereas question 4 empowers people to own their issue, this question activates their ownership. It translates the static problem toward dynamic resolution. You are giving them an opportunity to do something tangible toward solving their problem. You encourage by helping them be personally accountable for a first and immediate action step. They are verbally acknowledging, "I will do this." Their commitment to action becomes the launch point of your next conversation.

As mentioned before introducing these questions, you do not need to keep these eight quick questions in order, but they are designed to build upon the previous answers. Additionally, they serve to migrate the conversation from reflection toward action. If these questions do not capture your voice, then modify them to what best fits you. For example, if someone comes to you and bears her soul, then you might not jump directly into question 1, "Why are you telling me this?" That would likely feel threatening. Instead, you can affirm her and the complexity of her situation, and then you can transition into question 2, "Wow. I want to affirm you and acknowledge the huge burden that you are sharing. I would be interested in hearing how you decided to trust me enough to disclose this information." This allows you to gain a sense of her expectations that brought her into your office. Be aware that many times counselees' presenting issue is not the actual problem at all. The present problem is symptomatic of a deeper issue. However, it serves to bring them through your door. During the conversation, you gain clarity while simultaneously building their trust and confidence in your valued role as pastoral counselor.

4.4 Special Counseling Observations

Counselees regularly experience distress leading to significant personal and professional impairment. Chaplains frequently observe repetitive personality behaviors while conducting pastoral counseling. Is the response of counselees to issues relatively stable across time and situations? Is their response normative for their developmental stage or social environment? Is there an underlying cause, like substance abuse or a medical condition, contributing to this distress? In the context of pastoral care and counseling, *behavior* is not to be confused with *disorder*. A personality disorder is only diagnosable by a mental health professional. Chaplains are not qualified mental health professionals unless they have received specific education and earned appropriate certifications. To quote minister and professor Craig Barnes again, "I respect therapists too much to impersonate one."[16] Therefore, chaplains cannot diagnose personality disorders listed in the *Diagnostic and Statistical Manual of Mental Disorders* (*DSM-V*) or the fifth chapter of the International Classification of Diseases (ICD). However, the chaplain is often a gatekeeper[17] for referring counselees toward a mental health professional: "The majority of people with a personality disorder never come into contact with mental health services, and those who do usually do so in the context of another mental disorder or at a time of crisis, commonly after self-harming or breaking the law."[18]

Chaplains frequently find a recurrent pattern of three personality behaviors in their ministry. In fact, these behaviors are so common that we all do them at certain times to some degree.

Passive-Dependent Behavior

Behavior characterized by a pattern of neediness evident from an overreliance on others may be passive-dependent. The counselee frequently feels incompetent or helpless. Emotional and physical needs are met only by receiving care and reassurance from stronger figures. The result is a pattern of submissive and clinging behavior, often accompanied by a fear of separation or abandonment by important people in the counselee's life.

Individuals displaying passive-dependent behavior believe relationships with significant others, like their chaplain, are important for survival. They seek supportive relationships to manage their lives. To sustain these relationships, counselees will often avoid expressions of anger. They will volunteer for unpleasant tasks because that can bring the recognition they seek. They are frequently willing to accept extraordinary self-sacrifice in order to maintain valued bonds.

Which of the eight quick questions in the previous section do you think counselees expressing passive-dependent behavior will be most inclined to resist? It will likely be number 8: *With all of this going on, **what are you going to do now?*** When a passive-dependent person returns to your office for a future session and you ask him if he followed through, he will often respond, "No, I just can't get there." He can't seem to get it done. This is usually the starting point for the next counseling session and the one following. You will say, "Does it seem that we are at the same point we left the conversation last time we met?"

Our churches and chapels have many people fitting this pattern of behavior. These people are attracted to authority. Since there is no greater power than God—characterized in their life by a chaplain—they will make extraordinary self-sacrifices to maintain important bonds with you. Be aware that you are at risk of manipulating them. You allow them to volunteer for additional chapel responsibilities. You know they will be diligent in wanting to meet your expectations. You rationalize that their contribution will provide them a meaningful service opportunity. Yet you reinforce their perception that they exist for another person. Instead, you could support them in making their own choices and respecting their ability to act for themselves.

Sunday Christian worship services were held in the campus cafeteria immediately following breakfast. The cafeteria baker was a frequent counselee. Although he was never part of the Christian community, I appreciated the fact that he sought the chaplain. Yet it seemed he could never move forward toward resolving his problems. At first, I was flattered to be needed as a counselor. Yet after a while my sense of flattery moved to frustration. He was consuming much of my time with no apparent progress. He keenly discerned my growing anxiety. Without prompting, very early each Sunday morning he would bake fresh communion bread for the upcoming worship service. This became his weekly gift to the service. It took me too long to realize the communion bread was not being baked for the worshiping community. Nor was it being baked in service to Jesus. It was being baked as a way for him to sustain our relationship.

—College Chaplain

Keep a sharp lookout for people in your organization who keep investing more and more into the chapel program. Their goal may be to please you because they feel inadequate. There could be an unhealthy dependence on their chaplain. But note that this is not about you. Their attachment is positional and not personal. Passive-dependent behavior does not necessarily attach strongly to a specific individual. If you are reassigned and another chaplain follows you, the attachment will be forged to the new chaplain. Attachment figures are interchangeable.

You can't solve their issue. You can be enmeshed in it, as in the story of the chaplain and the baker in the preceding story, but you cannot do what they need to do themselves. They can't help telling you what you want to hear because they don't want to lose their relationship with you. Yet it won't solve their problem. You must set boundaries for your time and review the frequency of their appointment requests. After you've completed a series of short-term counseling sessions with them, it is likely time for a referral to a mental health specialist.

Passive-Aggressive Behavior

Passive-aggressive behavior was defined clinically by Brigadier General William Menninger during World War II. A psychiatrist, he studied soldiers' reactions to military compliance. Menninger described soldiers who were not openly insubordinate yet expressed their hostility "by passive measures, such as pouting, stubbornness, procrastination, inefficiency, and passive obstructionism."[19] Whatever context you serve as a chaplain, you will soon find yourself listening to people who express their behavior aggressively yet indirectly.

Many folks don't realize their behavior is passive-aggressive. Yet they end up in your office because their supervisor refers them to you with the expectation of a quick fix. The supervisor thinks the employee is sabotaging the mission. During your counseling, such people are pleasant and share how colleagues and management underappreciate them. They tell you that their supervisor finds it unacceptable to express anger at work. They say that the hierarchy of their workplace makes direct expression of anger seem like insubordination.

They develop indirect rather than direct communication methods. They become known for their hostile jokes, resentment, sullenness, and inefficiency. They may frequently find issues taking them away from work. It could be a sore muscle one week or a family problem the next. Others often feel sorry for their numerous problems and either shoulder their responsibilities or excuse them altogether. Their peers resent them because they offload work instead of sharing the workload. Procrastination and missed deadlines are fairly common. Ironically, they may blame the institution for not providing a "deserved" promotion.

Passive-aggressive employees create a toxic environment. Chaplains are helpful when observing the behavior and discussing with such employees why it is problematic. Chaplains can also help supervisors find ways to avoid intimidating people who disagree with them. As an example, chaplains can introduce relationship concepts like "disagree and commit." This principle stipulates that individuals are allowed to disagree while a decision is being made, but once a decision has been made, everyone must commit to it. The principle says disagreement is useful in early states of decision making while harmful after a decision is made. It allows supervisors to demonstrate willingness in receiving feedback. It also limits passive-aggressive behavior on the front end by encouraging open conflict with the expectation that once the decision is made, there is little need to complain, procrastinate, miss deadlines, or avoid others.

Immature Personality Behavior

People who are mature tend to be aware of their behavior within a framework of their culture and circumstances. They respond to their environment by displaying reasonable judgment as to when and how to act. This is a process of growth over time. A baby cries for food in the middle of the night and doesn't care if she wakes her parents. As she grows, she learns she will not get everything she wants whenever she wants it. Growing up includes understanding that the world does not revolve around you.

Persons behaving immaturely frequently lack this self-awareness and emotional stability. Behavioral characteristics include finding quick-fix solutions, sacrificing ethical or moral values, and lacking appreciation that actions have consequences. Immature persons find it difficult to accept responsibility for damaging behavior. Coping defenses commonly used by children continue into adulthood, including blaming others and lashing out verbally or physically.

This type of behavior frequently sacrifices long-term aspirations in order to avoid short-term pressures. Immature persons may do something illegal or unethical with an expectation that they will get caught. For example, a soldier avoids an upcoming assignment by intentionally ingesting an illegal drug prior to a mandatory urinalysis. He would rather receive a bad discharge from the military than fulfill his military obligation. He doesn't grasp that losing an honorable discharge will drastically reduce job opportunities following his military service.

I served as campus chaplain at a military college where students uniformly wore short-sleeve shirts. During harsh winter weather, they were given an option to wear a warm wool jacket. A small group of students embraced a stoic principle attributed to Marcus Aurelius, "You have power over your mind—not outside events. Realize this, and you will find strength." The group chose to act upon this principle by not wearing jackets no matter the temperature. Their immature decision led to a decrease in classroom attendance due to poor health.

—*Military Chaplain*

Immaturity has patterns of marked impulsivity and instability, frequently including impulsive behaviors such as substance or alcohol abuse, unprotected sex or sex with multiple partners, uncontrolled spending, reckless driving, and eating disorders. How can a chaplain provide these individuals with quality pastoral counseling? Chaplains can help people focus on their life's purpose and direction. Pastoral counseling contributes to a sense that life is meaningful. Behavior leading to self-harm and impulsivity may give people a feeling of immediate relief from their emotional pain, yet chaplains help them gain a clearer picture of their identity through what they value and believe. Chaplains also assist in bringing clarity to long-term aspirations and goals by helping people "keep the long look." College students and military personnel are a youthful population and therefore have more frequent issues with immaturity. A wise chaplain would refer someone exhibiting a pattern of these high-risk behaviors to a mental health professional.

Summary

As your knowledge level increases, your skill as a pastoral care provider grows. Keep in mind that these behavior patterns are often difficult to discern. When you find yourself frustrated because you feel unable to help a counselee or, conversely, are flattered by a counselee's continual affirmation and need for you, the problem may be your own. Both frustration and flattery are difficult for a chaplain to recognize. In a recent study of clergy, "91 percent in a survey of more than 1,200 admitted to people-pleasing tendencies to some degree in their ministries."[20] It seems clergy tend to be people pleasers and affirmation addicts, despite our overarching call to serve God.

All of us also have tendencies toward passive-dependent, passive-aggressive, and immature personality behavior. Understanding these three characterizations allows chaplains to better support counselees experiencing these behavior patterns. Pastor Andy Stanley helpfully distinguishes between "problems to be solved" and "tensions to be managed."[21] While you can address the problem, you are not likely to solve these behavioral issues. Chaplains are frequently called to support others in managing their tension. Chaplains also build strong referral networks because they have insufficient competencies to address certain types of problems.

4.5 Cognitive Focused Counseling and Distorted Thinking

When an employee, soldier, patient, prisoner, or college student comes to you for counseling, the person typically brings a presenting problem. As a pastoral counselor, you remain attentive by listening to the person's story, practicing SOLER, forming thoughts around the three-stage skilled-helper model, and asking some of the eight quick counseling questions. This framework forms a cognitive focused counseling methodology that is well suited to the work of chaplaincy. Chaplains encourage self-exploration and allow counselees to learn more about the impact of their thoughts and feelings upon their outward behavior. This type of counseling framework is designed to be short term, with the intent of helping counselees recognize their distorted thoughts and practice useful coping skills.

In the profession of psychotherapy, many mental health professionals, including psychiatrists, psychologists, clinical social workers, and family therapists, use a therapeutic approach called cognitive behavioral therapy (CBT).[22] This involves short-term and problem-specific counseling that emphasizes the present and not the past. It is designed to help patients understand thoughts that influence their behavior and is frequently used to treat a wide range of disorders, including anxiety, addictions, depression, and phobias. Counselees learn to identify and challenge automatic and distorted thought patterns that negatively influence their emotions and behavior. CBT concludes by helping counselees select specific strategies that address their problems: "In many studies, CBT has been demonstrated to be as effective as, or more effective than, other forms of psychological therapy or psychiatric medications."[23]

Chaplains are frequent first-line responders who challenge others to focus on their thoughts and behaviors. While chaplains are not CBT therapists, pastoral counseling appointments frequently position them to explore how thoughts and feelings influence counselee behavior. For example, a sailor who spends a lot of time thinking about aircraft crashes, flight deck accidents, and other air disasters may avoid assignment to an aircraft carrier. This avoidance can limit the sailor's career and advancement. It is not the responsibility of the chaplain to ensure that the sailor has a successful career. However, it would be helpful for the chaplain to assist the sailor in identifying the underlying thoughts leading to her avoidance of duty assignments.

Understanding and using problem-focused and action-oriented strategies are useful in pastoral counseling. Chaplains can help others recognize distorted thinking patterns that contribute to problems and support them in discovering fresh ways to cope with difficulties. Experienced chaplains refer people to mental health professionals when they discover deeper issues or anticipate a longer duration of counseling.

A student shared with me, "I always fail when I try to do something new. I fail at everything I try." I realized she was expressing "black or white" (polarized) thinking because she magnified her situation far beyond what actually happened. She got a poor grade on her final and concluded she was a horrible student and should quit school. This overgeneralization was based on a single incident. Distorted thinking makes you believe that if something bad happens just once, it will happen over and over again.

—Campus Chaplain

As a chaplain, you need to be aware of how your thought patterns create your reality and determine how you behave. Chaplains bring their own distorted thinking into the workplace. Our patterns of thinking are like wearing sunglasses before dawn. They limit what we see and slow our response.

Distorted thinking is a way that our mind convinces us that something is true when it is not true. There are at least fifteen common cognitive distortions.[24] These inaccurate thoughts keep us feeling bad about ourselves or reinforce negative opinions of others.

A distorted view can make you susceptible to mistakenly seeing situations as catastrophic, jumping to conclusions, or seeing things as either good or bad with nothing in between. Once you are aware of your pattern, you can practice refuting the negative pattern. By challenging the negative thinking over and over again, you can slowly diminish it and replace it with more reasonable and balanced thinking. Because these patterns are deeply ingrained, it would be helpful for prospective chaplains to personally experience CBT from a mental health professional before entering chaplaincy. Since "practicing what you preach" enhances credibility, CBT is a valuable precursor to serving as a chaplain.

4.6 Suicide Awareness and Prevention

Statistics regarding death by suicide in the United States are staggering: "Since 1999, the US suicide rate has risen by 30 percent. The plague hit the young hard. Between 2006 and 2016, suicide rates of those between age ten and seventeen rose by 70 percent. Roughly forty-five thousand Americans die by suicide every year."[25] In 2018, the Centers for Disease Control and Prevention (CDC) announced that the life span of the average American had declined for the third consecutive year.[26] And while a number of factors contribute to suicidal ideation, "religion plays a protective role against suicide in a majority of settings where suicide research is conducted."[27] Chaplains are at the forefront of offering practical theology to those they serve by focusing on the value of life as they help others discover their greater purpose.

Chaplains are frequent first responders to spiritual and emotional mishaps that face employees and others served by the institution. Where does someone safely go within an organization when confronted by crisis? Chaplains offer confidentiality and compassion. They also understand human behavior and develop an extended referral network. Many individuals will visit their chaplain simply to see if the chaplain can "do something for me." The chaplain is especially interested in serving those counselees bearing life-altering concerns. One of the more frequent and most lethal topics discussed with chaplains is suicide. The Department of Veterans Affairs health clinics now ask as part of the regular veteran physical, "Are you having any suicidal thoughts right now?" Chaplains were asking that question years before health-care systems integrated mental health into their patient intake assessment.

Chaplains are expected to provide three levels of suicide deterrence for their organization: prevention, intervention, and postvention. Karen Mason, a professor and psychologist who has been working in the mental health field since 1990, provides a helpful analogy to these three levels: "If suicide is like drowning, prevention is doing what you can to prevent drowning, like building a fence around a swimming pool and providing swimming lessons. Intervention is doing what you can once a person falls in the pool, like performing CPR. Postvention is doing what you can for the family after a drowning."[28]

Prevention

Chaplains are expected to develop training and present lectures on preventing suicide. The presentation is typically included in an orientation day for new personnel and as part of an annual cycle of mandated organizational training. Chaplains study suicide statistics, contributing factors, recognizable behaviors, appropriate responses, and interventions in order to build a training presentation unique to the culture of their organization. There are typically two types of prevention training: "An educational program informs an entire community about suicide and how to access help.... A gatekeeper training targets those who are in a position to recognize the warning signs of suicide and help people who may be suicidal."[29] There are also a number of standardized suicide intervention workshops developed for suicide prevention training, including LivingWorks ASIST two-day interactive workshop,[30] QPR Gatekeeper Training,[31] and Yellow Ribbon Suicide Prevention Program.[32]

Organizations emphasize the *quality* of life for the people they serve. They commit resources in time, money, and people addressing ways to increase the quality of life. Chaplains are in a unique position to discuss not only the quality of life but also the *value* of life. Within the context of their faith tradition, chaplains can share ancient narratives from Scripture pivoting around universal themes that support suicide prevention. There are multiple accounts of people who feel despair but do not choose death. There are also stories that affirm the value of every single person. Humans are not burdens. People who feel they are a burden are more vulnerable to suicidal thoughts.

Additionally, community support and connectedness protect individuals from suicidal thoughts.[33] Christians in particular belong to a community where people are called to love one another and care for one another. The apostle Paul admonishes, "So then, as we have opportunity, let us do good to everyone, and especially to those who are of the household of faith" (Gal. 6:10). The Christian community claims the worth of a person and the value of being in community. Chaplains affirm the value of life in others by naming their giftedness and allowing those gifts to flourish.

Prevention of suicides is the responsibility of everyone within an organization. Yet the chaplain is uniquely accessible to people with undisclosed psychological, sociological, biological, and spiritual issues. While chaplains do not have greater expertise than mental health professionals in the area of suicide, they are often the first person to hear of someone's suicidal thoughts. Suicidal contributing factors often include medical and biological issues such as depression and chronic illness; psychological issues, including self-hatred and failure; sociological issues, including loneliness, an inability to "fit in," and a family history of suicide; and spiritual issues described by overwhelming guilt or irreconcilable shame.

Intervention

The chaplain hears a multitude of issues and occasionally detects counselees who have a strong sense of worthlessness, hopelessness, and helplessness. When these three feelings merge, chaplains intentionally shift counseling conversations from prevention to intervention. The chaplain probes each of these three areas to ascertain the counselee's level of helplessness, hopelessness, and worthlessness. A chaplain listens for signs of being helpless ("I've nowhere to go"), hopeless ("It's no use anyway"), and worthless ("Nobody cares"). The more explicitly the counselee addresses each topic, the stronger the potential formation of a "suicide triangle." If all three are articulated and deeply felt by the counselee, the chaplain has a moral responsibility beyond the conversation to ensure that he is safe.

Can a chaplain ask a person directly if he is thinking about suicide as an option? It's a myth that if you ask, you're putting the idea in his mind. The counselee might be perplexed with suicidal thoughts and not know how to start this embarrassing conversation. Asking directly can be helpful. The more detailed the specifics, the greater the risk. An analogy is planning a vacation: You can dream about where you want to go for a while. If you start doing research online, it becomes a little more real. Once you buy plane tickets, you are committed to the vacation. The reason chaplains ask is that they want an answer to the question, "Has this person bought his ticket yet?" Chaplains should listen for articulated reasons for living. If a person is talking about his suicidal thoughts with you, then there is a part of him that has some reason for living. There is something that ties him to life with you.

The National Comorbidity Survey (NCS), a nationally representative general population survey, discovered that "one-quarter of those who ever sought treatment for mental disorders did so from a clergy member . . . and not by a physician or mental health professional." Principal findings led to the conclusion that "clergy continue to play a crucial role in the US mental healthcare delivery system."[34] Suicidal ideation exists among people in every community; therefore, being prepared is vital. Chaplains can help break the suicide triangle of helplessness, hopelessness, and worthlessness by initially offering help, hope, and worth, followed by ensuring that their counselee is safely with a health service provider. Organizations employing chaplains have established protocols that include due diligence responsibilities in caring for the counselee as well as protecting the institution.

Postvention

Not only are chaplains involved in the prevention and intervention of death by suicide, they also provide postvention pastoral care to families and organizations following a suicide. The sense of grief, mourning, and loss is unfathomably deep for those suffering relational loss due to suicide. Common responses include shock, disbelief, numbness, guilt, shame, and a sense of failure. Chaplains frequently hear, "I should have seen this coming," or "What could I have done differently?" Chaplains offer much-needed pastoral care by listening more than speaking. It is common for chaplains to discuss forgiveness. A theological question on many minds is whether suicide prevents eternal salvation.[35] Here are five related questions for prospective chaplains to consider before they find themselves in this situation:

1. What is your understanding of Scripture regarding suicide?
2. Is your understanding at variance from that of your faith group?
3. How will you provide pastoral counseling and care to someone you believe is contemplating suicide?
4. How will you approach and care for the survivors of someone who died by suicide?
5. How do you prepare to conduct a funeral or memorial service of someone who died by suicide, and what will you say at the event?

I served as the sole chaplain aboard a Navy ship. There were no medical or mental health professionals other than an enlisted hospital corpsman. A sailor knocked on my cabin door and requested I see him immediately. After talking for a few minutes, it was clear he was contemplating suicide due to a failed marriage. He was a highly decorated overachiever suffering abject failure as a husband. His despondency went beyond his words. He had a razor and told me his plan to slice his wrists at midnight. I asked him if I could bring the hospital corpsman into our conversation as his expertise might provide valuable insight into the situation and help reframe the situation. The sailor said, "I only trust you, Chaplain. I don't trust anyone else." Therefore, I didn't have his consent to bring external resources into the conversation. Nevertheless, this did not relieve me of my responsibility for the welfare of another human. Personal knowledge of his upcoming plan weighed heavy. I had a reasonable sense of responsibility for his care. I explained that even though I would not disclose his plan, I was now in a moral dilemma of ensuring he could remain safe. I told him that I would not stay true to my calling knowing that I didn't respond faithfully by caring for a hurting human. My next statement took him by surprise, "I won't leave you until your feelings resolve. I definitely won't separate from you until after midnight." We talked more, ate dinner together, and walked around the ship. By midnight the sailor had second thoughts on killing himself. He survived and completed his tour of service. This experience led me to conclude that suicide is never a permanent *solution* to a temporary crisis. Regrettably, it is a permanent *decision* to a temporary crisis.

—*Military Chaplain*

4.7 Confidentiality and Privileged Communication

It is important to understand your various responsibilities as a chaplain. One of the most crucial responsibilities is the handling of confidential and privileged communication.

Confidentiality

The office of the chaplain typically gives people the protection of confidentiality within the context of giving care. Counselees consulting you expect that you will respect the privacy of your conversations with them. Rooted in the sacred trust between an individual and a chaplain, the duty of confidentiality binds the chaplain to keep private what others share in confidence. Anything disclosed during the conversation, including the chaplain's responses, should be presumed confidential. This is because a relationship requires mutual engagement. The duty of confidentiality safeguards whatever counsel the chaplain provides to the counselee, just as it protects the information disclosed to the chaplain. The chaplain's duty of confidentiality protects the relationship, not just the interests of the person who comes to her.

Prospective chaplains should carefully study rules regarding the protection of confidential information. Confidentiality applies to anything the counselee reasonably believes is shared with the chaplain. The duty of confidentiality extends to any written communication as well. Confidentiality extends beyond the end of the care-giving relationship with the chaplain, and also beyond the death of the individual making the disclosure. As an example, in military chaplaincy, "All counseling records are considered confidential and must be safeguarded and destroyed when no longer needed."[36]

Hospital chaplains are governed by federal regulations that include very severe penalties for breaching confidentiality. Where chaplains are integrated into a medical treatment team, they have access to information protected by the Health Insurance Portability and Accountability Act (HIPAA).[37] Protected health information (PHI) includes information about the health status or provision of health care linked to a specific individual. It is incumbent upon a new hospital chaplain to study the rules for confidentiality.

Exceptions to Confidentiality

Although chaplains are generally barred from sharing information disclosed to them during caregiving, the safeguard is not absolute. Most contexts of chaplaincy include exceptions to confidentiality. Some common exceptions are directed toward the care of the individual. As an example, if a counselee expresses suicidal ideation, the chaplain would suggest that the two of them meet with a health-care specialist. If the counselee refuses, the chaplain would have the moral obligation of insisting that the two of them, chaplain and counselee, remain together until the ideation subsides.

Other exceptions to confidentiality go beyond self-harm. If a counselee intends to harm a third party, the chaplain may have a duty to warn the intended victim or the authorities. Specific exceptions to confidentiality can be found in the rules of a chaplain's institutional setting, such as a hospital, a college, or the military. In addition, exceptions to confidentiality may be mandated by the state in which the chaplain serves. Finally, exceptions may arise from the chaplain's own faith tradition or conscience. Chaplains

THE CHAPLAIN AS CAREGIVER

will want to discuss with their ecclesiastical endorser their faith group's position on pastoral confidentiality.

Mandated Reporting

Mandatory reporting of child abuse or neglect is another significant exception to confidentiality. By federal law, all states must have mandatory-reporting statutes that apply to certain professionals.[38] These include social workers, teachers, physicians, therapists, child-care providers, and law-enforcement officers. Many states also list clergy among the mandated reporters, although the scope of that duty differs significantly among these states.[39]

Privileged Communication

Chaplains should not confuse the professional duty of confidentiality with the legal term "privilege." This term comes out of the law of evidence, applicable in court proceedings. Some information that might otherwise be available for a legal proceeding may be treated as privileged, and one or more people may have the right to invoke the privilege and exclude that information. Courts and legislatures recognize a variety of privileged relationships, including spousal, attorney-client, physician-patient, and clergy-congregant. The concept here is simple yet important. Society sees value in these relationships and wants people to trust spouses, lawyers, doctors, and clergy.

Confidential communications made to a chaplain or another religious adviser are generally privileged. The privilege for religious communications covers both formal confessions conducted as part of ministerial practice and confidential communications made to chaplains in their professional role as spiritual advisers, caregivers, and counselors.

State laws and federal laws regarding privileged communication may differ. All branches of the US Armed Forces regard communications to clergy as privileged under federal law. Within the military court setting, Military Rule of Evidence 503 prohibits a chaplain or a chaplain's assistant from divulging a privileged communication without the consent of the military member. "While chaplains are not bound by mandatory reporting requirements in the Department of Defense . . . chaplains will always assist in guiding an individual to the appropriate resources."[40] A chaplain-soldier conversation in the context of a chaplain's military duties, whether on or off base, is privileged communication protected by federal law. Whereas state laws may differ, when chaplains serve in a military context they remain under federal and not state jurisdiction. Navy Fleet Admiral Chester A. Nimitz offered these remarks about military chaplains and their value of providing confidentiality and privileged communication to those who served during World War II: "By patient, sympathetic labors with the crew, day in, day out, and through many a night, every chaplain I know contributed immeasurably.... Most of it necessarily secret between pastor and confidant. It is for that toil, in the cause both of God and country, that I honor the chaplain most."[41]

Summary

There are very significant differences between the chaplain's duty of confidentiality and the evidentiary privilege. The scope of these legal concepts differs as well. Chaplains must review the federal and specific state laws that apply to their position regarding confidentiality, mandated reporting, additional exceptions to confidentiality, and privileged communication. Chaplains consider pastoral care a sacred responsibility and most strongly seek to retain the trust of their counselees and congregants.

Confidentiality protects the trust that a chaplain's role rightly engenders in those who reveal their deepest secrets. As a chaplain, you respect both confidentiality and privileged communication because you want to protect the people who rely on you and who make themselves vulnerable to you by disclosing concerns closest to their hearts.

4.8 Clinical Pastoral Education (CPE)

Clinical Pastoral Education (CPE) offers prospective chaplains a unique experience of theological and professional education for ministry. It provides the professional training needed for a career in chaplaincy. Often part of seminary education, CPE equips theological students, ordained clergy, members of religious orders, and qualified laypeople with tools for pastoral care through specific training in pastoral reflection, formation, and competence. While under supervision, CPE students minister to people in moments that matter. The training is typically in clinical settings such as hospitals and health-care centers.

Through intense involvement with people in crisis, peer students, supervisors, and other professionals, CPE students are challenged to increase the value of their pastoral relationships. Students are encouraged to develop caring pastoral relationships through written case studies, verbatims, seminars, supervised pastoral practice, and relevant reading resources. Throughout the process, students develop greater self-awareness as they enhance their pastoral care skills under close supervision. They learn how to engage patients and families on a daily basis and how to deliver care to them. They reflect on their own theological foundations as they seek to better understand those they serve. CPE equips chaplains to thrive by integrating their theology and clinical skills into the delivery of quality pastoral care.

All ministers have to start somewhere, and there are always growing pains no matter what the setting. Clinical Pastoral Education (CPE) gave me a ton of confidence in my pastoral identity. Sister Janet, my clinical pastoral supervisor, was a great mentor, and she was the one who encouraged me to volunteer at Attica State Prison. I wouldn't have entered the Federal Bureau of Prisons were it not for her influence on me.

—Correctional/Prison Chaplain

One unit of CPE typically includes:

- 400 hours (300 clinical and 100 instruction) spread over a period of twelve to thirty-six weeks
- Providing pastoral care to individuals and families
- Didactic and clinical seminars
- Mutually supporting, working, and sharing with other CPE students
- Preparing detailed reports and evaluating one's pastoral care
- Pastoral supervision and mentorship by a certified educator of CPE

For me, CPE was about practicing and learning to be a nonanxious presence. Also, learning to be comfortable with silence and not having to fill the void with unnecessary words. By reviewing pastoral conversations with my peer group, I learned to help others without interjecting my own "stuff" into the conversation.

—Correctional/Prison Chaplain

Many faith groups and ecclesiastical endorsers require at least two complete units of CPE or specialized ministry training before they will endorse their clergy as chaplains. Many full-time health-care chaplain positions require four completed CPE units and expect the chaplain to become board certified through the Association of Professional Chaplains (APC). Finding the right CPE program depends on the prospective chaplain's goals, timeline, and anticipated ministry setting. CPE associations with widespread recognition in Canada and the United States include the following:

1. Association of Clinical Pastoral Education (ACPE) is one of the most recognized and accepted CPE program providers in the United States. ACPE is recognized by the US Department of Education (USDE) to accredit over three hundred CPE programs offered in hospitals, prisons, churches, seminaries, and community-based organizations. These programs include internships, residencies, and hybrid resident or online programs. Units of ACPE meet the requirements for APC board certification.

2. Canadian Association for Spiritual Care (CASC) is currently the only professional chaplain certification and education organization in Canada. It is unique in that it offers both CPE and PCE (Pastoral Counseling Education). CASC has an agreement with ACPE and the APC to accept all units.

3. College of Pastoral Supervision and Psychotherapy (CPSP) is recognized in certain regions of the United States, such as the west and east coasts. One unit from CPSP may also be transferred for board certification through the APC.

4. The Institute for Clinical Pastoral Training (ICPT) relies on an online component featuring blended learning modules, videoconferencing, larger class sizes, and flexibility in allowing students to complete clinical hours in their current ministry setting. These units offer a standardized and evidenced-based CPE training program to chaplains and spiritual care providers. In January 2018, the HealthCare Chaplaincy Network (HCCN) and its affiliate, the Spiritual Care Association (SCA), partnered with the ICPT to deliver a standardized evidence-based CPE program.

Discussion Questions

1. How can you compassionately care for everyone within the institution, even those with no articulated faith?

2. What is meant by the statement "Everyone else is focused on the mission. I am the one person, chartered by the institution, to care for everyone else while they remain focused on the mission"?

3. What are some ways a chaplain translates care into active engagement?

4. How do proximity and availability become core values of flourishing chaplains?

5. Many organizations look to their chaplain as the person to deliver unwelcome news. What might be a better alternative and why?

6. What is the purpose of SOLER, and in what way does it communicate attentiveness?

7. When you provide pastoral counseling, how will you prepare your counseling space to safeguard counselees' privacy while ensuring full accountability and transparency?

8. Provide an example of how a chaplain can be responsible *to* but not *for* the counselee.

9. What are your automatic and distorted thinking patterns that negatively influence your emotions and behavior? As a prospective chaplain, how will you challenge this distorted thinking?

10. While organizations frequently address the *quality* of life, chaplains are in a unique position to emphasize the *value* of life. What is the difference and, as a chaplain, how might you do this?

11. What is the purpose of Clinical Pastoral Education? Why might it be valuable to prospective chaplains?

CHAPTER 5

The Chaplain as Adviser

> Without counsel plans fail, but with many advisers they
> succeed.
>
> —*Proverbs 15:22*

5.1 Prophetic Voice of Chaplain to the Institution

There are solid biblical foundations for the chaplain serving as an adviser. The writer of Proverbs affirmed the value of providing sound advice. Proverbs 15:22 could be the leadership quote of the decade, whether that decade was a thousand years before the birth of Jesus or two thousand years after. Wisdom on the value of advising is peppered throughout the book of Proverbs. For example, Proverbs 11:14 states,

> Where there is no guidance, a people falls,
>   but in an abundance of counselors there is safety.

Trusted and wise advisers are priceless, as Proverbs 24:6 adds:

> For by wise guidance you can wage your war,
>   and in abundance of counselors there is victory.

Such counsel is woven throughout the biblical narrative in practical applications of faith leaders providing advice to organizational leadership. Whether it be to protect the crown or the cargo, there is a legitimate place for the prophetic voice of the chaplain to various institutions.

Regarding the crown, Solomon's survival was directly influenced by a self-harming decision made by his adversarial brother Absalom. Both were sons of King David. Absalom usurped his father's throne and prepared to annihilate the remnant of those loyal to King David in order to consolidate his power. Prior to attacking the fleeing, disorganized, and embittered remnant, Absalom received counsel from two highly regarded advisers, Ahithophel and Hushai. If Absalom had acted on the counsel of Ahithophel instead of that of Hushai, Solomon would not have survived. The advice of Hushai slowed Absalom from an immediate attack, thereby allowing King David and his warriors to escape. Dejected, Ahithophel regarded the episode as a complete rejection of his fundamental role as adviser: "When Ahithophel saw that his counsel was not followed, he saddled his donkey and went off home to his own city. He set his house in order and hanged himself" (2 Sam. 17:23).

Chaplains, you must *never* go to that extreme! Please do not despair like Ahithophel if your advice is not taken. The point of chaplaincy is to offer your best advice. Leaders receive counsel from many sources, and it is unreasonable for you to expect leaders within your organization to take action on your advice alone. You are a principal adviser but typically not an organizational decision maker. Your input serves to influence but not mandate outcomes. It is priceless for chaplains to "be at the table" where decisions are made. There is great value in your voice being present, even when you don't have a vote. You complete due-diligence responsibilities as a chaplain once you offer your advice. Not all chaplains get to be at the table where decisions are made. Sometimes chaplains are at the table because of the positions they hold. Other times it is through certain relationships or because they are defined as an expert. Regrettably, many chaplains never find their voice for speaking truth to power. They remain timid and cloistered within the safety of their office instead of giving their best counsel to those desperately trying to make important decisions. Take note that you must persist in establishing a reputation where leaders recognize your voice and value your input. Receptivity to advice often comes from a trusting relationship built over time. Don't neglect the C-suite leaders who may indicate they are too busy to talk to their chaplain—your persistence in dropping by could lead to fruitful relationships, greater access, and stronger credibility.

Like Paul in the book of Acts, chaplains address a variety of concerns, from ordinary cargo issues to significant concerns for human survival. The experience of prisoner Paul at sea in Acts 27 offers a timely guide for chaplains desiring to speak truth to those in leadership roles. Paul is unflappable and indefatigable in his provision of wise counsel to his captors.

Yet the leader of Paul's prison ship to Rome refuses to heed Paul's advice once the sailing season turns stormy. "But the centurion paid more attention to the pilot and to the owner of the ship than to what Paul said. And because the harbor was not suitable to spend the winter in, the majority decided to put out to sea from there" (Acts 27:11–12). The centurion allows Paul's voice to be drowned out by the majority, and the Roman soldier's poor decision nearly drowns everyone at sea. Like a great leader, he learns from his mistake. The centurion completely flips by having overwhelming confidence in Paul. Later in the same voyage he refuses to listen to the majority, or the owner, or even the pilot. At the most dangerous moment, when the ship is near to foundering in heavy seas, the centurion heeds this wise advice of Paul: "Men, you should have listened to me and not have set sail from Crete and incurred this injury and loss. Yet now I urge you to take heart, for there will be no loss of life among you" (Acts 27:21–22). The centurion, who earlier refused Paul's counsel, now follows it above all other voices. Paul's counsel and the ensuing decision by the centurion save the lives of 276 sailors, soldiers, and prisoners.

If the centurion had rejected Paul again and instead acted on the counsel of anyone else, including the owner or the pilot of the vessel, the book of Acts would likely have ended at this chapter. Whereas earlier in the narrative the centurion listened to and acted on the opinion of the majority, he now completely rejects their counsel. "The soldiers' plan was to kill the prisoners, lest any should swim away and escape. But the centurion, wishing to save Paul, kept them from carrying out their plan" (Acts 27:42–43). The persistence Paul demonstrated led to a fruitful relationship, greater access, and stronger credibility. Whereas the first biblical narrative of Ahithophel, Hushai, and Absalom illustrates the remarkable value of providing advice to a leader, Paul's story communicates the need for persistence in messaging, even when the counsel is initially rejected.

There may be particularly high risk when advising senior leadership on their injustice and malfeasance. In 2 Samuel 12, we hear the prophetic voice of Nathan speaking to King David. Nathan rebukes David for his role in murdering Uriah. Expecting King David to become defensive and rationalize his unconscionable sin, Nathan wisely begins by illuminating David's crime through an indirect story, in which a rich man, self-absorbed by entitlement, acts unjustly toward a poor man. David "burns with anger" at the injustice and proclaims that the perpetrator must die. Nathan reveals the identity of the rich man while simultaneously disarming the king's wrath:

"You are the man!" (2 Sam. 12:7). King David is stunned. Whereas he could have Nathan killed for offending him, he realizes his crime, "I have sinned against the LORD" (2 Sam. 12:13).

Like Nathan, chaplains serve institutions where successful leaders may be poorly prepared for their success. Success often moves leaders toward complacency; they believe they are now "too big to fail." They devalue accountability by thinking normal rules no longer apply to them. Due to their position, they have a personal ability to manipulate outcomes. In the wake of success, managers and leaders—even those with a highly developed sense of ethics like David—can be seduced toward moral failures and ethical violations. A popular term describing the inability to cope with and respond to success is the "Bathsheba Syndrome."[1] Chaplains may be on the first line of defense against this syndrome by speaking truth to power, helping leaders clarify their motives, and reviewing structures, procedures, and practices that will help prevent supervisors from falling victim to their own success.

I have been working as a chaplain for almost twenty-five years, and I've had many roles in that time. I don't typically think of myself as an adviser, but it's an important part of my job. As manager of our spiritual care department I advise my staff on a daily basis, and formally once a year when we sit down together for a performance review. I also advise patients and families who are confronting difficult decisions, especially at the end of life. Finally, I advise staff, not only in spiritual matters but also, at times, in how they do their jobs.

—Hospital Chaplain

While modern-day chaplains do not serve in the same capacity as did Old Testament prophets such as Hushai and Nathan, they do have unique access to powerful leadership. As an example, Barry Black serves as the sixty-second chaplain of the United States Senate. He was elected to this position in 2003 after rising to the rank of rear admiral and completing his military career as the Navy Chief of Chaplains. Chaplain Black was named Becket's 2019 Canterbury medalist for his honorable defense of religious liberty for people of all faiths. He has gained a reputation of speaking truth to the powerful.

Chaplain Black opened the Senate in prayer by calling out his wayward flock of senators immediately before the US government shutdown in 2013. His fiery prayer asked God to give lawmakers courage. This prayer, known as the "save us from the madness" prayer,[2] was later spoofed on *Saturday*

Night Live. Chaplain Black commented on his role as adviser: "I think it's my responsibility to be engaged in what is going on. It's my responsibility to give a spiritual, biblical, ethical, and moral perspective to political issues and what our lawmakers are going through. . . . My typical prayers aren't that pointed. But when you have a government shutdown and the entire world is looking on and money is hemorrhaging and people are in need, I have to be a voice for those who cannot speak for themselves."[3]

When godly advice to key leaders is offered in the Bible, we typically find a combination of virtues embodied in the individuals offering advice. These virtues include credibility, trust, wisdom, perseverance, faithfulness, and a tolerance for risk. These are also core virtues for chaplaincy and align with the Association of Professional Chaplains Code of Ethics: "Public advocacy related to spiritual values and social justice concerns is promoted on behalf of persons in need,"[4] as well as with the Board of Chaplaincy Certification requirement to "Promote, facilitate, and support ethical decision-making in one's workplace."[5]

Advising is a very special and sacred role, deeply woven throughout the biblical narrative. Chaplains have a responsibility to be advisers to the institutions they serve. In many institutions, the chaplain plays a key role in interpreting the organization's mission and vision, as it relates to policies and procedures as well as to the broader community. At times, the chaplain may find that a personal position taken publicly may unintentionally be perceived as representative of institutional leadership.

> I once signed a petition sponsored by local clergy asking the school board to be more sensitive to when they scheduled their athletic events so that they would not conflict with weekly worship. I later got called into the CEO's office to remind me that when I did that, I put the organization into an uncomfortable situation, as the president of the school board had gone to him asking why his organization's chaplain had signed the petition.
>
> —*Continuing-Care Retirement Community Chaplain*

Be mindful that those serving in senior leadership are responsible for comments that could reflect upon the institution. Chaplains have a unique opportunity to speak truth to power, but if chaplains choose to ignore it, misuse it, or abuse it, they may have no credibility or have their access restricted when the moment of opportunity arrives. Advice can be ignored by leaders altogether if chaplains spontaneously provide advice too frequently. Chaplains can misuse advisement, and thereby lose credibility, by not adequately researching the issues they address. Advisement is abused when chaplains advocate for self-promoting outcomes. These are a few of the reasons why advising brings risk. A lot of chaplains refrain from exercising their advising role. It can bring unpredictable outcomes. It is not easy because of its potential for relational confrontation. Yet it is a core functional responsibility expected of chaplains. Advisement carries a great amount of influence. A chaplain who uses his voice judiciously gains the trust of his organization's leadership. When he does choose to speak, he is most likely to be taken seriously and credibly.

The biblical advisers Hushai, Paul, and Nathan speak to people in authority. As a chaplain, you also serve people in authority in your institution. It is important to understand and practice your prophetic voice within your organization. If you need comfort and courage as you respectfully practice speaking truth to power, remember God's words to the prophet Isaiah:

> Fear not, for I am with you;
>   be not dismayed, for I am your God;
> I will strengthen you, I will help you,
>   I will uphold you with my righteous right hand. (Isa. 41:10)

5.2 Definition of Advisement and Adviser

Organizational leaders expect chaplains to be subject-matter experts on religion and its influence both internally and externally to their domain. In response, chaplains assist the organization and strengthen development of their leadership at all levels. Chaplains serve as principal advisers on issues of faith to the highest echelons of leadership within an organization—depending on the institution, this might be the board, chair, president, director, CEO, COO, provost, official, warden, congressman, or commanding officer. This advice includes requirements for specific religions, the condition of morale, as well as ethical and moral relationships with the wider community. The chaplain has a valued voice with those in senior leadership positions, and she also delivers advice to individuals and groups at various levels within the organization regarding moral, ethical, spiritual, interpersonal, and humanitarian concerns. The chaplain serves as an advocate for the people she serves.

I served as command chaplain aboard one of the largest warships ever built. With over six thousand crew and aircrew, the carrier displaced 102,000 tons. It was a giant ship with an important mission. Providing the commanding officer advice was an essential part of my responsibilities. At the commanding officer's request, every morning the ship was at sea the commanding officer, executive officer, command master chief, and I met for fifteen minutes to discuss the tone of the ship. This meeting had nothing to do with the movement, hardware, or construction of the ship. It had everything to do with the morale of the crew. Once a day, the chaplain was invited to speak to the highest levels of leadership on the general character and attitude of the crew through a lens focused on ethics, morals, humanitarian, and spiritual well-being for everyone onboard.

—Military Chaplain

How do organizations make good decisions? Many institutional practices, if they are iterative in nature, develop into policies over time. At some point in this migration from practice to policy, the prospective policy is reviewed by lawyers to ensure that it is aligned with employee rights and employment law. Most organizations that employ chaplains also consult legal counsel. In-house counsel handles a range of legal issues affecting the company, among them employment, policy, tax, and regulatory matters. The attorney offers a legal opinion on whether a proposed initiative or decision is legal or illegal. Yet the complexity of decision making and policy writing frequently goes beyond this straightforward legal review.

When our organization developed a policy on advanced directives, the chaplains were invited to be part of the process, and because the organization was a Christian faith-based organization, area clergy were also invited to provide feedback. After reviewing the policy, all clergy involved—both local community and institutional chaplains—observed that "end of life" definitions within the advanced directives policy were based solely on a medical model provided by state and governmental guidelines. Organizational leadership decided to follow the recommendations of clergy and revise both the policy and the definitions to be more spiritually inclusive as per the organization's faith tradition.

—Skilled Nursing, Memory Support, and
Mental Health Services Chaplain

Determining whether a policy is legal or illegal serves as a baseline and is not the sole standard for decision making. Medical ethics boards have a defined role for ethical review as well. Bioethics is its own discipline, and chaplains regularly serve on these review boards. Hospitals with organ transplant programs need not only a medical review but also a legal review of all potential transplants. But criteria that align a good medical match between donor and recipient and ensure that the institution fulfills all legal due diligence requirements prior to transplant may still be insufficient. The chaplain is chartered by the institution to address moral or ethical implications for organ transplant decisions. As an example, what is the moral and pastoral response to a person who is no longer accepted as a transplant candidate? The chaplain brings an additional voice by identifying the nuances and ambiguities present in any given situation.

> One of my frustrations with many physicians is that they do not advise patients and families, but neutrally set options before them, like multiple-choice questions. Atul Gawande addresses this tendency in his book *Being Mortal*, and notes that "[this] is the increasingly common way for doctors to be" (Atul Gawande, *Being Mortal* [New York: Metropolitan Books, 2015], 200–201). This is the "informative" approach. Many of us do not want our doctors to take the paternalistic approach, the doctor-knows-best kind of thing, but this purely informative approach is also inadequate. Gawande suggests, having studied the work of medical ethicists, that what is needed is the "interpretive" approach. This is a shared decision-making approach and includes guidance and advice.
>
> —*Hospital Chaplain*

Chaplains serve as moral agents speaking into the goodness of decisions and the rightness of how they are made. Chaplains are clearheaded advocates for that which is right, true, and good. While attorneys serve institutions in order to offer opinions whether something is legal or illegal, chaplains are agents for moral issues and provide advice that avoids wrong, false, or malevolent behavior.

> I have an opportunity to advise physicians when I facilitate family meetings as goals of care are being discussed. Picture a small conference room with a table and a dozen family members and clinicians squeezed in. When the lead physician starts talking a mile a minute in clinical language—information mode—about the patient's medical condition, I can stop the physician and

advise that we step back and refocus the conversation on the patient's and the family's values. I can then ask the family or patient what they understand about the disease and what their hopes are for the future. Sometimes, I invite silence. I will say, "Stop. Let's sit for a moment with this news. This is really sad." Even when I am not facilitating the discussion—which is a role I have as ethics consultant—but am just part of a family meeting as chaplain, I can still speak up and direct the group's attention to all the voices at the table and the emotions in the room. I was recently in a meeting with a Pakistani Muslim man and a young physician who was explaining—through a phone interpreter—that his father's prognosis was poor and what the options were going forward. The physician was in information mode. The physician paused and I said, "This is hard." The man looked up and his eyes filled with tears. The conversation opened up after that as he told us how grieved he was that he could no longer converse with his father, to say how much he loved him. Such a simple intervention, to acknowledge the emotions in the room, is certainly not unique to the role of chaplain. Yet it is often the job of the chaplain to help clinicians see the whole person, as in creating a little space for a son's tears.

—Hospital Chaplain

When a complex issue is oversimplified, there is always risk of reductionist thinking. There are multiple considerations when solving problems. Whether a decision is simply legal or illegal remains a baseline and not a determining factor. Chaplains offer additional input valued and necessary for organizational decisions. Their counsel may slow the speed of decision making. Their words may not necessarily align with legal counsel.

Something may be legal and right from a societal example but not morally acceptable by the organization. At my organization, according to state standards, it was normally illegal and wrong to purposely disobey an advanced directive, but as a faith-based institution, the state allowed us to provide exemptions based on institutional convictions to not follow certain advanced directives as long as certain criteria were met. This often stood in opposition to socially accepted norms for training within certain disciplines of nursing and social work.

—Health-Care Chaplain

Organizational leadership should seek chaplain input as essential criteria for good decision making. The following table delineates primary advisers for making policy decisions. In each case, institutional leadership must ask if there is a place for the chaplain to contribute.

Issue	Adviser	Sample Types of Concerns: Where Was the Chaplain?
Legal / Illegal	Lawyer	Supervisor expecting gift from employee for a better job
Right / Wrong	Engineer	A car company rigging pollution emissions tests
True / False	Scientist	A dietary supplement caught using false advertising
Good / Malevolent	Doctor	Tobacco companies recruiting doctors to push smoking

What happens when an organization fails to bring its chaplain into the decision-making process? As an example, the process leading to a decision made by the US military to provide food for a desperately hungry Islamic community in Iraq didn't include a chaplain. Ingeniously preserved food packed in a self-contained plastic bag, called Meal, Ready-to-Eat (MRE), had been developed years earlier to allow military personnel to eat a full meal while in training or in combat. Military leaders assumed providing access to these MREs could be vital to starving Iraqi civilians during an emergency. Yet upon distribution, the indigenous population became angry and offended by what was intended to be a humanitarian gesture. It took a chaplain to communicate to leadership that the meal included religiously prohibited pork and also lacked halal certification.

Had a chaplain been consulted in the initial planning stages, the mistake of providing nonhalal products, including pork, would have been avoided. Eventually, the traditional MRE menu expanded to include the Meal Alternative Regionally Customized (MARC). This meal has found wider use in Southwest Asia. It is entirely vegetarian and provides an alternative for religiously prohibited food, such as pork for those practicing Islam and Judaism, or beef for practicing Hindus.

The chaplain's advisory role strengthens the organization and assists leaders in their individual development. A chaplain participates as a principal adviser to his organization on matters such as emerging religious requirements, the impact of religion on the organization, identifying lesser-known holy days in a majority-Christian culture, as well as personal and organizational ethical boundaries. Chaplains should not be afraid to speak truthfully and respectfully despite the risk of jeopardizing their relationship with leaders within the organization. It takes sound professional judgment to know when it is necessary to offer alternative advice that might be unpopular. These occasions will be rare, but the chaplain must be prepared to offer honest and frank advice. Receptivity to advice builds as the chaplain's relationship grows over time.

I also advise patients and families directly now. By this I mean that I share my values and my knowledge with people more readily than I used to. For example, families often have to face the decision about whether or not to consent to a feeding tube for their loved one, when their loved one is in end-stage dementia and can no longer safely eat. They may have religious reasons for believing that they must continue feeding Mom. They may be frightened about the decision because they had never talked about it with Mom. They may ask me my opinion. I tell them that my interpretation of my own sacred text—the Bible—does not require that I live as long as possible, using whatever technology is available. I also tell them that many others from my own tradition would interpret the Bible differently and disagree with me. I also tell them a feeding tube does not preclude aspiration pneumonia—from saliva—and that it does necessarily lengthen someone's life. I usually advise against it. I sometimes give people research articles, or religious articles about this topic. (See, for example, Daniel P. Sulmasy, "Terri Schiavo and the Roman Catholic Tradition of Forgoing Extraordinary Means of Care," *Journal of Law, Medicine & Ethics* 33, no. 2 [June 1, 2005]: 359–62, https://doi.org/10.1111/j.1748-720X.2005 .tb00500.x.) If I am respectful of other opinions and compassionate, then I am able to state my values openly. I am able to advise. Whether people take my advice or not is another story.

—Hospital Chaplain

An organization's leaders should appreciate counsel from someone who is approachable in a way that is unique among employees. In the course of personal counseling and ministry by walking around (MBWA), the chaplain will likely hear points of view unlikely to be expressed to managers within the organization. This is because the chaplain is known as someone who tends to have trust among a broad range of staff members, respects everyone's humanity, and is committed to maintain confidentiality. Organizations gain great benefit from the advice chaplains offer due to their unique ability to give voice to those who have none.

Institutions become comfortable securing legal advice, yet many are not conditioned to pursue moral advice. When an institution has questions about upcoming religious holidays, holy days, or observances, it should typically ask the chaplain for counsel. Yet chaplains should not let these questions be limited to religious expression. Leaders should be approaching chaplains for moral guidance as well, especially concerning issues shaped by cultural values. What may be defined as "right" in one culture is not necessarily universal. As an example, chaplains can help the institution remain sensitive to issues of gender and inclusivity.

> Our institution invited our chaplain staff to be part of a discussion that would allow for providing restrooms for transgender people, especially within the context of a locked psychiatric hospital. We were asked to consider all the moral and ethical questions that might evolve. This was significant because our organization's established faith group is relatively conservative.
>
> —Health-Care Chaplain

If the institution doesn't seek the chaplain, then the chaplain may approach leadership. Let the leadership team know that these questions are appropriate for them to ask. When they do not initiate the conversation, you need to approach them. The chaplain is a resident expert, demonstrating cross-cultural competencies as an institutional advocate for people as well as the institution.

> I served as a chaplain supervisor on a campus where the diversity of our student body required chaplains of various faiths. The rabbi chaplain came to me asking why his Jewish students were always prohibited from attending home football games. I didn't understand what he was talking about. He explained that in autumn, nearly every Saturday was dedicated to college football. He wondered why the Sabbath was targeted as the one day of the week for football. The Jewish students were prohibited from walking the long distance to the stadium, and there were no facilities for them to gather for kosher food during the game. He said that the college did not hold athletic games on Easter or Christmas but regularly did during Yom Kippur and Rosh Hashanah. I quickly realized that there remain a lot of Christian elements left in our culture, which took a rabbi to point them out to me. I also came to the conclusion that I wasn't being sensitive to the requirements of other faiths. I started planning better by looking at the institutional calendar two years in advance. I added holy days and holidays for the diverse faiths represented by our student body. It seems true that the first element of institutional change is awareness. The school still has Saturday football games, but our first Thursday night game was this year.
>
> —Campus Chaplain

In a way, Pulitzer Prize–winning author Thomas L. Friedman addresses cross-cultural competencies when he asks whether the world has gotten too small and too fast for human beings, organizations, and their political systems to adjust in a stable manner.[6] Friedman explains how our "flattening" of the world happened at the dawn of the twenty-first century. Historical and geographic divisions are becoming increasingly irrelevant. Open-sourcing, outsourcing, off-shoring, supply-chaining, and wireless technologies sparked massive collaboration and closer coordination among far-flung employees without regard to religion or geography. Governments, communities, organizations, companies, and individuals must adapt to these changes in order to remain viable.

Whether the chaplain is serving at an overseas health-care facility, a military deployment, a global cruise line, or an international business location, an enhanced understanding and appreciation of religion, to include the sensitivities and perspectives of other faiths, are a practical necessity. In a 2003 interview with PBS, General James Mattis shared an excellent example of how a chaplain serves as an adviser. The interviewer asked Mattis about the exceptionally good relationship between the Marines and the sheiks in the Iraqi province occupied by his Marines. He listed several factors involved in their successful mission, and then said, "I followed the advice of my chaplain." At one point tensions grew between the local civilian population and the Marines. "I feared violence. It reached such a point that during one of my staff meetings, I told my commanders to prepare to arm my Marines and, as a show of force, to have them circle the exterior of our base camp in full battle gear when the demonstration was set to occur later that week."[7]

His chaplain, Bill DeVine, proposed a plan he thought would be successful without resorting to a show of arms. Chaplain DeVine suggested that Marines mingle with demonstrators and offer them bottles of water. Mattis's initial reaction was to dismiss the chaplain and his bizarre plan. "But on second thought I called him in and asked him to explain."[8] Chaplain DeVine said that among the Iraqi people, it is a very friendly and hospitable gesture to offer people water. Providing water might be disarming for a crowd that came to demonstrate under a very hot sun.

General Mattis took his advice, not knowing what the result would be. The result was smiles all around, even some embraces, and friendly relations resumed on the spot. "On the suggestion of my Catholic chaplain, the Marines would take chilled drinking water in bottles and walk out amongst the protesters and hand it out. It is just hard to throw a rock at somebody who has given you a cold drink of water and it's 120 degrees outside."[9] Many times chaplains are a steady force in a very combustible world. Basic to a chaplain's effectiveness is honoring the dignity of every human being, whether ally or enemy, patient or doctor, prisoner or guard, seaman or admiral, student or provost, believer or nonbeliever.

This illustration highlights the need for chaplains to pay attention to cross-culturalism in foreign situations. Yet the general principle of acknowledging and advising leadership on cross-culturalism and religious accommodation is just as valuable domestically. Chaplains appreciate the result of globalization, specific to religious diversity, domestically as well as internationally. They are pivotal religious advisers as North American organizations and governments increasingly interact with cultures strongly influenced by non-Christian majority religions. As an example, the US Air Force reinforced their commitment to diversity and religious freedom in June 2019 when they graduated the first trainee ever granted permission to wear a "turban with uncut beard, uncut hair, necklace, and bracelet in observation of his Sikh faith."[10] Chaplains remain at the forefront of understanding this growing religious diversity in the United States. Globalization is no longer a foreign issue. The impact of globalization on domestic organizations is acknowledged personally and strongly through a variety of initiatives.

Under new patient- and family-centered care initiatives, we commit ourselves to creating opportunities for patients to exercise their religious expression and cultural traditions, even if it is inconvenient for the institution. Sometimes that is especially challenging for faith-based institutions coming from a different tradition. My advising role is to discover new ways of working "with" patients and families, rather than just doing "to" or "for" them.

—Hospital Chaplain

As you prepare for your role as an adviser, your contribution can start in the form of questions that gently guide toward deeper conversations. Your goal is to be constructive, not confrontational. Sample questions may include:

- What's your intent and goal?
- What does a win look like?
- What would you say to those who'd argue against that?
- But what if the facts were a little different?
- Do you want to be committed to this principle?

- Are you aware that you are establishing a precedent?
- Are you concerned that this might be unfair?
- It may work, but is it right?

If you bring a particular faith perspective to the issue, you should not suppress it. Yet don't try to force a single conclusion on everyone. If you advocate only from your faith perspective, your advisees might miss out on other angles. Most employees are never asked to offer counsel to their institutions or their leaders, yet chaplains are frequently consulted. This is a gift God entrusts to chaplains. Learn as much as you can about advisement. Remember, your source for authority is sustained by your personal integrity and pastoral identity. Avoid compromising either one.

5.3 Public Prayer: Worship Service and Civic Ceremony

The civic ceremony frequently places the chaplain in an advisory role because the chaplain is publicly offering a prayerful and prophetic voice. Although both faith-specific worship services and civic ceremonies may include prayer, the form of prayer is frequently different. This difference is not because the relationship between God and the chaplain has changed. It is because the chaplain is now representing the organization and intending to include all participants.

An organization may request that its chaplain participates in civic ceremonies that are not religious yet have elements of worship in them. The most frequent request is for the chaplain to offer public prayer at secular events. These civil events may be for those internal to the organization, such as a school graduation, an awards banquet, a promotion ceremony, an employee retirement, a sporting event kickoff, a building dedication, or a vessel christening. Civic events that are external to the chaplain's organization may include a city council meeting, a community luncheon, or a municipal memorial service. An increasingly frequent example is the blessing of the hands in health care. While originally designed for nurses, it now extends to numerous disciplines and crosses religious and cultural boundaries. Also, a company or civic institution may encourage staff and community to gather around a peace pole on significant days of the year, such as holidays and memorial times, for a chaplain-led prayer. Still another civil ritual practiced annually by many coastal communities is the blessing of the fleet. This event, called a "blessing," is not a religious service. It will typically include pageantry, feasting, dancing, and contests. It rarely includes a church service. Yet most events include a prayer for boats, hence the blessing of the fleet, from a local chaplain, priest, or pastor. The prayer is offered as a supplication for safe boating and bountiful fishing. While this is not a religious service, it clearly includes elements of faith within the civic ceremony.

Chaplains are frequently asked to provide prayers at civic ceremonies. Do you, as a prospective chaplain, see value in participating in such a ceremony? Would you turn down an invitation? Are you content being seen by some as a "religious ornament" at an otherwise civil, secular, and non-religious event? Do you view your invitation as an opportunity to "preach the word; be ready in season and out of season; reprove, rebuke, and exhort, with complete patience and teaching" (2 Tim. 4:2)? Do you view it as an occasion for others to hear God's name invoked in an otherwise secular event?

Not all events are as widespread as a blessing of the fleet. Some are restricted to certain groups and locations. However, they nonetheless offer the chaplain a prophetic voice and influential opportunity to the institution. As an example, this author had the opportunity to lead the United States Senate in the opening prayer at the second session of the 108th Congress, as documented by volume 150 of the *Congressional Record*:

> Lord, in this Chamber of leaders, who represent in their person, attitude, and vocation each of our 50 States in this great union, we now ask Your blessing, we invoke Your presence, we call upon Your wisdom, and we seek Your will for this great Nation.
>
> Use these Senators throughout this crucial time in our Nation's history. May their work, conducted both in and out of this Chamber, build and not tear down. May their relationships, both in session and thereafter, be ones of collegiality, friendship, and respect. May You be with them as they strive to keep America great.
>
> May You bless the 108th Congress and guide them as they continue to be compass points for our Nation and our world. May the direction they point keep them from temptation and evil, as they offer help and hope to those whose compass is adrift.
>
> We ask this in the name of the One who created us, who sustains us, and who delivers us. Amen.[11]

The intent of this prayer was to honor God while simultaneously affirming the conduct and relationships among Senate colleagues. The prayer used the analogy of a compass, asking our Lord to guide the Senate by providing direction to the nation and beyond. The prayer concluded by recognizing the attributes of God as creator, sustainer, and deliverer.

As a chaplain ministers to those within an institution, he will soon meet people not necessarily opposed to the *presence* of the chaplain but vehemently opposed to the *message* of the chaplain. These people are concerned the chaplain will unjustly use opportunities of prayer at civic ceremonies to proselytize. These concerns have merit.

> In some institutions, such as the jail I serve, chaplains are prohibited from proselytizing. This is partly because, given the captivity of the inmates, they are not necessarily in a position to be able to respond freely. They are not free from the dynamics of responding to the power and privilege that someone from the outside brings with the message of salvation.
> —*Corrections Chaplain*

Many believe a chaplain's position of offering public prayer is fraught with risk because the chaplain might leverage the opportunity to try to convert someone from one religion or belief to another. Chaplains, because they are given special trust granting them access to all people within the institution, must avoid any grounds for this assertion by seeking to include everyone in the prayer, unless it violates the chaplain's faith-group requirements. This aligns with the Association of Professional Chaplains Code of Ethics: "Members shall affirm the religious and spiritual freedom of all persons and refrain from imposing doctrinal positions or spiritual practices on persons whom they encounter in their professional role as chaplain."[12]

"Proselytizing" remains a hot-button term when it is defined as intentionally trying to convert someone to one's personal religious faith without an invitation. The Department of Defense advised, in March 2019, "Service members can share their faith (evangelize), but must not force unwanted, intrusive attempts to convert others of any faith or no faith to one's beliefs (proselytization)."[13] Therefore, proselytizing is *not* included within the capability of advisement. It would be unethical for a chaplain to say without prior consent, "I advise you to join my faith group." Instead, chaplains seek to find common ground through conversation and relationship building. Start by asking people what they do and invite them to share a story of how their work contributes to the mission of the organization. Follow up with, "Can you say more about that?" Chaplains form relationships that build trust and encourage respect. One safe way to initiate a potential faith-focused conversation is using the phrase given by a Jewish chaplain, "I don't want *my* faith to change you. I want *your* faith to change you." Chaplains help people find meaning and purpose in their existence. Chaplains seek to cooperate with all people without compromising their faith standards and personal integrity.

Regarding public prayer at secular civic ceremonies, one big issue among some Christian chaplains is the closing formula. One reason a simple "amen" is appropriate is because many organizational ceremonies require mandatory attendance. This is vastly different from a publicized worship service that is invitational, voluntary, and noncompulsory. If prayer is offered at an event where attendance is compulsory, then chaplains should be sensitive to all people in attendance. Does their required attendance outweigh a particular Christian chaplain's felt need to invoke the name of Jesus? Would a Jewish chaplain be required to quote Hebrew prayer from a public platform?

Some of my colleagues are convicted that all prayers end in the name of Jesus. I also close my prayers during worship services "in Jesus's name," even though my denomination doesn't require it. When Jesus teaches us to pray in his name, it's a call to pray in his authority and under his sovereignty. This means we are free to say "in Jesus's name" during worship. However, when I am asked to pray at a mandatory ceremony, I end my prayer saying simply, "amen" or "in your holy name, amen." I realize that other chaplains may have different practices, and I respect their convictions even if I don't share them.

—*Veterans Affairs Chaplain*

The point is, consider the context each time you are asked to pray. At mandatory events that include public prayer, many attendees subscribe to different faiths or no faith at all. Might some attendees feel intimidated or offended by a chaplain partaking in an obligatory public presentation? Would it not be wiser to find a way of inviting everyone to be included in the "amen"? In the public domain, when an event requires mandatory participation, many chaplains offer a modified Aaronic blessing (Num. 6:24–26) or read an appropriate prayer from the Psalms. Here is a sample closing prayer from a recent retirement ceremony: "Bless her as she prepares to transition from the years of employment to now embark on a new path of life. Guide her to know your will and purpose at all times. As we bid her fair winds and following seas, may the Lord bless her and keep her. May the Lord make his face to shine upon her and be gracious to her. May the Lord lift up his countenance upon her and give her peace."

The tension and anxiety faced by chaplains when providing prayer at mandated events are part of the institutional duality of their position. Most local church pastors don't regularly face this challenge. Dr. Janet McCormack, associate professor of chaplaincy and pastoral counseling at Denver Seminary and coauthor of the acclaimed book *The Work of the Chaplain*, commented about public prayers at civic ceremonies: "I worked harder on those prayers than I did on my sermons. For many people, this was the only time they heard anything from a Christian. I was careful not to push people away, but also careful to represent myself as a Christian chaplain. You're representing a specific group, and you're the ambassador for that group. I was never asked to do something outside of my faith." Dr. McCormack offered further wisdom regarding prayer preparation for civic ceremonies: "One of the things we can always do is pull in attributes of God: creator, love, light, beginning, end, and sustainer. I don't think we need to use a template such as 'in Jesus' name' to make it real prayer. That phrase is more about our comfort level. That's what we grew up with, that's what we think we're supposed to be doing. I find it's more important that the people out there are invited into prayer."[14]

This echoes a comment by Dr. Mark D. Roberts, executive director for the Max De Pree Center for Leadership at Fuller Theological Seminary: "Ironically, it is my commitment to following Jesus that leads me to pray without saying 'in Jesus' name.' Jesus, after all, welcomed to himself those who hadn't the faintest idea who he really was. They were drawn to his truth, his kindness, and his love. People did not flock to Jesus because he hammered them with religious language, but because he welcomed them with God's own love. In this context he was able to speak of the truth of God's kingdom and its implications for people, which included calling them to repentance."[15] This could have significant implications when a chaplain is employed by a faith-based institution. It is reasonable for organizational leaders to expect their chaplain to live by the values of the organization. Yet what happens when a faith-based organization hires a chaplain with the assumption that he will pray "in Jesus's name" with dying residents, even though many of the residents are not of a Christian tradition? Will the chaplain advise the leadership of this problem or acquiesce to their expectation?

In closing, when praying for mandatory gatherings, consider including as many hearers in the prayer as possible. Whereas the focus in these paragraphs is toward untrained but well-meaning chaplains, experienced chaplains already know how to design prayers that will be respectful of their audiences. Would it not be wonderful if all who gathered could pray in one accord and join the "amen" without hesitation?

As Dr. McCormack said, "No one is going to trust what I say if they don't trust that I care for them."[16] Relationships have to be genuine, and so must our prayers. People will know you're a chaplain by the way you treat them through your words, your actions, and your humility. Chaplaincy is all about relationships. The role of adviser must be undergirded by solid relationships in order to be respected and honored.

Discussion Questions

1. How do you, as a chaplain, advise institutional leaders on ethics, character, and moral decision making?
2. What does it mean to have a prophetic voice?
3. How does the institutional expectation of receiving advice from the chaplain align with the chaplain's role?
4. How might a chaplain lose credibility as an organizational adviser?
5. In what ways do chaplains serve as advocates for the people they serve?
6. If an inmate in the county jail asks for religious literature that includes racist ideology in order to practice his religion, does religious freedom or institutional safety and security "win"? How might the institution help support the inmate while not distributing literature that can incite violence?
7. What options does a chaplain have when it is necessary to offer alternative advice that might be unpopular?
8. When is it appropriate for a chaplain to initiate a conversation with institutional leadership about employee advocacy? What advocacy topics might be appropriate?
9. In what way can a chaplain, having a wide appreciation of religious diversity, contribute to an organizational understanding of cross-culturalism?
10. In what ways can the chaplain's role in a civic ceremony have an advisory role?

11. Why would you, as a chaplain, bring value by participating in a civic ceremony?

12. What concerns do you have in offering prayer at an otherwise civil, secular, and nonreligious event?

13. What is meant by proselytizing? Why is it a hot-button term? Under what conditions is it ethical?

14. What elements of prayer are you required to include no matter the circumstance? Would your faith group concur and support you in this decision?

15. What is meant by this statement: "I don't want *my* faith to change you—I want *your* faith to change you"?

CHAPTER 6

Bringing It All Together

> I believe that when all is said and done, all you can do is to show up for someone in crisis, which seems so inadequate. But then when you do, it can radically change everything. Your there-ness ... can be life giving, because often everyone else is in hiding.
>
> —*Anne Lamott*

6.1 Integration

You are soon ready to step out and serve as a chaplain. Your goal is to gain deeper appreciation for your calling and find the organization that allows you to express your ministry gifts. This chapter sets out how to find the right fit by aligning your ministerial giftedness with organizational values. It identifies what you can expect in the first three months of chaplaincy; it also offers helpful introductory tips on ministering to your family during the process.

Showing Up

A chaplain's work is to be present with people. Some days this work can feel discouraging, like what you have to offer is inadequate to the situation, especially when responding to crisis and tragedy. But a chaplain's ministry of presence provides immeasurable (and sometimes measurable) value for the people she serves and for her institution. As Anne Lamott wrote, a chaplain's "there-ness" and availability to step into the chaos of others' lives is life giving to the people around her. Christian chaplains radically change the people they serve and the situations they encounter by being incarnationally present and bearing the grace of Jesus to all who will receive. As a chaplain, you bring "Christ in you, the hope of glory" (Col. 1:27).

A chaplain knows that it isn't ministry programs or religious policies that change lives. It is you showing up and being available for others. You bear no armaments for war. You carry no keys to the prison cell. You have neither the stethoscope nor the gown of the medical doctor. Your tools are not to be used upon people—they are offered among people. Hospitality is freely shared. The word of God, entrusted to inadequate chaplains, is first proclaimed in the silence of simply showing up.

> Jesus told us to "go out." I said, "Here I am, Lord, send me!" and he put me into the wilderness for two and a half years. I learned to "wait" in the wilderness. Waiting is one of the foundations of chaplaincy. In the wilderness I also learned to love the sound of the wind, which has no sound until it encounters something. Chaplaincy is a ministry of presence, which is most notable by its presence and absence, like the wind or the water. It is way different than being a pastor in a church. It is something different every moment. I was having dinner with one of my dearest friends the other day, who is a pastor. She is all about working within church walls—predictability, organization of ministries—the model of "church" as we know it. I am all about escaping the walls and getting out with people.
>
> —*Police Chaplain*

Finding the Right Organization

Finding the right organization to employ you as a chaplain may be challenging, but it is not as difficult as it used to be. Many people are looking for meaningful help and support structures in their communities and are more frequently turning to their workplaces. As a result, workplace chaplaincy is expanding. An article in the *Atlantic* notes, "For many people, particularly in the United States, religious leaders and institutions often offer that support structure. For those who don't have that kind of independent community, work is a logical place to look for help—and some employers seem to be recognizing that."[1] More institutions are seeking to add chaplains to their staff. Since chaplaincy is growing, there are likely chaplains currently in your surrounding area. You do not have to travel far to connect with a chaplain.

Appendix A of this book contains a brief overview of what it's like to work as a chaplain for different types of institutions, each summary written by a chaplain serving in a particular field. Particularly useful in exploring potential employment is initiating an informational interview. Contact a chaplain in potential areas of your interest to see if he'd be willing to talk on the phone or allow you to visit his workplace. As an example, if you are interested in health care, then talk to chaplains in hospital, hospice, VA, continuing-care retirement community (CCRC), memory care, and skilled nursing chaplaincies. The variety of these conversations will help you gain an appreciation for the diversity of ministry opportunities. Visit their workplaces and listen to their stories. Learn about their calling to chaplaincy, philosophy for institutional ministry, and style of pastoral care. Sample questions during your interviews might include:

- What kind of ministry experience turned you toward chaplaincy?
- How did you affirm your call to chaplaincy?
- What are some frequent issues that come up in counseling?
- What is it like working alongside people of different faiths?
- Where do you go for mentoring?
- How do you stay connected with your faith group?
- What kinds of restrictions or restraints are placed on chaplains?
- What do you do to practice self-care?
- What does a perfect day look like as a chaplain?
- What was the worst day of your ministry?
- How did you recover from that event?
- What is your relationship with local churches and clergy?
- Why is chaplaincy the right fit for you?
- What would be my next steps in pursuing ministry in chaplaincy?

People love to talk about what they do and how they serve. It is fundamental to who we are as humans. These informational interviews potentially offer you two outcomes. First, you listen to these chaplains' answers to see if you resonate with them. Whereas the initial chapter of this book discussed your calling to ministry, these interviews offer the personal perspectives of other chaplains. Trust God to open the door to the right organization and use these interviews to explore your calling. Ask the Lord to make you receptive to his possibilities for you. The second outcome to your interviews is more specific. Meeting with various chaplains will serve to raise their awareness of your interest in chaplaincy. As you ask questions, the chaplain will observe you and form an impression whether you would do well in chaplaincy.

It is important to prepare a follow-up to your informational interview. Your last question to the chaplain would likely be, "What would be my next steps in pursuing ministry in chaplaincy?" This open-ended question allows you to reengage by sending a written thank-you expressing your appreciation for the chaplain's counsel. If you sense the meeting went well, ask for a second appointment specifically focusing on your preparation for chaplaincy. You already know from prior chapters in this textbook that the chaplain belongs to a faith group and is accountable to his own ecclesiastical endorser. Further, he may belong to a professional association of chaplains unique to his type of chaplaincy. You might request him to provide a referral that will connect you to both his ecclesial endorser and his professional association. There could even be a time when you ask this chaplain for a recommendation.

Many chaplains enjoy connecting prospective chaplains to resources and people who might help them along the way as they discern their calling. Your goal is to gain deeper appreciation for your potential calling into chaplaincy and also find the right organization that will allow you to express your ministry gifts.

Matching and Aligning Organizational Values

Once your call to chaplaincy has been affirmed and confirmed, your goal is not simply getting a chaplain position but getting the *right* chaplain position for you. Many clergy serve in places where they sense they don't belong. They are in a rural setting yet seek a less isolated urban church. They serve on a staff that tasks one area of their talents, but the ministry remains unidimensional and they have other pastoral strengths begging to be exercised. They are in a ministry but not the right ministry for them. Consequently, their unhappiness leaves them vulnerable. They risk projecting their disappointment and frustration upon their congregation as well as their own family.

The risk of ministry misalignment is not limited to the parish. It includes chaplaincy but with one significant difference. Like other pastoral ministries, chaplains are most healthy when individual giftedness is aligned with organizational values. Whereas church mission statements tend to be unremarkably similar, corporate mission statements are diverse.

Prospective chaplains can choose from a variety of organizational settings for ministry, and each one has its unique mission and set of values. More variety means greater opportunity to find one uniquely fit to the chaplain's competencies. It is the prospective chaplain's responsibility to review the vision, mission, and value statements of the organization during the employment candidacy process. Seek organizations that allow talents to be valued as strengths. If a chaplain is at odds with her organization's goals, it will likely bring confusion to those she serves.

> As a pre-Christian student at a service academy, I voluntarily enrolled in a Christian confirmation class taught by chaplains. My hope was to hear from a chaplain what might make Christianity appealing. In the third session he dropped a bombshell. He said that being in the military was incompatible with Christian faith. His previous combat trauma had shifted his view to active pacifism. Already struggling to matriculate from the service academy, I resented this pressure he put on me to immediately resign. I was confused and hurt by this interaction, and I stopped attending his confirmation class. It took another five years before I talked again to a chaplain.
>
> —*Military Officer*

Instead of embracing their chaplain ministry, chaplains who are misaligned with their organizational mission grow to resent their position. Instead of serving people, they risk using people. You can avoid this negative behavior by first identifying and aligning your aspirations with organizational values that resonate with you. God does not desire for you to jump on the first chaplain opportunity that comes along. Realize that not every opportunity is a calling. If you have not identified your strengths, consider CliftonStrengths.[2] It is a great tool for identifying, matching, and aligning your unique strengths to your chaplain position.

> I took the CliftonStrengths online assessment to discover my top talents. It identified five out of thirty-four strengths that I unwittingly and naturally use. I've learned a lot about these five areas of connectedness, learning, adaptability, maximizing, and belief. Upon deeper review of these talents, I now realize how the military chaplaincy embraces organizational values that align with my strengths. For example, a military chaplain must quickly connect with others due to the "revolving door" nature of her ministry. It requires someone to learn a culture and be adaptable to change because of frequent deployments and moves. It seeks to maximize members by frequent career

milestones resulting in promotion. It also has a strong sense of core values undergirding the profession of arms. Joining the military as a chaplain aligned my strengths with healthy organizational values that now allow me to flourish in my job.

—Military Chaplain

The First Ninety Days

What are the initial steps for an energetic, fully prepared, newly appointed chaplain arriving at his first chaplain position? Chaplains are vulnerable at the start of a new job because they lack context for their ministry. They do not yet have in-depth knowledge of the challenges facing them. The early days are critical because small differences in a chaplain's actions can have a huge impact on long-term effectiveness. Failure to create momentum will result in stalling an otherwise high-potential ministry. There are effective methods to accelerate closing the gap between being a new employee who consumes resources from the organization and being a reliable and valuable resource contributor. Michael Watkins, in his book *The First 90 Days*, offers some ideas that will help new chaplains get up to speed faster.

Watkins writes about the "break-even point," when a chaplain stops consuming resources from an organization and commences creating value. His book's title refers to this time frame, approximately three months. During the first three months of a job, the chaplain becomes oriented to the organization. He engages its leadership and culture. He builds relationships. He seeks to build initial coalitions with others and develops early credibility.

Effective ministry is accelerated as the new chaplain inspires and mobilizes the energy of others within the organization. This leveraging of ministry multiplies the impact of faith, ethics, morals, and virtues upon the overall execution of an organization's mission. Leaders grow in awareness of the chaplain's role through frequent dialogue with her as well as hearing from other key influencers about her value. As Watkins notes, "Displaying a genuine ability to listen often translates into increased credibility and influence."[3] As the new chaplain integrates herself into the culture, she builds knowledge that will help her make better decisions sooner. Good decision making moves her to much sooner reach the break-even point, where she will bring personal value creation to the organization.

Instead of immediately building programs, the first ninety days are best suited for meeting people and allowing them to get to know you and your approach to chaplain ministry. First, focus on briefly sharing your story, the values and goals you represent, and your method of being available for others. Second, ask people about their background, family, and interests. Finally, educate yourself about your organization. Raise questions with people that will help you better understand the organization from their vantage point. Consider asking them about the biggest challenges they face and why they have these challenges. Follow up by asking where they see promising opportunities for growth, where they find underdeveloped or undeveloped opportunities for change, and what they believe needs to occur in order to bring these opportunities to fruition. End your conversation by asking them how you, as their chaplain, can best support them. What do they need from you? Where do they need your focused attention?

What made you successful in your previous ministry experience may not work now. Doing what you know and avoiding what you don't know will likely not work. Be cautious not to overpromise results. It is better to underpromise and overdeliver. In these initial conversations, be deliberate, not hurried. Many chaplains confuse motion with progress. Building momentum through a targeted approach is wiser than scattering your time through diffused ministry programming.

Your goal as a new chaplain is to build personal credibility by gaining respect as a solid contributor and team player. Within the first ninety days, pursue initiatives that will excite and energize people, establish key relationships, and get people to talk about ministry expectations. Seek to gain greater access to people throughout the organization and find high-potential opportunities for short-term ministry improvements. If this is done well, you will build momentum, deepen your impact upon the organization, and gain credibility as an accessible chaplain.

Chaplain and Family

Chaplaincy goes beyond the workplace. It is a whole-family ministry, since the job has enormous impact on the families of those the chaplain serves. Spouses and children of beneficiaries often connect with the chaplain for a variety of purposes, including premarital counseling, wedding officiating, marriage enrichment programs, child baptisms and dedications, organizational holiday gatherings, weekly chapel worship services, as well as funerals and memorial services. Chaplains are often the only clergy they know. These spouses and children are not the only family members affected by chaplaincy. The chaplain's own spouse and children are also directly impacted by the chaplain's ministry, in ways unlike what happens in the local parish.

Unlike my experience as a pastor's wife in the church, I was never expected to accompany my husband up front. I don't play the piano. I don't sing in the choir. I don't lead women's Bible studies. Instead, put me in the chapel nursery with the two-year-olds or invite me to help with vacation Bible school. Don't pigeonhole a spouse, even in the chaplaincy. It became a standing joke among chaplain spouses that we are now done being piano players and choir directors. Instead, as a chaplain spouse, I felt I could serve where my gifts were strong. If there was a need, I could lend a hand. Yet there were no expectations that I had to do anything.

—Chaplain Spouse

Not all chaplaincies are the same. Most provide a great amount of stability. Some require frequent mobility because of deployment. The military chaplaincy is noted for its frequent moves. While military chaplains can request upcoming assignments, the needs of the military service may supersede their request. There is an ebb and flow to military chaplaincy. Some assignments anticipate unpredictable contingencies that require a chaplain to be mobile. Yet a follow-on assignment may call for the chaplain to be geographically stable.

In military chaplain families, we tend to be "tumbleweeds." We moved eighteen times in thirty years. Frequent moves forced us to grow and rely on each other. Our kids were usually easy with moves and very adaptable. However, the teen years were particularly difficult. It was strange for them to find other high school students who had spent their entire lives in one place. Our children couldn't understand how that could happen. Moving, making new friends, and the unexpected situations that occurred when uprooting a family made them resilient.

—Chaplain Spouse

The military allows chaplains with exceptional family needs to remain in locations that provide for those specific needs. If the family seeks an overseas assignment, an initial assessment is conducted to confirm the availability of required medical or educational resources. Each branch of service is mandated by the US Department of Defense to provide comprehensive and coordinated community support for all military families with special needs. This includes housing, educational, medical, and personnel services. Families requiring specialized services for physical, developmental, emotional, or mental disabilities can request that their active duty member be enrolled in the program.

Being a military kid, you learn about sacrifice and duty. Being a pastor's kid, you learn about integrity and hospitality. Being a chaplain's kid, I believe you learn a third and even more important skill set: you learn about empathy, diversity, and the value of widening your circle to include more people in your community than might be comfortable at first. Every two or three years when we'd have to move and start the process over again, I got to see proof that inclusion, mutual respect, and kindness can create a community from scratch.

—*Chaplain Family Member*

While chaplains listen to many people, information disclosed during counseling cannot be shared with family members. A chaplain's confidentiality is not extended to a spouse. There is no appropriate circumstance for a chaplain to share with his family what is spoken under the clergy-penitent relationship. Sharing a story in which a counselee's information is disclosed to someone in the chaplain's family represents a breach of duty.

One of the greatest gifts provided to families of chaplains is the enduring friendships that develop among chaplain colleagues. No other professional ministry combines so many faith groups working together for a common cause. Protestants representing a multitude of denominations work alongside Roman Catholic and Orthodox priests. Christian, Jewish, and Muslim chaplains frequently serve in the same organization.

Growing up as a military kid and a Protestant chaplain's kid, I often had to pull double duty. Not only did I know military acronyms and customs, like what that stripe or insignia meant on someone's uniform, but I also knew church history and traditions, like to expect the altar cloth to turn purple every Ash Wednesday. The thing that set me apart as a chaplain's kid, however, was how I also learned why there's a curtain covering the Torah scrolls and how those small bowls of holy water relate to the Sign of the Cross. Until early adulthood, I had no idea that my ecumenical upbringing was unique—I thought everyone's church choir sang at both Catholic Mass and Protestant worship, and that all kids got to play dreidel in December.

—*Chaplain Family Member*

Chaplain families network and tend to build relationships on the commonalities of faith that are also shared by their respective chaplains. When they focus on the differences in faith traditions, they do so to learn from one another and understand that diversity leads to inclusion and not exclusion. Chaplains in the military share a common background of having shallow roots. Chaplains serving health-care, college, or prison communities focus on growing deeper relationships within their local region. Their spouse and families move less often, so they don't incur the frequent stress of relocation.

In mobile institutions such as the military, disaster-relief, or first-responder chaplaincy, chaplains are still needed to serve the families remaining behind. These chaplains help confront the stress of separation by helping families network with others who share the anxiety of having distant loved ones. As caregivers during these vulnerable times of family separation, chaplains embrace the challenges caused by the deployment with creative solutions. They design programs and initiate activities focused on helping those most challenged by the separation.

Family tensions can be frustratingly high during separations. As an example, when a military member visits a unique place and sends photos to her husband and children back home, it can unexpectedly bring feelings of envy. A common question is, "Why do you get to explore the world while I take care of the kids?" Chaplains help validate these feelings of loss and separation by affirming the parent who stays behind carrying a dual role of filling in where he can for the traveling parent.

Chaplains are not always deploying in military, disaster-relief, or first-responder ministry. They cycle through a season of deployment followed by stability at home. This allows them to fully engage in family activities. Like an accordion expanding and contracting, the work of the chaplain assigned to deploying and traveling institutions also expands and contracts. If you enjoy being adaptable, there is no other ministry as unique as chaplaincy.

6.2 Self-Care

Self-care is essential if a chaplain intends to sustain inspirational and healthy ministry. It is important to think about cycles of stress and risks of burnout. Chaplains are particularly susceptible to compassion fatigue. As Proverbs 4:23 says,

> Keep your heart with all vigilance,
>   for from it flow the springs of life.

Boundaries

Self-care starts with developing healthy personal boundaries. Boundaries are there for mutual protection, and they provide accountability for both chaplain and counselee. Boundaries define limits and avoid awkward situations. Development of standard protocols is invaluable. For example, when you talk with someone in your office, leave the door open and ask a third party to be in the vicinity. Even with protocols, there will still be unexpected gray areas where standards are not clearly stated.

> I am an industrial chaplain in a manufacturing plant. The assembly line is very noisy, and employees spend long hours at their workstations adding parts to the semifinished product. A team assembler left the line for a brief pastoral care conversation. Three minutes into our conversation, she told me she was uncomfortable because I was standing too close to her. This surprised me. I realized my relational boundary couldn't be the benchmark for others. In order to decrease any perception of intimidation, I must be aware of space and sensitive to proximity. I always need to maintain appropriate distance between the counselee and me. I now frequently sit at a small round table, stocked with several water bottles, with an available chair for the counselee. The table serves to provide a nonthreatening boundary and isn't distracting to our conversation. It provides a measured distance while not becoming a barrier.
>
> —Workplace Chaplain

Touching people without permission, no matter how innocent, is never allowed, with the exception of shaking hands. A pat on the back or a touch on the shoulder is a boundary violation. You must respect the boundaries of the person you're working with, and you also have to maintain your own boundaries. This will create awkwardness if you do not establish boundary protocols at the beginning of your chaplaincy.

> My stepfather was a hospital chaplain. He was always a calm, patient, and kind man. He did not pressure or push himself on anyone but was always available. He was the first person I knew who greeted everyone he met with a hug as long as they seemed receptive. He could strike up a conversation with a stranger in the grocery line and minutes later, they would be telling him about their sick parent or recent job loss. There was something about him that just invited people to share their stories with him. But one of the defining characteristics of my stepfather as a "hugger" could have been something that got him into trouble.
>
> —Prospective Chaplain

Maintaining physical safeguards is essential. Rooms scheduled for counseling should have an unobstructed window built into the door. If no window, the door remains open. Play soft background music. Ensure that an office administrator is outside the office in physical proximity and close enough to hear should anyone call out. Precautions are always taken to maintain privacy while ensuring the dignity and safety of both counselee and chaplain.

Self-Awareness

Chaplains can choose to be available twenty-four hours a day. At some point they realize there is an endless ocean of suffering and human need. You cannot address it all. As a chaplain, what empowers and energizes you? What's your motivation? What's driving you? Do you long for creativity? Do you like to work inside or outside? What depletes you? What are your signs of depletion? What keeps you going in a challenging job? If you are an introvert, will you relish isolation after a busy day with people? If you are a strong "J" on the Myers-Briggs Type Indicator, how will you feel not bringing counselees to resolution?

> When I first became a chaplain, I thought I could do it all. When someone would come to my office for counseling, I fixed a Velcro sign on the door that said Counseling in Progress—Please Do Not Disturb. After five or six sessions per day, I became so exhausted that I would leave that sign up long after each prisoner left. I needed time to myself. I was "counseling" myself by exploring ways to establish realistic and much-needed time boundaries.
>
> —*Correctional/Prison Chaplain*

Two concepts that might be helpful for chaplains when thinking about self-awareness are *transference* and *countertransference*. Sigmund Freud developed these labels to describe the way patients transfer feelings from important persons in their early lives onto their psychoanalyst. Most chaplains are not psychoanalysts. Nonetheless, this concept is valuable in chaplaincy. For example, a counselee may expect his chaplain to be holy in everything he does because of cherished childhood memories, just as he might expect a police officer to uphold the law at all times and a doctor to cure any ailment. Transference can be very positive, as the counselee is more likely to trust someone serving in a role he cherished in the past.

Countertransference is defined as redirecting a therapist's feelings to-

BRINGING IT ALL TOGETHER

ward a patient. A chaplain may be nicer to a counselee when the chaplain feels the counselee holds her in high esteem. A chaplain's awareness of her own countertransference is very important for self-care. Countertransference feelings can serve as a sensitive interpersonal barometer. For example, a chaplain may not be aware when a counselee's manner resembles the chaplain's sibling. Before the chaplain realizes what is happening, he is increasingly confident in providing a specific, yet misdirected, solution to the issue based on an altogether different relationship.

Here is a mental checklist for chaplains seeking to grow in their awareness of possible countertransference: (1) Is this feeling happening frequently? If so, it may say a lot about the chaplain but probably nothing about the counselee. (2) Is the feeling triggered by something unrelated to the counselee, such as hunger, overcaffeination, stress, or fatigue? (3) Is the feeling related to the counselee in an obvious way? Maybe the counselee looks like your sister or an ex-boyfriend. (4) Is the feeling uncharacteristic of the chaplain, a reaction to one particular counselee, and yet an exact trigger is not immediately obvious? These feelings often shed light on subtle yet important dynamics between you and the counselee.

Countertransference is not usually helpful when unexamined or unrecognized. It can interfere with the chaplain's ability to help someone. This occurs when a chaplain is so entertained by a counselee's humor that the underlying bitterness is ignored or never named. It can occur when an attractive counselee is never challenged because the chaplain is unwittingly seeking affirmation. It is experienced when a chaplain feels bored, irked, or paralyzed in the presence of a particular counselee. It is the chaplain's job to recognize these feelings and address them. A wise chaplain will refer the counselee to another colleague when these feelings emerge.

For example, when counseling a member of the opposite sex, chaplains may unintentionally feed the person what she acutely seeks in a romantic relationship. The counselee may nonverbally think, "I wish my spouse gave me the kind of attention that you're giving me right now." Yet you're thinking, "This is a forty-five-minute professional conversation that I provide as a service." The counselee is nonverbally processing, "I've always wanted someone who will listen to me and relate with me like you." The counselee places greater confidence in you because she is transferring an attachment she wishes she had with her spouse. Because of her willingness to be vulnerable and disclose deeper needs, you suddenly see something in her that sparks you toward a countertransference attachment. This spirals quickly and obviously becomes unhealthy. Be cautious. This is not where anyone wants to end their vocation as a chaplain. Your best response is to hold yourself accountable. Tell a colleague about your experience while maintaining the confidentiality of the conversation. Refer the counselee to someone else as soon as you can. If you believe you are the best person to give her help, then you've already crossed over the edge of helping. You've compromised your ability to remain impartial. The potential of harming her is higher than the potential for helping her. Practicing self-awareness is part of self-care.

Safety

Some chaplaincies have inherent risk. Yet chaplains can prepare themselves for those moments when they and those they serve face issues of safety and potential danger. Law-enforcement chaplains cope with the possibility of dangerous suspects and high-speed vehicle chases. Health-care chaplains risk being around communicable diseases, exposing themselves to low-level radiation, and meeting potentially hostile family members. Sports chaplains deal with injuries, accidents, and athletes with strong egos. Industrial chaplains face high levels of noise, workplace machinery, and occasionally contaminated waste. Correctional chaplains deal with potential fights, riots, and violence. Crisis intervention chaplains tackle a spectrum of hazards, from flooding to domestic terrorism. Military chaplains are faced with war, bombings, and funerals for young people. Ask yourself: What am I willing to do? Where am I willing to go? Who am I willing to see? As you ask these questions, pray for God to guide you to a ministry where you can be fully present "to will and to work for his good pleasure" (Phil. 2:13).

Ethics

Ethics integrates personal boundaries, self-awareness, decision making, and safety. Many institutions consider ethical violations to include dating another employee, accepting gifts from a counselee, providing legal advice to an inmate, or carrying a weapon. Chaplains must accept the ethical standards of the institution. If chaplains violate these standards, they will be held accountable and will likely suffer personal consequences. Others within the organization often idealize the position of chaplain. This is one reason why chaplains are held to a higher standard than others. Personal misconduct is a betrayal of sacred trust and denigrates the role of chaplaincy. By holding yourself accountable, you minimize the possibility of doing something unethical.

Health and Wellness

Your personal health is an important aspect of self-care. Christian chaplains strive to sustain healthy habits because God created the body for his own purpose: "Do you not know that your body is a temple of the Holy Spirit within you, whom you have from God? You are not your own" (1 Cor. 6:19). Basic building blocks for one's body include getting adequate sleep, getting regular physical exercise, eating a well-balanced diet, maintaining significant relationships, having an active prayer and devotional life, and sustaining connection with one's ecclesiastical body.

When I was doing seriously intense pastoral counseling, I would have six or seven soldiers per day. It was a lot because I was doing everything else a chaplain does: Bible studies, Sunday preaching, worship preparations, small groups, and premarital preps. I started spacing more time between appointments and filled the gaps in between with all the other expectations.

—*Military Chaplain*

How do you keep your bucket full of energy and compassion? Perhaps you start your day by pouring energy and compassion out of your bucket after encountering and addressing an injustice. You still have a half bucket after meeting with a grieving family at noon. Yet the afternoon consumes the rest of your energy as you work on next year's budget. Your bucket of empathy and energy is now empty, and you still have a small-group meeting at night. Burnout is a common reaction to long-term stresses such as professional isolation, ambiguous successes (e.g., "That was a great sermon, but the twenty hours you spent preparing didn't count"), an unrealistic and unsustainable pace, undefined boundaries, and a messiah complex believing you need to save the world.

A chaplain colleague of mine overeats when depleted. He realizes he starts eating more even though he's not hungry. My trigger is avoidance. As an extrovert, I am energized by being around people. Yet when exhausted,

I avoid people and seek time by myself. If I am walking through the hospital corridor, I won't make eye contact with other people. There are situations when this is completely appropriate. There are other times when this isn't acceptable behavior.

—*Hospital Chaplain*

Burnout makes you feel apathetic, pessimistic, indifferent, irritable, and negative. These are typical symptoms of compassion fatigue frequently experienced by caregivers. You are not tired *of* being compassionate but tired *from* being compassionate. Chaplains and other caregivers become emotionally depleted after hearing about pain suffered by victims. The emotional and physical distress caused by serving those deeply in need can desensitize a chaplain's ability to express empathy. This may result in no longer having the emotional energy to be "present."

You also may encounter secondary trauma by exposure to people who have been traumatized themselves. Their disturbing description of traumatic events raises your level of compassion fatigue because your empathy collides with your inability to solve or cure the issue. Prolonged burnout and compassion fatigue result in stress-related diseases, like high blood pressure, as well as moral ambiguity if what you hold as sacred has been violated. Your perspective changes. You may experience doubt and uncertainty regarding your calling, your ministry value, and your faith.

It took me years to learn that there was something called compassion fatigue. It only affects those of us who are caregivers, including those who are chaplains. We've given pieces of our heart away in order to care for others. So we need to be filled again. I go to my faith first. I find places of respite, places where I feel safe, places where I can commune with God, that might not look religious. I often turn to water. I go scuba diving when I'm really upset. I soak in a tub and listen to soft music. Don't limit yourself to only the things you read about in books. These work for somebody else. Find out what works for you and then do it. Know that God is going to be in it if you're connected to him in what you're doing.

—*Hospice Chaplain*

Fill your empty bucket through intentional self-care. Experience an annual retreat with your denomination. Go away for spiritual direction and guidance. Encounter a silent retreat. As you practice care for the caregiver, you develop resiliency. Your ministry of compassion and caring comes from the full bucket of God's compassion for you and his caring of your life. You can only give what you've received. This is a wonderful, grace-filled gift.

All your natural abilities of inspiring, influencing, relationship building, and strategic thinking can go only so far unless you build resilience. How can you develop the capacity to recover quickly from difficulties? A number of resources are available to help chaplains sustain a forward-looking and uplifting presence.[4] Remember that you are called, not just driven: "Driven people often project a bravado of confidence as they forge ahead with their achievement-oriented life plan. . . . Called people, on the other hand, possess strength from within, a quality of perseverance and power that are impervious to the blows from without."[5] May God use you as a person responding to what he is calling you to do, and may you do it in a way that gives you satisfaction—soul-expanding, bucket-filling life. Survival skills for healthy chaplains include:

- Setting appropriate boundaries
- Learning to delegate
- Maintaining a personal support system
- Learning the power of saying no
- Personal prayer, meditation, and worship

Decompression

How long does a chaplain meet with an individual for pastoral counseling? Although we block off sixty minutes for a session, the standard practice is to meet for around fifty minutes.[6] This offers a few minutes to reset for another individual by the start of the following hour. If you remain longer in conversation and relinquish your reset time, you will likely be fatigued for the next person. Instead, you need to maintain time boundaries. Be practical in setting expectations by hanging a clock that's visible to the counselee and you. The ten minutes between appointments is priceless. What will you do immediately after the counselee walks out of the office? Start by collecting your thoughts and calming them during this ten-minute Sabbath. It is a pause between the last conversation and the upcoming one. Relax and tell yourself, "I need to take a minivacation right now to decompress myself. Otherwise, the next person coming through the door will receive both my fatigue and my unresolved anxiety from the past fifty minutes."

When I have several intense counseling appointments in a row, and the next person is waiting, I realize my level of exhaustion is growing and my attention span is shrinking. I might say, "I've had a really tough morning. Right now, I don't think I have the energy you deserve. Could we reschedule our session for later?" Invariably they will almost always say yes, because they want me at my best, not my depleted.

—Corporate Chaplain

What does a brief decompression session look like? It can be prayer. It can be silence. It can be reflecting on a Bible verse. It can focus on doing something recreational. Turn on music. Do a dozen push-ups. Play a harmonica. Solve a quick sudoku or crossword puzzle. Light a candle. Get energy back into your system.

There are seasons where you can expect intense pastoral counseling. It may be due to a crisis in the organization, such as a layoff, employee reduction in force, or relocation. It can be seasonal, such as an approaching holiday when people are typically with their families but unusual circumstances prohibit time together. It can be global: during the COVID-19 pandemic, "religious leaders are expected to provide counseling, lead prayer groups and minister personally to people with special needs. For many, that aspect of their work has never been more important, or more difficult, at a time when communities are struggling to contain the coronavirus."[7]

My typical decompression prayer goes like this, "Lord, I need to release this person to you because I cannot carry their load. I am not healthy enough. I am not smart enough. I am not wise enough to be trying to manage this person's life, but I come to the only person in the universe who can, and that is you, Lord." It is a freedom-cleansing time. I release what I received. I hand over to God the violence, oppression, pain, weakness, and grief.

—Correctional/Prison Chaplain

It is helpful to be aware of your high-energy moments. Chaplains often shift counseling appointments to afternoons in order to use creative morning time for sermon preparation. Exercising time management and prioritizing events are part of building intentional decompression into the structure of a chaplain's workday. Having established a pattern of practicing decompression prepares the chaplain for an appropriate response to unexpected crises. A new chaplain soon discovers that people often bring issues to discuss that may not actually be a crisis. Yet it feels like a crisis to them, so they come to their chaplain with a sense of overemphasized urgency.

> One thing I would always try to do is immediately respond to their crisis. I became exhausted. My health and inadequate rest concerned me. I couldn't drink enough coffee to stay alert with the number of mounting problems. They kept coming. I had to find an alternative. I remembered a medical examiner taking my vital signs and asking, "What is your pain on a scale of one to nine?" I modified the question for counselees: "What is your urgency on a scale of one to nine?" If they said eight or nine, I dropped everything. If they said anything less, I asked if they would be willing to make an appointment. This was a turning point for me. I captured my life back.
>
> —*Disaster Relief Chaplain*

There are times when pastoral decompression conflicts with human crisis. During emergencies, you drop your expectations for decompression. Yet most pastoral conversations aren't urgent. You can ask if counselees are willing to make an appointment. By giving them a specific dedicated time, you hopefully achieve two beneficial outcomes. First, by delaying the pastoral counseling appointment, they will receive the "fully present" you and not the "depleted" you. Second, their presenting issue may be resolved before the appointment due to their retaining ownership of the problem and potential solutions. By placing a buffer of time between their initiation and your availability, you provide a brief period for them to reframe their problem.

There are legitimate crises. Medical triage is a process of sorting people based on limited resources. Those with immediate medical needs receive quicker treatment. This concept applies to pastoral counseling. If you receive the news, "My husband was just rushed into ICU," then drop everything and go. Few mental health professionals will see clients without a prior appointment. It is reasonable for psychologists, counselors, clinicians, therapists, clinical social workers, and mental health nurse practitioners to schedule appointments unless they are on duty. Yet chaplains frequently do not consider the benefit of setting up appointments because they see their role as accessible urgent care providers. Practice accessibility by being intentional in planning and scheduling.

Pastoral-counseling triage is a legitimate process for discerning the urgency of the request. Including the counselee helps that person recognize the magnitude of the situation and requisite need for assistance. When the counselee is prompted to classify the urgency of his crisis, it may become obvious that his framework needs recalibration. A chaplain might hear, for example, "I need to talk to you right away because I have this terrible problem. I have to figure out where I am going to grad school next year." If a chaplain doesn't first ask a counselee to rate the urgency of his issue on a pastoral-counseling triage scale, then the chaplain risks coming across as cynical. The chaplain might think to herself, "One of our students just died by suicide, and you are worried about your future school mascot?" Jumping into an immediate counseling session in response to a noncrisis can result not only in cynicism but also in burnout.

Remember, the chaplain is frequently the most accessible counselor. If you are too accessible, you risk not being emotionally available to those who require your full pastoral competencies. Consider developing strategies and avenues of decompression that support you and your energy level.

> There have also been times when, on a beautiful day, I asked the student if he didn't mind being seen with his chaplain outside. If he supported the idea, I said let's take a walk around campus and talk. Let's go get a coffee or a slice of pizza. It changed the venue. It was relaxed. I still gave my time to them even though it was shoulder-to-shoulder and not face-to-face.
>
> —*Campus Chaplain*

Detachment

Tim Keller, in *The Reason for God*, writes about the emotional exhaustion that sometimes accompanies simply talking with people: "It requires very little of you to love a person who is pulled together and happy. Think, however, of emotionally wounded people. There is no way to listen and love people like that and stay completely emotionally intact yourself. It may be that they may feel stronger and more affirmed as you talk, but that won't happen without you being quite emotionally drained yourself. It's them or you. To bring them up emotionally you must be willing to be drained emotionally."[8] Chaplains need to care while at the same time remaining appropriately detached. A silent prayer between the chaplain and God could be, "Lord, I give this to you. This is beyond anything I can do. Help me keep going and moving forward."

We can then detach because we've handed it over to God. We still care. We will still follow up. But we don't carry the burden with us. We all have limits. Chaplains practice staying within their limits. There are enormous demands on chaplains. Detachment goes beyond decompression when the suffering of others is handed to God. In this way you honor your limits in order to truly fulfill who God called you to be.

Assigned to a combat unit with another chaplain, the two of us cared for four thousand marines. In their "tent city" in the desert, the two of us set up a humble tent and placed two chairs at each end. Word soon got around that the chaplains were available and nearby. The initiative worked beyond our expectations. Many lined up for counseling. There was a constant flow. My chaplain colleague, who had a counseling degree, balanced care with detachment. He tirelessly invested in each counselee. Yet I seemed to emotionally overattach to each person. Soon I was counseling only six a day compared to his twelve a day. He remained healthy. I felt exhausted. He then offered me this gift, "Hey, it looks like you are getting too invested in these people. You can't solve their problems. Yet they love coming to you because you emote all over them. This is great for them. They want you even more. But you need to stay healthy." He increased his counseling load and gave me priceless time to do what I needed to stay healthy: go jog, go read, go clear my head, so I could come back fresh again.

—*Military Chaplain*

If you find that you dread upcoming pastoral counseling sessions, don't ignore that important feeling. Your response can be withdrawal, backing off, and referring in order to avoid burnout. This is legitimate detachment. Yet replace the emptiness with healthy practices. Nature loves a vacuum, and you would clearly benefit from soul care.

For Christians, soul care grows deeper with personal confession. Those who provide pastoral counseling stay emotionally and spiritually healthy by receiving pastoral counseling, which includes regular confession. Dietrich Bonhoeffer, in *Life Together*, recognizes the power of confession and encourages all Christians to confess to one another, including pastors who provide counseling: "Every person should refrain from listening to confession who does not himself practice it."[9] In Bonhoeffer's opinion, you shouldn't confess to someone who isn't herself confessing to someone else. This takes on special significance for Christians who have a unique understanding of the power of forgiveness: "The most experienced psychologist or observer of human nature knows infinitely less of the human heart than the simplest Christian who lives beneath the cross of Jesus. . . . Worldly wisdom knows what distress and weakness and failure are, but it does not know the godlessness of men. And so it also does not know that man is destroyed only by his sin and can be healed only by forgiveness."[10] As chaplains seek to maintain a healthy soul, they can avoid burnout and fill the gaps of distress with care for the soul.

It's an indictment of twenty-first-century Christianity that pastors and chaplains are frequently placed on a pedestal where they have no safe place to turn. This leads to an excessively high burnout rate. There are few places to create either an informal or formal relationship where chaplains can be real with colleagues and friends who will offer them prayer support, a hug, or a kick in the pants. We all need that, probably at a formal level, but it is easier on the informal level.

> I am with the parents of two children—their daughter died in late teens from a disease. Their son just died by suicide. I get the call and am walking through the pain with them. After the funeral, the parents are decompressing, and I'm absorbing. Suddenly I'm overwhelmed. I don't know where to go with it. I didn't realize how deep I was into this until my exhaustion. I've been too busy with caring for others and ignored my own self-care.
>
> —*Hospital Chaplain*

6.3 Final Thoughts

We close with a few thoughts on mentorship and a few words of encouragement as you fulfill your calling as chaplains.

Mentorship

Finding a mentor is one of the most important activities a new chaplain can do. The Talmud speaks of the value of having both a mentor and a friend. A quote commonly referred to in mentoring is, "Find yourself a Rabbi, and find yourself a friend."[11] Why should a chaplain seek a mentor? Because it would be helpful and life-giving to have someone in your life who is adroit in matters of leadership, skill, patience, presence, integrity, and restoration. W. Brad Johnson and Charles R. Ridley, in their book *The Elements of Mentoring: The 65 Key Elements of Mentoring,* offer the following observations about mentoring: "What are the outcomes of mentoring? . . . Greater professional competence, increased career satisfaction, greater acceptance within the organization or profession, and decreased job stress and role conflict. Mentored individuals also are more likely to mentor others."[12] Mentoring is a valued form of empowerment. It is also an innovative way to tie one's ministry together into a whole. It helps you discern your ministry while distilling your talents. As chaplains are mentored, they further shape their calling and unique contribution to the organization they serve.

There can be mutuality in mentoring. It often works best if mentor and mentee are not constrained to one another through a supervisor-subordinate working relationship. Otherwise, transparency and authenticity—critical values for mentoring—conflict with their positional roles in the organization. Seek a mentor outside your employing organization. Mentoring that begins informally through a relationship is more effective than mentors who are arranged or brokered. There is also evidence indicating that "employees—especially women—prefer mentorships with a more reciprocal and mutual character."[13] A safe place to ask for a mentor might be within your own faith group. Your ecclesiastical endorser or faith-group supervisor of chaplain ministries will likely be able to connect you with a seasoned chaplain mentor. This can lead to meaningful relationships for new chaplains who don't know where to start.

Lois Zachary, in *Creating a Mentoring Culture: The Organization's Guide*, notes that expectations for mentoring have matured since the formal concept came into vogue during the 1970s. During the past half century, the focus has shifted from knowledge transfer, by an older and more experienced sage, to the present-day appreciation of mentoring as a valued time of process-oriented reflection that encompasses life beyond the work itself. The transition from *knowledge as the product* to *reflection as a process* serves to make mentoring even more reflective, innovative, and beneficial. According to Zachary's definition, "Mentoring is best described as a reciprocal and collaborative learning relationship between two (or more) individuals who share mutual responsibility and accountability for helping a mentee work toward achievement of clear and mutually defined learning goals."[14]

Mentors are able to reflect on their experiences in relationship with God. They provide compassion, appropriate self-disclosure, transparency, authenticity, and maturity, and are committed to keep conversations confidential. When these values are practiced, there is great gain to mentoring because the mentee can discern the movement of the Spirit within the mentee's heart. Any correction the mentor needs to offer can be preceded by a high degree of encouragement. A good mentor provides correction by first preparing in advance for those awkward and painful moments. Johnson and Ridley write, "Good mentors address subpar performance and lack of attention to detail.... Early in the mentorship, effective correction should be preceded by a healthy dose of affirmation and encouragement."[15] Yet it is important not to cheapen the value of the mentoring relationship through insincere praise. It is clear that before mentees can hear constructive feedback, they must first know it comes from a place of love and advocacy for them.

Chaplains who have a mentoring relationship with another chaplain can focus on their mutuality of ministry. There can be a shared commitment between the mentor and the mentee to the following:

1. *Commit to learning about your profession.* As you develop your pastoral identity, continue to ask the following questions: What are the anchor points to my understanding of theology? How do I approach counseling? How do I approach preaching? How do I approach worship?
2. *Commit to learning about your culture.* Chaplaincy is often transient. Cultivate becoming an observer of your organization, culture, and society. How can you be adaptable to your organization while sustaining your commitment to lifelong learning?
3. *Commit to the practice of leadership.* Your influence as an ordained clergy gives you rare access to leaders both within and outside your organization. Does your position as a chaplain somehow make you feel marginalized? How might your perspective change when you affirm that God placed you in your chaplain ministry and your role is pivotal to those within the organization?
4. *Commit to ministry in a variety of contexts.* As you look at your culture, discover your context for ministry. How can you best deliver ministry according to your faith-group requirements and traditions?

Keep the Long Look

Chaplains are innovators in their organizations. They inspire others to become better versions of themselves. Chaplains bring meaningful change to institutions due to their commitment to people within the organization. For those who are prospective chaplains, I hope this book has provided an inspiring glimpse into the pivotal role of chaplaincy. For those who are currently serving as chaplains, I want to take this opportunity to thank you for your dedicated commitment to your constituents, whether they are employees, their families, or others receiving services from your organization. Moreover, I want to thank you for your unwavering commitment to your faith that is foundational to your calling to serve in the ministry of chaplaincy.

You are chartered by your organization to stand as both bridge and buffer between the institution and its people. At times, you encourage those entrusted to you to "keep the long look" and help them to not wane in either their character or their hope. Other times you serve as a buffer between the organization and its people, ensuring that those entrusted with power will listen to what they must hear. You do this in spite, and often in trepidation, of personal consequences to you. The beauty and wonder of your calling as a chaplain are that the institution expects no less from you. You are recognized as someone who cares for everyone, even when others cannot. You are entrusted with carrying the presence of God into malevolent and hostile situations. You are called upon to advocate for those who suffer. You are concerned for those who are ill or injured. You serve the dying and honor the dead. As you continue your vital ministry, I want to include a few final thoughts as a chaplain mentor.

1. *Be faithful.* Your public faith in God sets you apart from other professionals. Ensure that you stay anchored to your experience of God through your unique faith group.

2. *Be a leader.* Chaplaincy swims in the current of institutional leadership. Your moral and ethical compass supports others in the myriad decisions they must make. You are expected to learn from leaders around you. Imitate the best. Strive to be an admirable example to all. Also, be open to mentoring a less experienced chaplain.

3. *Be not afraid to ask the hard questions.* If you don't ask the tough questions, no one will. Speak truth to power. You have credibility and access to places and people others can only dream about. Don't be timid, because you have too much to offer. Yet remember to listen twice as much as you speak.

4. *Be compassionate yet strong.* Constantly seek opportunities to engage those you serve. Chaplains are occasionally perceived to be pushovers. Surprise them by maintaining high standards tempered by humility and forgiveness.

5. *Be focused on excellence.* People are looking at you to be spiritually savvy, morally upright, ethically sound, mentally alert, and physically healthy. Strive toward holistic excellence without being crushed by the weight of other people's expectations. Be sure to give yourself an extra dose of grace, because we all feel incapable of measuring up.

6. *Be vision casting.* Look ahead to what needs to be done. Most people in your organization are busy executing the everyday mission. You have an opportunity to look beyond the mundane. Most of you are educated with academic degrees beyond your contemporaries. Communicate to those surrounding you that there is more to life than what meets the eye.

7. *Be willing to take intelligent risks.* Chaplaincy often challenges the status quo through disruptive innovation. Yet don't be a risk-taker without first being informed. Seek wise counsel and avoid jumping to conclusions. Weigh the options and then make the decision. If you end up making a mistake, be first to admit it. Your credibility will sky-rocket. First, you will gain credibility as a leader for taking intelligent risk. Second, even if you are wrong, your credibility will soar simply because you are willing to admit you are a fallen human while at the same time accepting that you are accountable for your actions.

8. *Be involved.* You are vital to your organization. You are unique. You are respected. Great chaplaincy requires involvement, forethought, and bearing a ministry of presence. I urge you to carry forward the honorable and distinctive legacy of others who have served before you as chaplains. Lead the way for future generations of chaplains.

Discussion Questions

1. What is meant by the "inadequacy" of chaplaincy?
2. How does a prospective chaplain find the right organization? What questions would you ask during an informational interview with a chaplain?
3. What are the risks of serving as chaplain in an institution that is misaligned with the chaplain's values?
4. How can your family connect with your ministry as a chaplain?
5. What are potential positive and negative impacts upon families for each type of chaplaincy (e.g., health care, military, campus, first responder, etc.)?
6. What self-care practices do you value? Prioritize them and share why they are helpful in sustaining an inspirational and healthy ministry.
7. What is compassion fatigue, and what are its signs in your life?
8. What are the differences between decompression and detachment? In what ways are they valuable?
9. How will you find a mentor? Are there any people that come to mind? What assumptions and outcomes do you expect from this relationship?

Acknowledgments

Thank you, readers, for letting me be a part of your journey toward chaplaincy. I hope this book is a helpful guide to this unique ministry as well as a resource for those difficult days when you need a reminder of why your presence matters so deeply to the people in your organization.

Thank you to the incredible team at Eerdmans who made this book a reality. I am grateful for James Ernest and the energy he brought to our early conversations; he opened the door and inspired me to walk through it. Jenny Hoffman confidently guided this project through the publishing process, and this book might be unreadable without the copyediting work of Tom Raabe. Big thanks also to Laura Bardolph Hubers, Alexis Cutler, Mike Debowski, and Shane White.

Thanks to my seminary students from courses taught at Fuller, Gordon-Conwell, and Wesley. I appreciated your thoughtful feedback and discussion in class. You all inspired me to write this book, and I hope you find yourselves reflected in these pages.

Thank you to many wise colleagues and friends who generously gave their time to read and comment on early drafts. Thanks especially to those among you who freely shared your own stories and professional insights for this book; many of these appear on the pages throughout and make this book much more interesting and useful than I could have ever offered on my own. Thanks also to those of you who made enormous contributions with your edits. You shaped this book to be infinitely better, and you encouraged me more than you realize: John D. Barry, Jim Knol, Norm Brown, Liz Milner, Jan McCormack, Annie Abbott Foerster, Drew Brennan, Jon Cooper, Julie Jones, Kate Meyer, Melody Meeter, Irv Elson, Rob Coyle, Cathleen Wolff, Sharon Knibbe, Mornier Rich, Jake Marvel, Lindsay Bona, Madison Carter, Judy Nelson, Bert Moore, Jeff Watson, Ken Sampson, Dianna Smith, Jim De Hoog, Ken Kolenbrander, Darcy Lovgren Pavich, Timothy Dunn, Caryn Baham, Andy Wood, Tom Verner, W. Brad Johnson, and Shaun Kennedy. Legal sections of the text were written in consultation with Professor Robert Tuttle, Berz Research Professor of Law and Religion, George Washington University Law School; he asked me to please note that this book is not intended to provide legal advice to anyone. I am thankful for the encouragers who inspired me along the path of chaplaincy and supported me in this process of writing: Brad Ableson, Joe Estabrook, Harold Baker, Jay Coker, John Luke, Scott Redd, Rod Rempt, Michael Sears, Joe Leidig, Michael Good, Jim Critchlow, Rob Stevenson, John Bishop, Joey Tomassoni, and Ali Ghaffari.

Thanks to the Reformed Church in America (RCA) for shepherding me along the way over the past thirty-five years. I write a lot about the importance of a chaplain's faith group, and I'm grateful to have my home with the RCA.

Thank you to all who have been praying faithfully for this book, especially Art Athens, Harry Guthmuller, and Ken Stevens. Throughout this whole experience, I've learned more about prayer than any other activity. This journey taught me that the practice of listening exceeds my need for speaking. I am thankful for God's faithfulness.

To my brilliant, talented, and deeply loved daughters, Rebekah Wallin and Hannah Nance, and their loving husbands, Jason and Bryan: Thank you for reading the manuscript, for challenging my thinking, for polishing my writing, and for sharing your editorial gifts with your dad.

And to my number-one prayer warrior and all-star wife, Marla: Thank you for all your encouragement and patience and love. I truly couldn't have done this without you.

Organizations and Settings
Typically Served by Chaplains

Although the functions and duties of chaplains are similar, each organization forms a unique culture due to its purpose, mission, values, norms, incentives, and symbols. Prospective chaplains would be wise to study the various ministry contexts of the following organizations and settings before determining which domain will best allow them to flourish. All these positions include prerequisite education, training, and preparation. While each setting has its own expectations for employment, many will require:

- MDiv from accredited seminary, divinity school, or equivalent educational background
- Clinical Pastoral Education (CPE)
- Ordination, licensure, or credentialing from faith group
- Board certification as a board-certified chaplain (BCC)
- Ecclesiastical endorsement
- Internship or residency in chaplaincy setting

The following types of institutions provide skilled chaplaincy. While this list is not exhaustive, it identifies the most common types of organizations that value chaplaincy as organic to their mission. In the sections below, many experienced chaplains serving within each institutional context will amplify their specific areas of chaplaincy, describing their unique ministries from the vantage point of serving inside their organization.

1. Hospital Chaplaincy

Prepared in consultation with Chaplains Cathleen J. Wolff, BCC, and Julie Jones, BCC.

Chaplain quote: "Chaplains make their feet stick where others may wish to run. Chaplains accompany others through life's celebrations, as well as the darkest nights of the soul, without any agenda beyond the persons we are serving."

Inspiring verse: "Be still, and know that I am God" (Ps. 46:10 NIV).

Environment and culture: Many hospitals offer acute-care facilities that provide comprehensive, state-of-the-art medical care. Hospitals often include psychiatric services. A core value is "Patients come first," and spirituality is considered part of holistic care. Chaplains in the Department of Spiritual Care participate in patient care rounds as part of the interdisciplinary care team. Chaplains form part of the interwoven fabric of providing exceptional patient- and family-centered care.

Typical responsibilities: Chaplains provide spiritual and emotional care to all patients, families, and staff in an environment of anxiety, sickness, pain, birth, and death. Chaplains are typically present at any announced hospital emergency code, death, and multiple trauma that occurs at medical centers. Chaplains frequently are included in the multidisciplinary trauma team. Many chaplains support decedent care (i.e., release to funeral home) and serve as designated requesters for tissue and organ donation. This requires specialized training and fits within the chaplain's ethics to honor the whole person and his end-of-life wishes. Chaplains may provide occasional healing services (i.e., group burial for miscarriages four times per year), may provide weekly spiritual groups within the mental health services department encouraging patients to access their spirituality as part of healing, may offer invocations at large hospital events, and may interact with local faith group leaders to assist in meeting the spiritual needs of patients. Chaplains may offer complementary holistic care, including stress management, palliative care, healing touch, or guided imagery, which often assist with positive pain management and relaxation. Chaplains typically serve on interdisciplinary boards and committees. As an example, a bioethics committee draws individuals from all elements of health-care services, including chaplains, who advise the administration on ethical issues within the organization's clinical, educational, and research mission.

Unique factors, concerns, or challenges: Patients do not enter the hospital with the specific need or intent of spiritual care. Therefore the patient is captive and vulnerable. Chaplains are viewed as available, open, approachable, nonjudgmental, and representing God. An unrequested visit, or "cold calling," requires sensitivity. Because of the emergency nature of health care, emergency situations will occasionally challenge chaplains to offer services that may be foreign to their theological tradition. This often requires consultation with chaplains of various spiritual traditions or specific education from the patient the chaplain is serving.

Recipient comments on value of chaplaincy: "When things went wrong, and relationships became broken, my need for reconciliation was facilitated by your ministry. As a patient, my core spiritual needs emerged in my health crisis."

Additional information and resources:
 ACPE—the standard for spiritual care and education: www
  .acpe.edu
 Association of Professional Chaplains: www.professionalchap
  lains.org
 National Association of Catholic Chaplains: www.nacc.org
 Neshama: Association of Jewish Chaplains: www.jewishchap
  lain.net

---

2. Hospice Chaplaincy

Prepared in consultation with Chaplains Kate Meyer, LPC, and Caryn Baham, BCC.

Chaplain quote: "I have the opportunity to walk with people in the most holy of moments. I've come to see God's grace in new and abundant ways as patients and families allow me into their story during a time filled with vulnerability, loss, hope, and peace. One of the things that I love about hospice ministry is that I don't know what each patient used to be. This allows me the unique opportunity to meet them where they are without the added weight of their history."

Inspiring verse: "Peace I leave with you; my peace I give to you. I do not give to you as the world gives. Do not let your hearts be troubled, and do not let them be afraid" (John 14:27 NRSV).

Environment and culture: Hospice patients are located at home, in extended-care facilities, hospitals, or inpatient hospice units. Hospice chaplains frequently work exclusively with families if the patient is comatose, unconscious, or sedated. Hospice is conducted with a team, therefore the chaplain works closely with a home health aide, nurse, and social worker; the chaplain will also have regular interaction with volunteers. Hospice chaplains enter into the home environment of those they serve; this means a chaplain must be prepared to enter homes of people at all economic levels, all education levels, and among a variety of races and cultures. A helpful movie to explore the subject of death in a different culture is the 2008 Japanese dramatic film *Departures* (Japanese: *Okuribito*). Hospice chaplains frequently enter a wide variety of extended-care facilities and must be prepared to advocate for the care of their patient upon the occasional finding of an unacceptable level of care.

Typical responsibilities: Regardless of personal faith, when a hospice chaplain meets with a patient, that patient's spiritual identity is all that matters; the overarching goal is for patients to have a sense of peace regarding whatever they believe will occur after death. It is not the job of the chaplain to challenge or change what a person believes, but to assist the person in finding peace and acceptance of his own spiritual beliefs and journey. A hospice chaplain can expect to be assigned a geographical area and to visit patients on a standard basis twice monthly. The hospice chaplain can expect to have both long- and short-term relationships, assist in processes of reconciliation, be the liaison between a patient and the faith community, and perform funerals and weddings, baptize, and offer sacraments.

Unique factors, concerns, or challenges: Professional palliative care/ hospice chaplains bring expertise for end-of-life care as well as care of those with life-limiting conditions. Hospice is unique because death is always on the table of discussion. Whether a patient is accepting of it, fighting it, afraid of it, or simply naming it, death is there. Unlike other areas of chaplaincy, hospice chaplains often build rapport quickly because of this fact. The chaplain frequently demonstrates the competency of advisement by providing ethical mediation on futile care, while diffusing the moral distress for care recipients, their families, and hospice staff. Hospice chaplains can be called upon to provide grief support to family members in the months following a death.

Recipient comments on value of chaplaincy: "Your soothing, inspiring manner and quiet nature left Dad peaceful and calm."

Additional information and resources:
Egan, Kerry. *On Living*. New York: Riverhead Books, 2017.

3. Continuing-Care Retirement Community (CCRC), Older Adults, Senior Independent and Assisted Living, Memory Care, Skilled Nursing Chaplaincy

Prepared in consultation with Chaplains Bert Moore and Jeff Watson.

> *Chaplain quote:* "Moses taught us to pass on what our 'eyes have seen' to the coming generations. Sometimes, CCRC ministry is less about preaching and more about listening, more about facilitating the wisdom of the elders to the younger staff, volunteers, or family members."

> *Inspiring verse:* "Don't let anyone think less of you because you are young. Be an example to all believers in what you say, in the way you live, in your love, your faith, and your purity" (1 Tim. 4:12 NLT).

> *Environment and culture:* Chaplains minister to older adults in a community setting. The minimum eligible age to move into a CCRC is usually around 62, but the average age of the residents is the mid-80s, with many who are 100 or more. Life in a CCRC resembles that on a college campus, since the majority of residents live independently. Activities on campus involve opportunities for learning, group or individual travel, and a variety of clubs and groups. The residents have a diverse background of education and work/life experiences providing a wealth of wisdom. Many share in common the loss of a spouse and now find themselves in a new environment. Most enjoy being sociable and fill their days with a variety of activities, including eating a meal with others in a campus restaurant. As the residents age, they may experience some loss of mobility, perhaps some decline in one or more of their senses, and often the incremental loss of independence. They may eventually move into a care facility that provides inpatient rehabilitation, assisted living, memory care, or skilled nursing. This transition presents a life adjustment that may be difficult to accept. As seniors living in a caring community, each will continue to experience the passing of friends who have been close to them during their time at the CCRC. One resident referred to moving into a CCRC as moving into "God's waiting room."

Typical responsibilities: Chaplains provide spiritual care and counseling to residents, staff, and family, all of whom possess a variety of worldviews. These responsibilities include coordinating and facilitating worship opportunities for the various faith communities and myriad activities for spiritual growth of residents and staff via Scripture studies, spiritual gatherings, and special observances. In an interfaith setting, gatherings such as prayer breakfasts or Memorial Day services provide opportunities for people of various faiths to interact. When a resident passes away, there is a special time of ministry to her family and friends during a critical time of need.

Unique factors, concerns, or challenges: The residents of a CCRC have had successful careers and their own unique life experiences. These backgrounds provide for interesting conversations and discussions. Most residents also have experienced loss and are dealing with a variety of health issues. The unknown possibility of living their final days in some way incapacitated, in pain, or suffering from dementia can often cause great concern and anxiety. Being sensitive to the individual's needs and her openness to spirituality requires a great deal of discernment and wisdom.

Recipient comments on value of chaplaincy: "You were a warm presence in my mother's life throughout her residence there, and a great emotional support to me during her time of illness. Your kind words and prayers were a consolation to us."

Additional information and resources:
Cole, Thomas R. *The Journey of Life: A Cultural History of Aging in America*. New York: Cambridge University Press, 1992.
Gentzler, Richard H., Jr. *Designing an Older Adult Ministry*. Nashville: Discipleship Resources, 2000, 2006.
Kimble, Melvin A., Susan H. McFadden, James W. Ellor, and James J. Seeber, eds. *Aging, Spirituality, and Religion*. Minneapolis: Fortress, 1995.
Koenig, Harold G., and Andrew J. Weaver. *Counseling Troubled Older Adults: A Handbook for Pastors and Religious Caregivers*. Nashville: Abingdon, 1997.
Mace, Nancy L., and Peter V. Rabins. *The 36-Hour Day: A Family*

Guide to Caring for Persons with Alzheimer Disease, Related Dementias, and Memory Loss. 5th ed. Baltimore: Johns Hopkins University Press, 2011.

---

4. Military Chaplaincy (Active Duty, Guard, and Reserve)

Prepared in consultation with Chaplain (Colonel) Ken Sampson, US Army (Ret.).

Chaplain quote: "Mingled with sadness and heartache were tears of profound joy as we celebrated a God who, through the very chaos and carnage of war, had revealed himself to us—his love, his power, and his plan for our lives."[1]

Inspiring verse: "Go after a life of love as if your life depended on it—because it does. Give yourselves to the gifts God gives you" (1 Cor. 14:1 *The Message*).

Environment and culture: The focus of chaplaincy to the broad armed forces community is on providing ministry to eighteen-to-twenty-five-year-olds, their leaders, and their families. The military setting is energizing, forward looking, and positive. The potential to maximize personal development is without peer.

Typical responsibilities: The government has legitimate interest in protecting the religious liberty of those under its jurisdiction. An important part of the government's accommodation of these individuals is through chaplaincy. Chaplains are at the forefront of advocating for military members and other authorized beneficiaries by offering a ministry of presence. Public law permits chaplains to conduct public worship for personnel assigned to their commands.[2] They provide or facilitate pastoral responsibilities, including rites, sacraments, counseling, education, and care for all. It is essential and expected that chaplains are immersed in their unit's activities and mission.

Unique factors, concerns, or challenges: The military seeks theologically trained, spiritually motivated, and fully qualified ministers to serve as chaplains. Chaplains are credentialed religious leaders and also commissioned officers who are noncombatants. They are employed by and receive salary from the federal government. They wear uniform and hold rank. Requirements include commitment—military service "is a 24/7/365 relationship . . . that involves the highest possible stakes—life and death, killing and dying."[3] Chaplains recognize that their calling can be fulfilling and adventuresome, yet also costly, and often necessitates tensions of unit/family responsibilities, war/peace issues, or faith/patriotism ties. Chaplains "cooperate without compromise" to provide spiritual guidance in a pluralistic society. They provide for human needs and hold the welfare of their personnel as their chief concern. Chaplains directly contribute to the moral and ethical framework of the military community. Ministry is deeply embedded in the undertakings of their units, rather than in the confines of a sanctuary pulpit.

Recipient comments on value of chaplaincy: From a 2/14 Infantry Battalion soldier: "Thank you for all the motivation you gave to every soldier in this combat unit. Just the thought of you being around motivates me. Thanks for being a faith-filled rock for all of us to build on and for your encouragement."

Additional information and resources:
> Bergen, Doris. *The Sword of the Lord: Military Chaplains from the First to the Twenty-First Century.* South Bend, IN: University of Notre Dame Press, 2004.
> Carroll, Andrew. *Grace under Fire: Letters of Faith in Times of War.* Colorado Springs: Waterbrook, 2007.

---

5. Correctional Chaplaincy (Federal, State, and Local)

Prepared in consultation with Chaplains Liz Milner and Jon Cooper.

Chaplain quote: "It is humbling to see those whom society has deemed unfit in some way express hope, faith, and compassion. Often our society will extend care to those it sees as 'worthy.' When we enter into and care for those society deems 'other,' we find God in a powerful way that helps us see the common humanity we all share and the face of God in 'the least of these.'"

Inspiring verse: "Truly I tell you, whatever you did for one of the least of these brothers and sisters of mine, you did for me" (Matt. 25:40 NIV).

Environment and culture: Chaplains work with adults and juveniles who endure long periods of isolation, uncertainty, loss, shame, and limited choices. A high percentage of incarcerated women have been victims of sexual assault and trauma, and most inmates have witnessed much violence. Many inmates struggle with addiction or mental illness. In many locations, the jails are de facto mental health institutions. People of color tend to be disproportionately represented in these mass incarceration facilities. The environment and culture of correctional institutions can vary greatly depending on whether the chaplain serves in a county jail, a state prison, or a federal institution. New chaplains may experience an initial claustrophobic feeling working in a prison, similar to how new sailors feel isolated on a ship at sea, but the feeling is temporary and dissipates. A bigger adjustment occurs with the restriction of social media devices inside the prison. It can be challenging for chaplains to leave their smart phones at the entrance. Juvenile facilities are run differently than adult institutions, with distinctive command structures and rules.

Typical responsibilities: Chaplains provide spiritual care and regular religious services to the incarcerated. This can include worship services, small-group services, individual services, pastoral counseling, grief counseling, referral to appropriate religious resources, as well as religious diet evaluation and approval. Chaplains also advise the institution on religious questions and concerns, such as the wearing or displaying of specific religious items and their potential impact on the institutional mission. Prison staff members typically work their eight-hour shift and depart. Therefore it is unusual for prison staff to attend religious services while on duty. Nevertheless, chaplains offer pastoral counseling to staff both during and after critical incidents. They also plan and participate in memorial services when a staff member dies and organize other events such as the annual National Correctional Officers and Employees Week.

Unique factors, concerns, or challenges: The population in many correctional institutions tends to be from marginalized and socioeconomically disadvantaged communities. This makes it essential that chaplains and volunteers serving in these contexts are aware of their own social location, racism, and privilege. They must be able to intentionally address disparities that arise and understand the human condition, notions of punishment and reform, and the nature of God. Awareness of manipulative behaviors and how best to engage others while maintaining strong boundaries is essential. They should not advise others on court or legal issues but offer a compassionate and restorative presence. Additional training in suicide intervention, the criminal justice system, restorative justice issues, victimology, substance abuse counseling, cycles of violence, domestic violence counseling, and conflict resolution is helpful.

Recipient comments on value of chaplaincy: "Chaps, everyone knows all about my hell, but now in my heart I know there's a heaven."

Additional information and resources:
> Beckner, Thomas. *Correctional Chaplains: Keepers of the Cloak.* Orlando: Cappella, 2012.
> Ekblad, Bob. *Reading the Bible with the Damned.* Louisville: Westminster John Knox, 2005.
> Gilliard, Dominique. *Rethinking Incarceration: Advocating for Justice That Restores.* Downers Grove, IL: InterVarsity Press, 2018.
> Lamb, Wally. *Couldn't Keep It to Myself: Wally Lamb and the Women of York Correctional Institution.* New York: Harper Perennial, 2003.

---

6. Workplace, Industrial, Corporate, and Community Chaplaincy

Prepared in consultation with Chaplain Judy Nelson.

Chaplain quote: "As a workplace chaplain, I have the opportunity to touch many lives the institutional church will never touch. It is a ministry of presence, being the face of Christ in places that can be very dark."

Inspiring verse:

"Do not withhold good from those to whom it is due,
    when it is in your power to do it.
Do not say to your neighbor, 'Go, and come again,
    tomorrow I will give it'—when you have it with you."

(Prov. 3:27–28)

Environment and culture: The Associated Press reports that in 2020, more than 20 percent of the Fortune 100 companies established faith-based employee resource groups. Included are some of America's best-known businesses, like Tyson Foods, Target, Facebook, American Airlines, Apple, Dell, American Express, Goldman Sachs, and Google's parent company, Alphabet. Workplace, industrial, corporate, and community chaplains serve in fields such as trucking, food processing, auto assembly, beverage bottling, packaging and distribution, transportation, offshore deepwater oil production, and beyond. Employees focus on certain tasks to be completed, products produced, and quotas met. While each workplace intends to establish and maintain a culture built upon the corporate ethic, the actual culture is frequently formed by the standards that team members (employees) bring with them and practice. The factory floor often is peopled with hundreds of employees who feel they are unable to get "better" jobs. Many do not have a high school diploma. For a large percentage, English is their second language. Factories also tend to attract those whose employment track records may have been inconsistent at best. Depending on the type of facility, employees may work in conditions that lack temperature regulation, are unclean, and are prone to safety hazards. These surroundings tend to further deplete employees.

Typical responsibilities: The chaplain provides compassionate presence and spiritual care to all employees and their families, respecting the diversity of all. A chaplain makes regular pastoral rounds, visiting the production floor, break rooms, and cafeterias, as well as administrative offices. He forms relationships with employees at every level and often coordinates with the human resources manager. He ensures that employees are being supported during individual crises, illnesses, hospitalization, special occasions, and recognition of significant accomplishments. Workplace chaplains are asked to officiate weddings and funerals for employees or their families who have no church or specific faith background. Chaplains may also find themselves in the middle of employment/union/management issues, advocating for the proper care of employees. The chaplain should be aware of community agencies and service providers that serve the various needs of employees outside the realm of the chaplain's responsibility or training.

Unique factors, concerns, or challenges: Depending on the environment, culture, and location, the workplace population may come from socioeconomically disadvantaged communities where drug and alcohol abuse is common. Chaplains hear life stories filled with childhood trauma, loss, divorce, and abuse. Chaplains should employ gracious understanding, extreme hospitality, and compassion while maintaining professional and personal boundaries. A focus for companies employing chaplains is to elevate employee satisfaction, reduce turnover rate, increase levels of focus, reduce stress-related illnesses, promote productivity, and lower absenteeism. Chaplains understand that people are spending more time at work than at any other location; increasing the level of support at work thereby can positively affect all of life.

Recipient comments on value of chaplaincy: "When they told us we were getting a chaplain, I wondered, what on earth for? Now I don't know what we would do without you. You have changed everything. I am staying here based on the fact that this company cared enough about their employees to have a chaplain."

Additional information and resources:
Crary, David. "More US Firms Are Boosting Faith-Based Support for Employees." *Business Insider* (website), February 11, 2020. https://www.businessinsider.com/more-us-firms-are-boosting-faith-based-support-for-employees-2020-2.

Green, Emma. "Finding Jesus at Work." *Atlantic*, February 17, 2016. https://www.theatlantic.com/business/archive/2016 /02/work-secularization-chaplaincies/462987/.

7. College and Educational Chaplaincy

Prepared in consultation with Chaplain Dianna Smith.

Chaplain quote: "As a professional working in higher education, I find creative approaches toward ensuring the religious commitment of students is compatible with intellectual inquiry."

Inspiring verse: "May we know what this new teaching is that you are presenting? For you bring some strange things to our ears. We wish to know therefore what these things mean" (Acts 17:19b–20).

Environment and culture: Large state universities, for example, may have ten thousand students or more. There is a mix of residential, off-campus, veteran, first-generation, and international students. Accordingly, college is a very diverse community.

Typical responsibilities: There is a material difference between a *college chaplain* and a *campus pastor.* Many Christian colleges employ a campus pastor to manage the various weekly and seasonal Christian activities expected by Christian students and faculty. A college chaplain, while frequently serving Christians as their pastor, also advocates for the spiritual welfare of all students, whether they express another faith or no faith. A chaplain enhances the development of students' spiritual lives, promotes the understanding of spiritual practices and religious traditions, and provides holistic support to students, faculty, coaches, and staff. Chaplains often serve as the public voice of religious and spiritual life through ceremonies, convocations, celebrations, vigils, and memorials. They exercise moral leadership by representing the various expressions of religious life and spirituality across the college. Chaplains also serve as ambassadors for the spiritual dimension of the college to the external community, including not-for-profit organizations, local congregations, and faith groups that may have interest in the college.

Unique factors, concerns, or challenges: Freshman homesickness is common. Chaplains address the loneliness and help students navigate the transition from teen to young adult. College chaplains frequently find themselves in the middle of sexuality issues, especially for students exploring their sexual identity, gender expression, gender identity, or first sexual experiences. Chaplains can expect frequent relational conflict among students now seeking the chaplain for counsel and resolution. Additionally, vocational counseling is typical because chaplains minister to graduating seniors who may question where God is calling them next. Chaplains in denominational schools will need to uphold the requirements, theology, and ethics of their faith group while simultaneously experiencing pressure when students challenge their position. Every graduation is a time of joy but also a time of reorganization for a new incoming class. In 2018, nearly one-quarter of incoming freshmen were challenged by food insecurity.[4] As a college chaplain who also coordinates the student food pantry, Chaplain Dianna Smith comments, "My biggest challenge is building awareness and capacity to serve a growing number of hungry and homeless students. Much of my time, in between semesters, is focused toward raising awareness with the college administration of their students' physical and spiritual needs."

Recipient comments on value of chaplaincy: "I will miss you so much. These past four years working with the Student Christian Center have meant so much to me. Thank you for all the time you spent with me, especially when I was in crisis mode."

Additional information and resources: The National Association of College and University Chaplains is a multifaith professional community supporting spiritual and ethical life in higher education. See https://nacuc.net.

8. Pediatric and/or Adults with Disabilities Chaplaincy

Prepared in consultation with Chaplain Jim De Hoog.

Chaplain quote: "Being present with those who are often forgotten by society is a great privilege as I share with them God's love, goodness, and grace. I often receive more from them as compared to what I give to them."

Inspiring verse: "Pure and genuine religion in the sight of God the Father means caring for orphans and widows in their distress and refusing to let the world corrupt you" (James 1:27 NLT).

Environment and culture: Chaplains working with children and adults with intellectual developmental disabilities (IDD) operate in a variety of workplace environments. They serve at gathering places, such as job and life-skills training centers, day activity programs, and group homes, as well as in individual living spaces. They interact with people who communicate in various ways. Some people will talk freely about themselves. Many have difficulty using their verbal language skills. Others communicate through their body language. Along with professional caregivers and staff, chaplains help people with IDD maintain their independence, productivity, and inclusion. All staff, including case managers, nurses, and program directors, are responsible for the care, welfare, safety, and security of the people served.

Typical responsibilities: Chaplains provide spiritual care in various ways. They may lead worship services, funerals, weddings, small groups, and educational training sessions, and they may visit hospitals and engage in pastoral counseling. Chaplains may be responsible for overseeing and working with volunteers who support the organization in various ways. Some chaplains serve on boards and committees, such as a human rights committee chartered to ensure that personal rights are not violated through medications or programs.

Unique factors, concerns, or challenges: People with IDD are often looked down upon or forgotten by society. They are the last ones hired and the first ones released from employment. Pastoral care to the fringe of society can be trying and rewarding at the same time. These chaplains, more than others, require a solid foundation in their identity as humans created in the image of God. They need to educate themselves on a wide variety and spectrum of disabilities. For example, Dr. Stephen Shore of the Organization for Autism Research wittily said, "If you've met one person with autism, you've met one person with autism," simply to emphasize diversity within the autism spectrum. Chaplains are sensitive to balance the learning accommodations, verbal and nonverbal communications, sensory receptivity, social interaction, and individual interests of those they serve. Knowledge of Americans with Disabilities Act (ADA) law and requirements is helpful. The chaplain will provide services to people with a wide range of disabilities. Funding sources to support individuals with IDD vary from state to state. Opportunities for chaplain positions are advertised through nonprofit and governmental agencies.

Recipient comments on value of chaplaincy: "Thank you for your sensitive care and advocacy in addressing stereotypes, assumptions, and gaps in their support. Anyone can be a recipient of faith so long as faith is something we are given by God and not something we do."

Additional information and resources:
> Nouwen, Henri J. M. *The Road to Daybreak: A Spiritual Journey.* New York: Doubleday, 1988.
> Swinton, John. *Dementia: Living in the Memories of God.* Grand Rapids: Eerdmans, 2012.
> Vanier, Jean. *Becoming Human.* Toronto: House of Anansi Press, 2008.
> Vanier, Jean, and John Swinton. *Mental Health: The Inclusive Church Resource.* London: Darton, Longman & Todd, 2014.

9. Veterans Affairs (VA) Chaplaincy

Prepared in consultation with Chaplain (LTC) Kenneth Kolenbrander, US Army (Ret.) and VA Chaplain.

Chaplain quote: "My goal is to bring quality pastoral care to those who sacrificed for our great nation in time of war or peace—serving those who have served."

Inspiring verse:
"Though one may be overpowered,
  two can defend themselves.
A cord of three strands is not quickly broken." (Eccles. 4:12 NIV)

Environment and culture: A VA chaplain serves as a clinical provider in a health-care setting on an interdisciplinary treatment team. The chaplain hears the veteran's story and honors the faith of the veteran. Veteran patients come from all branches of the US military. Veterans' family members often accompany them throughout their stay. VA health care also encompasses long-term care and mental health clinics as well as many types of recovery groups and settings.

Typical responsibilities: VA chaplains' ministry and involvement engage veterans from the time they enter the facility until their discharge. Chaplains offer bedside visits and deliver care as requested by the patient or medical personnel. They also provide worship services, Bible study groups, and memorial services. Most of all, they listen to patients' stories. For VA chaplains who previously served as military chaplains, there is an immediate bridge of trust.

Unique factors, concerns, or challenges: VA chaplains care for those who bore the battle and carry compassion for patients who often feel hopeless and without a voice. Many chaplains are trained in palliative care and grief ministry. Just as important as this training is a caring heart for veterans and their unique struggles. Chaplains need patience to listen to them and hear their stories. Most of the chaplain visits to veterans are "cold calls," with patients the chaplain does not know. Since most patients are prior military, they bring their unique cultural bias and background to the VA health-care setting. A civilian chaplain may be at a loss in understanding rank and power in the military setting. Interservice rivalry among the armed forces frequently lasts throughout a lifetime. A former Navy chaplain now serving as a VA chaplain may not be accepted by a former Army patient. Yet, no matter the chaplain's background, VA chaplains strive to maintain a continuity of chaplain care to veterans as they come and go.

Recipient comments on value of chaplaincy: "Thanks for being my trusted friend, because all of my family and friends are gone. You are invaluable during this current health battle!"

Additional information and resources:

Adsit, Chris. *The Combat Trauma Healing Manual: Christ-Centered Solutions for Combat Trauma.* Newport News, VA: Military Ministry Press, 2008.

Keller, Timothy. *Walking with God through Pain and Suffering.* New York: Riverhead Books, 2013.

Sittser, Gerald L. *A Grace Disguised.* Expanded ed. Grand Rapids: Zondervan, 2004.

---

10. Residential Treatment Chaplaincy

Prepared in consultation with Chaplains Darcy Lovgren Pavich and Timothy Dunn, LCADC, LCSW.

Chaplain quote: A chaplain at a state-licensed drug and alcohol rehabilitation center that serves men and women military veterans said, "Most of the veterans I serve were wounded by life long before they were wounded by war. These are today's lepers, discarded on our streets. These are war heroes with substance use disorders, posttraumatic stress, untreated mental health concerns, and homelessness. We must not pass by on the other side of the street!"

Inspiring verse: "For the Son of man is come to save that which was lost" (Matt. 18:11 KJV).

Environment and culture: In residential treatment facilities, the chaplain frequently serves former homeless now living in a full-service, state-licensed, residential substance-use disorder, and mental-health treatment facility. The end goals are sobriety, training, employment, managed health care, and housing. Many are court mandated to the program. For others it is a safe haven because it is off the streets. Coincidental to an opioid epidemic, an increase of alcoholism and prescription medication abuse among the elderly, and an ongoing use of illicit drugs in society, chaplains serving in any field can identify the signs of substance abuse and make referrals to substance-abuse treatment programs.

Typical responsibilities: Chaplains provide and facilitate the free exercise of all religions or none. No services other than community memorial services are held on site. Chaplains engage in one-on-one religious studies, teach classes on spiritual growth using the twelve-step model of recovery, provide grief counseling, and care for all residents and staff. The twelve-step approach used by Alcoholics Anonymous follows a set of "steps" toward recovery. The final step is, "Having had a spiritual awakening as the result of these Steps, we tried to carry this message to alcoholics, and to practice these principles in all our affairs." With the wide acceptance of the twelve-step program in addiction treatment, chaplains have frequent opportunities to play an important role in leading recovering persons toward discovering their spirituality and belief in a "higher power" that is accessed by prayer and meditation.

Unique factors, concerns, or challenges: Prior experience working with homeless having posttraumatic stress disorder and traumatic brain injury is valuable. This is a complex setting, combining prison, mental institution, hospital, and street ministry. Chaplains must be comfortable enough with their own faith not to force it on others, yet diligently practice their faith without typically speaking about it. Residential treatment chaplains model self-care, balance, honesty, and being true to their beliefs. The residents will expect it to be displayed consistently, though not perfectly. Although you will not be one of them, you will also not be above them. "As a psychiatric chaplain, I have found instructing patients in learning and practicing mindfulness meditation, which is widely accepted with supporting research, to be a means for patients to access, tolerate, and cope with moods while developing an openness to spirituality."

Recipient comments on value of chaplaincy: A self-confirmed atheist and hater of anything religious said: "You challenged me to read the Bible. Not as a religious pursuit but an intellectual activity.

I read the Bible. Hollywood has nothing on those writers. I read it, cover to cover. Of all the people that crossed my wake, you inspired this godless soul."

Additional information and resources:
> *Alcoholics Anonymous: The Story of How Many Thousands of Men and Women Have Recovered from Alcoholism.* 4th ed. Alcoholics Anonymous World Services, Inc., 2002.
> Mahedy, William P. *Out of the Night: The Spiritual Journey of Vietnam Veterans.* Knoxville, TN: Radix, 2004.

11. Public Safety: Law-Enforcement, Firefighting, and First-Responder Chaplaincy

Prepared in consultation with Chaplain Annie Abbott Foerster.

Chaplain quote: "One must have the long-term vision of constantly building up relationships and trust in a stress-filled environment. Chaplains come alongside people under constant tension who themselves seek to protect a city full of strangers."

Inspiring verse: "Those of us who are strong and able in the faith need to step in and lend a hand to those who falter, and not just do what is most convenient for us. Strength is for service, not status. Each one of us needs to look after the good of the people around us, asking ourselves, 'How can I help?'" (Rom. 15:1–2 *The Message*).

Environment and culture: The daily routines of a law-enforcement officer do not coincide with the work of any other profession in our society, and the work is not "normal" work. One does not go to the office nor get holidays off. The day is never predictable and often dangerous. These job characteristics are actually what keep many of the officers on the job; a repetitive job would kill the soul of most in the career of law enforcement. But a patrol officer's day is filled with negativity. Every call is a complaint; bodily threats, mental harm, relational disruptions, theft and robbery, parking and traffic offenses, trespassing, mental illness, and serving warrants are all common. Officers may patrol for hours just observing, waiting for something to happen, which is followed by high rushes of adrenaline. There is seemingly endless report writing and court attendance. Detectives have cases of sex crimes, elder and child abuse, and cyber or financial crimes. The opportunity for depression and hopelessness is obvious. Officers need to figure out how to decompress and discuss "the daily grind." Consequently, law-enforcement chaplaincy has a unique calling and particular concerns. Officers are reluctant to admit they are anything but "All good, Chap!" Therefore, gaining trust with each individual in the chaplain's care is paramount.

Typical responsibilities: Daily chaplaincy work includes respectful and creative ways to help first responders discover areas where they may need to reflect or decompress, and encouraging them to be in touch with their own spirituality (whatever that may be). Chaplains should be available and approachable as a nonjudgmental sounding board, proactively reaching out to their agency's men and women. Chaplains may "ride along" with police officers (observing proper etiquette) and may accompany law-enforcement personnel, assisting with giving in-person notifications of death or serious injuries. Attendance at awards and promotions ceremonies, recruit graduations, community events when law enforcement is involved, and law-enforcement fund-raisers is common, as is performing funerals and weddings. It is important to constantly let the law-enforcement and first-responder communities know that you care about them. This builds the trust that is needed to do the chaplain's work. Without trust, very little can be accomplished in this traditionally "closed" and conservative community. In times of traumatic incidents, chaplains may work up to eighty hours a week. They must be equipped to be resilient and quietly present, and to listen without giving advice, refraining from recounting or comparing their own experiences or giving "spiritual insights."

Unique factors, concerns, or challenges: Law-enforcement (including police, other government agencies, and corrections) and first-responder occupations (fire and EMS [emergency medical services]) are very high-stress jobs. They are filled by people who serve the public selflessly, often under visually and mentally horrid conditions, whose jobs often lack the support of the public. They have a critical need for spiritual care. Many public safety chaplains receive specialized training and are expected to meet specific standards. Some chaplains have advanced training in suicide prevention and critical incident stress management (CISM), and teach classes in resiliency training. Chaplains frequently observe CISM debriefings after officer-involved shootings. First-responder chaplains need a strong commitment to the practice of spiritual self-care. A burned-out chaplain will do more harm than good. Receiving certified spiritual direction, talking with trusted friends who understand the stresses, and participating in a community of spiritual companions (church, temple, synagogue) are essential to the mental and spiritual health of first-responder chaplains. Chaplains should be currently certified in basic first aid, including cardiopulmonary resuscitation (CPR) and operation of an automated external defibrillator (AED).

Recipient comments on value of chaplaincy: "The value of chaplains cannot be overstated. Police work is frequently underappreciated. It rapidly shifts from long periods of boredom to moments of genuine fear. Having someone on my team to talk to, not as a fellow cop but as a genuine listener, is invaluable."

Additional information and resources:
Federation of Fire Chaplains: https://ffc.wildapricot.org.
Gilmartin, Kevin. *Emotional Survival for Law Enforcement: A Guide for Officers and Their Families.* Tucson, AZ: E-S Press, 2002.
International Conference of Police Chaplains: http://www.icpc 4cops.org.
International Critical Incident Stress Foundation: https://icisf .org.
Kirschman, Ellen. *I Love a Cop: What Police Families Need to Know.* Rev. ed. New York: Guilford, 2018.

12. Sports Chaplaincy

Prepared in consultation with Chaplain Madison Carter.

Chaplain quote: "My focus is biblical. I know who I am because God's Word tells me I belong to him. I am a sinner saved by grace. I am not afraid to engage with anyone. If an athlete has faith, or no

faith, I am still their chaplain. Everyone has a story to tell. I want
to be part of their story."

Inspiring verse: "The LORD is my light and my salvation; whom shall
I fear? The LORD is the strength of my life; of whom shall I be
afraid?" (Ps. 27:1 KJV).

Environment and culture: Sports chaplaincy has a tribal mentality. Fra-
ternal competition is sports chaplaincy's foundation. There are
soaring heights of fame and gain. There are also deep canyons of
loss and rejection. Each athlete and coach is expected to abide
by a code of conduct as well as a code of ethics. A coach can
bolster physical strength. A coach can enhance mental tough-
ness. The chaplain helps stretch the spiritual grit, which encourages men and women of moral convictions. The chaplain is frequently identified as a key resource to help define and model
sportsmanship.

Typical responsibilities: The typical responsibilities for sports chaplaincy include counseling athletes and staff along with conducting religious services during the week and prior to games. The
best sports chaplains make hospital visits when an athlete is injured, and they sit with family and friends when the doctor gives
MRI results. Sports chaplains understand the art of chaplaincy
while appreciating the need for continued training. They never
stop sharpening their craft.

Unique factors, concerns, or challenges: Don't coach. A person who
loves people does not need to be a sports aficionado to be a sports
chaplain. At the same time, having a requisite knowledge of the
sport your team plays is a plus. The best way to prepare is spending time in meetings and developing the central focus for the
program's leadership. The travel schedule and eclectic personal-
ities make the role challenging; therefore, chaplains must have
a plan for self-care that they fiercely protect. Sports chaplains
should have a pastoral background. They should view the entire
team, staff, and leadership as their congregation. Their ministry
should foster grit and growth. Sports chaplaincy also requires
agility. Members of a team may not share their religious, moral,

political, or social views. Elite athletes lean on their chaplains in order to focus their full energies on their craft. Physical troubles lead to spiritual trouble. Emotional troubles challenge the spiritual framework. Keeping the spirit strong keeps the mind and body focused. As a sports chaplain, it is imperative to strengthen counseling skills. Sports teams are tight-knit groups. Chaplains do not encroach in their space without permission. When the athletes trust that their chaplain is concerned about them as people, not as stars, not as celebrities, not as gods, and not as free meal tickets, they will invite their chaplain inside their circle.

Recipient comments on value of chaplaincy: After a difficult game, a head coach said, "Chaplain, when you are around, I feel at peace." This quote ranks at the top of my list. Another quote affirmed my long-term value to the athletes as I listened to these delightful words on my voice mail, "Chaplain, I found someone I want to spend the rest of my life with, but I need you to meet them first."

Additional information and resources: Cede Sports is a Christian organization that mobilizes chaplains through sports. Information is available at https://cedesports.org.

13. Crisis Intervention and Disaster-Relief Chaplaincy

Chaplain quote: "Providing compassion requires stepping out of my comfort zone and intentionally entering a place of crisis—danger, pain, loss, or grief—during the spiritual and emotional catastrophes of life."

Inspiring verse: "Blessed be the God and Father of our Lord Jesus Christ, the Father of mercies and God of all comfort, who comforts us in all our affliction, so that we may be able to comfort those who are in any affliction, with the comfort with which we ourselves are comforted by God" (2 Cor. 1:3–4).

Environment and culture: Chaplains provide spiritual resources, emotional "first aid," and comfort to victims, survivors, and first responders in the aftermath of a critical incident. These disasters can be either small-scale or mass-casualty, including wide-area natural disasters such as hurricanes, tornadoes, earthquakes, and fires; multiple-victim crimes of violence such as mass shootings; or an accident such as a civilian aircraft crash.

Typical responsibilities: Chaplains provide disaster-relief and trauma mitigation to survivors of mass-casualty events or natural disasters in the form of pastoral care. Oftentimes a response team is formed to care for the "walking worried"—victims of criminal, man-made, or natural crises. Through their faith, chaplains help victims and survivors understand and normalize their reactions to increasingly abnormal situations and help them to begin their spiritual, physical, and emotional recovery. These "spiritual paramedics" provide practical acts of compassion, including feeding the hungry, clothing the naked, providing water for the thirsty, and sheltering the exposed. Disaster-relief chaplains may be board certified with experience in crisis management and traumatic stress. A background in critical incident stress management, suicide intervention, traumatic stress, grief after crisis, pastoral crisis intervention, and response to aviation incidents is also helpful.

Unique factors, concerns, or challenges: Disaster-relief chaplaincy has a high rate of compassion fatigue. Chaplains become emotionally depleted after hearing about the suffering of victims. They are not tired *of* being compassionate but tired *from* being compassionate. They need to practice self-care in order to have the emotional energy required to be available for people. In disasters, spiritual care is often pictured as providing a calm presence, listening nonjudgmentally, intervening with care, and offering the hope one can find through faith. A vital aspect of disaster chaplaincy is "the ministry of presence." Providing a simple, empathic, listening ear is a primary pastoral act. The chaplain in disaster relief shares God's presence with victims and offers words of assurance that "I am with you." A unique factor of this sort of chaplaincy is that the chaplain frequently experiences loss from the same precipitating circumstance. The hurricane that destroyed victims' property may have destroyed the chaplain's as well. The chaplain cannot deny the reality of the crisis, should not minimize the sense of loss it causes, and may not be able to diminish any of the pain. But the chaplain offers the comfort of God's presence through words of comfort and assurance. Being present may invite a sense of community within the crisis, may lead to healing reconciliation, or may reconnect a survivor with God.

Recipient comments on value of chaplaincy: A medical worker in Haiti said, "My medical staff commented that having you present made a difference in their personal attitude while they served. Some even said they could not have completed their service without your support due to the emotional trauma while working in the cholera clinics."

Additional information and resources: The Emotional and Spiritual Care Committee of the National Voluntary Organizations Active in Disaster (NVOAD) is an association of organizations that mitigate and alleviate the impact of disasters and also focus on identifying specific emotional and spiritual issues impacting disaster response. Additionally, various governmental and non-profit agencies typically support disaster-relief efforts, including the International Critical Incident Stress Foundation (ICISF), the American Red Cross, the Salvation Army, the National Organization for Victim Assistance (NOVA), the Southern Baptist North American Mission Board (NAMB) Disaster Relief teams, the National Transportation Safety Board (NTSB), the FBI, and the US Coast Guard. Many of these organizations cooperate with various faith communities by providing chaplaincy training in preparation of delivering effective disaster-relief services.

Scenarios and Case Studies

Review the following case studies from actual chaplaincy situations. Reflect on what you've learned in this book as you process through these questions. Choose a scenario that aligns with your specific area of chaplain interest and explore it in depth. Try to account for the theological underpinning of chaplaincy and how it intersects with the question, issue, or problem. As you use these case studies, consider the following framework:

Ministry challenge: What is the challenge you are facing?
- What are the theological, relational, and personal issues that are before you?
- What issues and experiences from your own life do you need to be aware of as you meet and respond to this challenge?
- Why is this a challenge that you need to address?
- What are the possible implications of your actions and response?
- What ought to be going on?
- What are the outcomes that you would hope for?
- What are the theological principles of pastoral ministry that inform your reflection on this challenge?

Ministry action: How might you respond?
- What theological resources could be brought to bear in this situation?
- What additional resources could be utilized in addressing this situation (e.g., books, articles, people, technology, etc.)?
- What are the next steps that you will take?

Health-Care Chaplain Scenarios

1. Ron is a young patient under your care who was just admitted to hospice. He has a progressive disease that will slowly take his ability

to speak and swallow, but throughout, he will be completely awake and aware of what is going on with his body. He cannot eat anything by mouth but eats through a tube, and eventually he wishes to stop this so that he can pass peacefully, believing that God has decided his day on earth. The tube feedings are preventing him from passing peacefully and naturally, and are making it too difficult for his family. If you were his chaplain, how would you offer support to this patient, his family, and the staff?

2. You are paged one evening to the bedside of a mother who has just given birth. Her baby was fine when she was born, but about thirty minutes afterward the nurse tending to the mom notices that the child is not breathing. The child is rushed off and the mom and dad are left behind. In consulting with the nurse on the way in, you discover that this patient's doctor is "renowned" in the hospital for contracts with foreign national patients who pay him a lump sum to come to the United States to deliver their babies. (He passes some cash on to the hospital for their services.) As such, it is not clear who will pay for these extra complications, as they were not included in the original contract. The nurses have been upset with this doctor for some time over this matter, but there have never been complications like this before. Meanwhile, the mother is away from home, away from family, aware that her daughter will likely die, and there is uncertainty about their status and funding. Her English is limited. How do you proceed?

3. You have a former patient who recently passed away. Her family now asks you to officiate her funeral with no mention of God, Christ, or the Holy Spirit, as she did not want any mention of a faith tradition. How would you go about creating a funeral service that meets the expectations of the patient and family while still honoring your own faith? What is your theology of inclusivity/generosity, knowing the person you are remembering did not want to mention God in her service?

4. You meet Jennifer in the neonatal intensive care unit at the bedside of her daughter, Joy, who is premature (twenty-four weeks) and has many anomalies. The doctors do not anticipate that Joy will live more than a week. They have asked you to see Jennifer because she refuses to have any negative talk or conversations in Joy's room. Jennifer identifies as Christian, specifically Word of Faith movement. How do you provide support for the medical team and Jennifer?

5. Andrea is the mother of a three-year-old son, Tom. You meet her

and her boyfriend, Ryan, in the waiting room of the pediatric intensive care unit. You know that Tom is at the hospital for nonaccidental trauma (abuse). Ryan is the primary suspect in the crime. Andrea is very upset and does not believe that Ryan hurt Tom. As the chaplain, how would you support Andrea, Tom, Ryan, and the medical team?

6. You are a hospice chaplain, and during your visit the patient requests immediate baptism. You ask whether she has ever been baptized. With tears in her eyes, she says her former baptism was insufficient because it was based on a Trinitarian formula. However, new teachings from a church podcast convince her that her prior baptism in the name of the Father and the Son and the Holy Spirit is blasphemy. She grabs your hand and begs you to baptize her with a new baptism using "in Jesus' name" so she can have salvation. What do you say? What do you do? What does your faith group say about this?

Military Chaplain Scenarios

1. Jack and Annie, a military couple, come to you for marriage counseling. They are struggling in their relationship with trusting one another. Jack met Annie at a local strip club where she was working as a stripper. After falling in love and getting married within a few weeks of meeting, Jack has now decided he doesn't want his wife to be a stripper any longer (partly because many of his friends attend the strip club); however, Annie enjoys the attention she gets from others at the club and likes the extra money she makes to buy nice things. They have come to you to help them work on their relationship.

2. Susan, a military woman, comes to you to work on her marriage. As you counsel her, you soon realize that her spouse is another woman, Sarah. Crying and upset, Susan explains how her partner of the past ten years now wants to leave her for a male friend with whom she is now having an affair. Susan and Sarah also have a child together who legally belongs to Sarah from a prior relationship. They together have raised this child for the past ten years, ever since the child was a baby. How do you help support this family?

3. While deployed in a combat environment, a soldier named Sean comes to you for counseling. Sean is visibly angry, shaking, and showing aggressive signs of being upset . . . all while still holding his M-4 carbine (which soldiers carry at all times during combat). Sean explains to you that he just heard from a colleague back home that

Sean's wife has been cheating on him with his best friend while Sean has been deployed. Sean frantically comes to you for help in what he should do in the situation.

4. While deployed, you receive an emergency call at 2:00 a.m. from a frantic military member. Soon thereafter you arrive at your chapel office and discover that he is actually a high-ranking commander on the base. The commander is delusional and upset, claiming that he is "surrounded by demons and devils," and has asked to talk with a chaplain to help him cope with the spiritual things he claims he has been seeing. As you meet with the commander, he becomes irrational and quite literally "crazy." He accuses you of being a "tool of the devil" and one of Satan's "demons in disguise." Upset and aggravated, he tries to storm out of your office. What do you do?

5. For the past several months, you've been developing a mentoring relationship with a fellow service member named Marty. The unit you are both assigned to is suddenly deployed to war. Not long after deploying together, Marty is mortally wounded while on a combat patrol, and you are summoned to the makeshift medical clinic. There you see Marty covered in blood and bullet wounds, with most of one leg missing. He only has seconds to live. The military medical staff and other members wounded on the patrol are all next to him in the room with you. You are there to be a visible sign of the Holy. How do you comfort your friend and the others?

6. While deployed to a combat location, you are conducting a weekly Bible study for military members. During the study, a soldier named Jerome bursts in and tells the group that he was just on patrol and inadvertently stepped on a land mine. It launched into the air but didn't detonate. If it had, he would have surely been killed. He is not a Christian, but he believes that God has just spared his life and wants to be baptized immediately. What do you do?

Correctional/Prison Chaplain Scenarios

1. James, a twenty-eight-year-old inmate at the prison where you work, comes to your office to discuss his plans to marry Sheila, a woman he met before his incarceration. Together they have a seven-year-old son. James has five years left on a ten-year sentence for selling drugs. He came to know the Lord in prison, and you, as his chaplain, have been instrumental in his faith development. Sheila and her whole family are Jehovah's Witnesses. They would like for you to perform

the ceremony in the prison visiting room, which is allowed by prison policy. Although it is possible for you to meet with both of them together in the visiting room, regular contact between staff and inmate family members is discouraged. Also, conjugal visits are not allowed at your prison.

2. An inmate requests to see you. When you arrive, he says, "I am a Satanist and I would like a copy of the satanic bible." Your contract is with a government institution, and that means you are bound to serve those of all religions and faiths. The man looks sheepish but determined, and seems somber. How do you proceed?

3. Bill, a twenty-two-year-old inmate serving a twenty-year sentence for armed bank robbery, comes to your office to discuss being baptized by you. He says he has known the Lord since he was young and used to sing in the church choir. He was baptized when he was thirteen prior to coming to prison, but he feels it "didn't count" because he continued in the life of criminal activity. He has been active for two years in the Sunday evening Protestant service, and he says this time he is serious, and he wants to "set an example for others" by being baptized. How do you respond to Bill's request to be baptized?

4. Two chaplains serve at the same prison. You are the senior one answering the phone. It's a call from the warden. "One of my senior staff members, the deputy warden, has a little problem. He's the best person we've got." You say, "I'll be pleased to help if I can." "Well, the deputy warden's daughter wants to get married this weekend. He said she talked with your junior chaplain, Chaplain Jones, about performing the ceremony, but Jones said that he couldn't do it—or he wouldn't do it." You say, "Several days' notice on performing a wedding ceremony isn't much time, Warden, and there are requirements and sometimes restrictions placed on chaplains by their churches, by their faith groups." He explodes: "What do you mean restrictions and requirements of the church? Jones is a state correctional chaplain, isn't he? Who certifies his pay? He'll do what you and I tell him to do." You are feeling very tense. What is your answer?

College and Educational Chaplain Scenarios

1. You are a college chaplain. An associate professor stops by your office with a concern. Her religious practice prohibits her vegetarian lunch to be in the same faculty lounge refrigerator as her colleague's

bologna meat sandwiches. She wants to know what you can do for her as chaplain. Is this an issue of religious facilitation? Should chaplains get involved in this issue? What are the pros and cons of potential solutions?

2. A student approaches you and says, "I'm pregnant, but I'm getting an abortion today. Can you pray with me that God will forgive me?" What do you say?

3. A student comes to you and says, "I'm a Muslim student, and I have to fast for Ramadan. But the campus doctor tells me I have to eat regularly. I have the right to practice my religion, and I need you to explain that to her. And I don't want a female doctor . . . it is shameful to be seen by any woman who is not my wife." How do you respond?

Workplace, Industrial, Corporate, and Community Chaplain Scenario

1. You are a chaplain, and another employee approaches you, saying, "I am grateful our company is giving us Christmas and New Year's Day off from work. But I'm Jewish, and those days don't mean anything to me. Can I have Yom Kippur and Rosh Hashanah off instead?" What do you say? Can you, as a chaplain, advocate for an employee's orthopraxy while disagreeing with, or not appreciating, his orthodoxy? As a chaplain, do you want to see his religious needs met? Would you feel different if he asked time off for Eid Al-Fitr and Eid Al-Adha? Why or why not?

Sample Clinical Pastoral Education Verbatim

CPE verbatims are a fairly common practice in chaplaincy. They are integrated and presented to the group alongside other residents. As soon after visiting a patient as possible, a chaplain writes down what he remembers from the conversation. A complete verbatim would be followed by theological, sociological, and psychological analysis. The main focus of the verbatim is to allow the group to review what the chaplain did, ask questions, and discuss the pastoral visit from different angles. The writing and reflecting afterward are also helpful to CPE development. Chaplains can find something interesting in every visit they make. This sample verbatim has had names and locations changed. More information on the common qualifications and competencies of the chaplaincy profession can be found at the Association of Professional Chaplains website.

"I Have Been Craving a Frankfurter"

Context: I have known Rena for several years, mainly because she attends worship services on Tuesday mornings and Sunday afternoons at a nursing home in the same system as my hospital. She is Catholic but enjoys coming to the ecumenical Protestant services. I know that Rena is reserved and quiet and sometimes slow to respond when you speak to her. This may be in large part because she can't see well and her hearing is also impaired. I know that she also is more forgetful than she used to be and has lost some short-term memory.

C1: (I come close to R and bend down to her ear and touch her hand.) Hello, Rena. It's M, chaplain from Augustana. I see that you have been here for a couple of days and you were in the emergency department for almost two days. I'm sorry it took so long to get to a room. How's it going?

R1:   (Begins tearing up) Hello. I don't know what's happening. Nobody is telling me anything. You are the first person to talk to me.

C2:   I'm sorry, R. That sounds very lonely.

R2:   (Begins crying) Nobody is telling me anything. I don't know why I am here. What are they going to do to me?

C3:   R, they won't do anything to you without talking to you first. They won't give you tests or do surgery or anything like that without asking your permission. They have to get your permission for whatever things they do.

R3:   Oh, okay. That's good. (She looks relieved, but as if to prove me a liar, a nurse comes in and hooks her up to oxygen, places the two prongs in her nostrils, and says, "This is oxygen, R, to help you breathe." The nurse leaves.) Do I have to have these in?

C4:   The nurse said it's to help you breathe. Does it feel like it's helping you breathe easier?

R4:   I don't know. I can breathe fine except when I get nervous. I don't have any problem breathing.

C5:   Is it hurting your nose? Is it painful?

R5:   No, it's more like irritating. I don't like all of this. I feel like such a burden.

C6:   It's hard to feel like that. (Silence) You are not a burden to me. I like to be with you.

R6:   I'm glad. Thank you. (She cries.) I just want to go home.

C7:   Where is home, R? (She points silently to the ceiling.) So home is in heaven, with God?

R7:   Yes. I just want to be with God.

C8: I am sorry you are suffering so much. May I say a psalm and prayer for you?

R8: Yes, please.

C9: (I put my hand on Rena's forehead, say Psalm 23, followed by a personal prayer, then the Lord's Prayer.) Dear R, you are a good person and you don't deserve this suffering. I will come back tomorrow and see you again. Is there anything else I can do for you?

R9: No, thanks for coming.

In the next couple of days, I speak to the director of nursing at the nursing home to tell her what R had said about wanting to go to heaven and to see if there had been any conversation regarding R's current treatment choices and goals of care. I also speak to R's nurse and tell her about the hearing loss and vision loss. The next day there was a sign above her bed indicating these things and instructing that she needs help with eating.

Rena was in a good mood the next two times I visited her. When I asked if there was anything I could do for her, she said, "I have been craving a frankfurter."

Checklist for New Chaplains:
Moving from Parish Ministry to Chaplaincy

This checklist was written by John D. Barry while he was transitioning from parish ministry to chaplaincy. Whereas the author of this textbook writes from the perspective of a long-term career chaplain, this practical advice comes from someone crossing over the threshold. The following provides another viewpoint for readers to consider in preparation for their own entry into chaplaincy.

It has been said that learning is moving from one point of ignorance to another. There are few times in life that will force you to admit ignorance more than switching careers. If you're going straight from an MDiv to chaplaincy, chance has it that your degree program and practicum work prepared you to pastor a congregation—not for chaplaincy. If you're moving from parish (congregation-based) ministry into chaplaincy, it is vital to realize that "one of these things is not like the other." While chaplaincy and parish ministry have much in common, they can be rightfully classified as two different careers. Both are pastoring, but they are certainly not the same career of pastoring.

If you're moving from parish (congregation-based) ministry into chaplaincy, this checklist is for you. Here's how you can increase the speed at which you move from ignorance to competency—or at least turn the "unknowns" of your new career into "knowns." There are three major spheres of life to consider when making your transition: mental/spiritual, relational, and contextual. Each area requires a unique type of preparation, and neglect of any particular area can (and likely will) affect the others.

1. Prepare Yourself Mentally and Spiritually

- Find a mentor who has at least a decade of experience in the same type of chaplaincy as you, and start asking questions. There are two vital questions: (1) "What advice would you give someone just start-ing out—what can I learn from you that took you years to learn?" and (2) "What ethical issues did you encounter that you found to be challenging as a minister?" If you're wondering how to get a mentor, then work your network, especially your contacts within your faith community—tell anyone and everyone who will listen about what you plan to do next with your life. Chance has it that someone in your network knows someone else who has had a career like the one you envision. Your mentor is also your go-to person whom you will call later, when you encounter that odd situation you could have never imagined.

- Conduct informational interviews. This is similar to the previous step, in the sense that you will ask the same questions. The differ-ence is that you are not developing ongoing relationships (as in mentorship) but are learning what you can about your new career from a wide variety of people who have lived the type of life you plan to live.

- Read (or listen to) books by chaplains who have had similar careers. As you read or listen, note especially the spiritual and mental hard-ships the author has faced. Then, imagine experiencing the same hardship. How would you react? How can mentally working through the hardship now prepare you for a similar hardship when you face it? There are also some "must read" books for every chaplain, regard-less of field. See the bibliography for some recommendations and continue your reading journey.

- Read (or listen to) books about the field you plan to enter (e.g., books by military generals if you're going to be a military chaplain, books by ER doctors if you're going to be a hospital chaplain). At this stage, you are going a level beyond your particular career path to try to understand the ethos (culture) of those with whom you will be serv-ing. It is equally helpful to consider books about the particular and ongoing problems in your field (e.g., for military chaplaincy, books about posttraumatic stress; for hospital chaplains, books about ad-diction and end-of-life care).

- Listen to addresses and talks about your particular type of chap-laincy. Hearing stories is more valuable than reading a bullet list. You will later be able to mentally reference a particular story, as if it were your own experience, and it will inform you as you go about your new occupation.

- Above all, pray. Mental preparedness is a spiritual journey. Be in conversation with God during the whole process. And be sure that not all your conversations with God are about your career. Spending time with God, in his presence, is not just a necessary part of your preparedness but will be a critical practice to learn right now. That's how you will maintain mental stamina when life gets hard later.

2. Prepare Yourself Relationally

- Start doing the type of ministry you plan to do right now. Chance has it that if you're truly honest with yourself, there is an area in your next career that makes you uncomfortable. For example, you may have never had someone confess to you a grievous wrongdoing, describe a trauma, or talk about her repeated and ongoing addiction. It could also be that you're comfortable in all those areas but you're uncomfortable in a pulpit or leading a Scripture-based study with a small group of people; or maybe you've never been with a family whose loved one is about to die. Whatever it may be, you need to experience that next step as soon as possible. Getting uncomfortable now will make your next career easier because you will be able to say to yourself, when the pressure is on, "I've got this." The key is to have confidence in your competency, not just your calling.
- Start counseling in extreme settings. This is similar to the previous step but is necessary to single out because our risk-averse brains will seek to avoid it. Pastoral counseling is a chaplain's bread and butter—and doing so when it's all on the line is what we do. But counseling in a parish these days is fairly "safe"—for lack of a better word. If you've never counseled regularly at a homeless rescue mission, a recovery house, or with the dying, now is the time to do so. Do everything you can to experience the extreme now; once again, this will make your career transition smoother. You can also take this one step further by having a regular recap process built into your personal learning plan. This is similar to the verbatim process required in Clinical Pastoral Education (CPE) but is less formal. Simply talk about the difficulties you're facing with your mentor.
- Get new training to prepare yourself. Related to both of the last points is the need to identify your personal growth areas and obtain necessary training. Think about what your next career will require and compare that to the subject areas in which you've had the least

formal education. You can fill in some of these gaps with reading, but interactive learning settings—like weeklong or weekend seminars from experts—are far more conducive to skill-based learning. The goal here is to learn the relational skills you will need in a setting where you can receive immediate feedback. You need someone who will say something to you like, "You know, you seem really cold when you do *this*" or "Your body language is telling me *this*" or "That question could be better asked *this way*."

- Above all, in the relational category, if you're married, talk with your spouse about the potential issues you imagine facing in your new career. Now is the time to develop appropriate boundaries between your work life and your home life. It is also the time to consider how your relationship will function in your new context (e.g., deployments for military personnel; the ongoing secondary trauma experienced by hospital chaplains; the emotional burden of counseling addicts and preventing suicides). The best thing you can do for this step is to consider getting marriage coaching before you make your transition—especially if that coaching is conducted by someone specializing in clergy-related issues. An investment in your marriage will pay dividends for years to come. The goal is to know your areas of ignorance now—"What are we not seeing about our marriage?"—so that you can address the areas of ignorance before the problem is exponentially more difficult in your new context. If you're not married, have these conversations with your accountability partner or your best friend. The assumption here is that you already have accountability relationships in place; if you don't, you could add that step and make sure to talk about personal issues and individual trauma that you have not discussed in detail before.

3. Prepare Yourself Contextually

- Ask questions, all the time. In the first ninety days of your new career, you will want to learn everything you can. The key here is again asking questions. Who knows what you don't know? Ask your supervisor questions. Tell her you're learning—and then admit ignorance—and ask for guidance. Don't assume you know anything, because you know what "assumptions" do.
- Consider the financial reality of your new occupation. To think that finances don't affect you as a chaplain is a type of ignorance that will

not be bliss. The priorities of your new organization, whether spoken or unspoken, are set by the budget. Just as your parish may have put funding the new building over international missions by making that building project the biggest item in the budget, your new context likely puts something before people. Learn what the priority is, because it will affect you. Also, consider if you have the resources you need to do your job. If you don't, what proposal could you write to change your allocated budget? Who makes the financial decisions? In the business sector, this is called "knowing your real customer" and "knowing who the stakeholders are." Remember that there are many people who have incredible influence, even if their title does not say so (e.g., administrative assistants, VPs over other areas, resource managers in military chaplaincy). In every institution, there is the organizational chart of relative ranks and there is the real chain of influence. This influencer hierarchy includes the people who prioritize resources to include fiscal and human capital.

- Learn the structure of your new organization. Who will decide if you're doing your job well? Who will write your performance reviews? When will those take place? What do those people care most about? Here's where taking people to coffee or showing up in their office to say hello makes a big difference. Every place has its politics and power structures—to think otherwise will cost you many opportunities. You will want to learn the structure as quickly as possible.
- Mentally note cultural norms. In every organization, there are the written codes (e.g., employee manuals, bylaws, slide decks) and there are unwritten norms. What's the oral history of your organization? What do people say about how things work? Especially observe phrases like "Well, that's the [organization name] way," and "That's how we've always done things," and "That reminds me of when [x event] happened." These are part of the cultural (or oral) memory of an organization and its people. Often, the oral tradition is more important than the written one. If you don't know the oral tradition, you may easily walk into a situation that makes no sense to you personally but is significant throughout the organization. The key is to learn how to react when you run into these walls.
- Learn from your predecessor. Your predecessor may have been great at his job or terrible at it. Either way, he has something to teach you. Ideally, you can learn this information before he moves on. After he

departs, it remains likely that he will still correspond with you. Make sure you read your predecessor's work. Note, though, that there is a fine line between comparing yourself to your predecessor and learning from him. Learning is the goal, not comparison. Especially ask your predecessor, "What went well and smoothly?" and "What was difficult?"

- Above all, in the contextual category, remember your personal goals. What matters to you in your new job? How can you frame those goals in a way that fits with the organization? How can you live out God's calling on your life, in this context, at this point in time? Here's where regularly checking in and maintaining your relationship with your faith community is critical to your success. That's how you stay grounded in your identity as a person of a particular faith tradition in a pluralistic context. That's how you remember why you do what you do. At the end of the day, you report to God first.

It is okay to be ignorant. In reality, ignorance is essential for growth. Everyone was ignorant once. But lack of preparation will ultimately punish you and those you serve. Prepare yourself mentally, spiritually, relationally, and contextually. You won't regret it.

Helping Churches and Employers Understand the Difference between Chaplains and Pastors

What is the fundamental difference between a chaplain and a pastor? Many highly committed and well-trained clergy serve as chaplains rather than as pastors. They are ambassadors of faith and God's loving care beyond the walls of the local church, and they minister to those who might not otherwise meet a pastor. While chaplains do many of the same things pastors do, their job descriptions are as diverse as the people they minister to.

1. Chaplains are called to specialized ministry by organizations, not traditional congregations. Rather than working in churches, chaplains minister in hospitals, mental health centers, nursing homes, residences for children and adults with disabilities, hospices, college campuses, sports locker rooms, police cars, fire stations, prison cells, aircraft carriers, and military barracks, just to name a few locations.

2. Chaplains extend care to people of all faiths and people of no faith. Chaplaincy reaches a broad spectrum of religious preferences, beliefs, and theologies. If chaplains cannot themselves provide appropriate religious services or meet the needs of those in their care, they find someone who can facilitate.

3. Chaplains frequently work with a multifaith team. While grounded in their own theological tradition, chaplains adapt to secular and multifaith environments. They have a joyful and unapologetic faith commitment, a healthy pastoral identity, and a sense of mission to those they serve.

4. Chaplains rarely dress like clergy. You may not recognize a chaplain by the way she dresses. Most often chaplains do not wear a clergy collar. You will see a chaplain wearing a simple facility ID badge, a unique vest, or a uniform.

5. Chaplains receive specialized training. Many have specialty training in pastoral counseling and advanced education in ethics. Clinical Pastoral Education (CPE) is an essential element of a chaplain's education and provides practical, on-site, pastoral care training.

6. Chaplains are called. A chaplain's certification, appointment, and continuation in his role are contingent upon maintaining good and regular standing with the faith group along with a current ecclesiastical endorsement.

7. Chaplains function as ministers. They provide worship, liturgical, and sacramental ministry, including baptisms and the Lord's Supper, as well as preach, perform weddings, and officiate funerals. They bring the same educational requirements as a minister and have a well-rounded pastoral identity. Prior experience in a church prepares chaplains to minister to a diverse population.

8. Chaplains embody their faith. They remain faithful without proselytizing. While chaplains minister in diverse and unexpected places to people who are not necessarily Christian, they nevertheless share the good news of God's love. They serve in organizations and communities throughout the world, inviting people to meet God wherever they are.

Glossary

Access   The ability for people within an organization to engage in religious activities and form associations external to the organization. In chaplaincy, religious access goes in one direction. People within the organization can reach out. Outside religious groups cannot reach in or have access without prior permission.

Accommodation   An institution's response to specific religious and faith-based requests by employees and other beneficiaries. The ability of an institution to respond may be based on issues of access due to isolation; the unique character of organizational activity, such as first responders or the military; and the availability of the chaplain to communicate the religious needs of individuals back to the institution. The chaplain helps the institution accommodate the religious needs of those who serve, or are located within, the institution and supports those representing non-majority faith groups having unique religious requirements.

Board-certified chaplain   A person who has demonstrated professional excellence as a chaplain, meeting all eligibility requirements, including a bachelor's degree, a graduate theological degree from an accredited school, four units of Clinical Pastoral Education (CPE), and endorsement/support by a recognized faith group. Various associations board-certify chaplains. A widely known and accepted board-certification process is through the Board of Chaplaincy Certification, an affiliate of the Association of Professional Chaplains (APC). Chaplains seeking board certification must meet common qualifications and competencies of the chaplaincy profession. The process of certification includes recommendation by a certification committee, review by the Commission on Certification, and ratification by the Board of Directors.

Chaplain   A clergy member specifically designated by his faith group and employing institution to perform the capabilities of providing religious ministry according to his faith tradition, facilitating the diverse religious needs of others, caring for all within the institution, and advising organizational leadership at all levels of management.

Clinical Pastoral Education (CPE)   A unique experience of theological and professional education that serves as a prerequisite for chaplaincy. Often part of seminary education, CPE equips theological students, ordained clergy, members of religious orders, and qualified laypeople with tools for pastoral care through specific training in pastoral reflection, formation, and competence.

Compassion fatigue   The state of being tired not *of* being compassionate but *from* being compassionate. It entails becoming emotionally depleted after hearing about pain suffered by victims. The emotional and physical distress caused by serving those deeply in need can desensitize a chaplain's ability to express empathy. This may result in the chaplain no longer having the emotional energy to be "present." Self-awareness leads to healthy activities.

Cooperative pluralism   The acceptable and supportable coexistence between adherents of different religions or faith groups. Cooperative pluralism does not typically occur in local churches.

Ecclesiastical   Related to religious organizations.

Ecclesiastical endorsement   A signed document from a religious organization certifying and permitting the prospective chaplain to serve as a chaplain in the name of the particular faith group. This endorsement satisfies the administrative requirements of the employing institution. First, the endorsement verifies that the applicant is professionally qualified to perform all offices, functions, sacraments, ordinances, and ceremonies required of a minister for that religious organization. Second, it states that the person is capable and authorized to minister as required in a pluralistic environment. Third, the endorsement verifies that the applicant meets the graduate education and religious leadership requirements of the faith group.

Ecclesiastical endorsing agent   An individual authorized by the religious organization to provide or withdraw ecclesiastical endorsements. Endorsing agents represent their religious organizations and possess ecclesiastical authority to endorse and withdraw endorsement for their chaplains.

Endorsement   An institutional process internal to religious organizations used to confirm the ability of their clergy to conduct religious observances or ceremonies in the context of chaplaincy.

Facilitation   Religious support and assistance given to others not sharing the same theology or faith expressions as the chaplain.

Incarnational ministry   A term coined specifically for Christian chaplains, but the idea extends to all chaplains no matter their faith tradition. It exemplifies the ministry of Jesus by deliberate movement and direction of chaplains toward where people live and work. Some chaplains call it simply ministry by walking around (MBWA). They dedicate time on their calendar several times a week for MBWA in order to be among those they serve. It provides them intentional opportunity to be away from their office and the distractions of e-mail, research, and projects in order to meet and engage people where they are.

Institutional duality   The status of being simultaneously in two institutions. The chaplain is not half clergy and half employee but a full member in both the faith group and the employing organization. Simultaneous participation requires adaptability and awareness of the differences.

Loitering with intent   Providing a nonanxious presence.

MBWA   Ministry by walking around. This is an intentional decision to be out of the office and the distractions of e-mail, research, and projects for the specific purpose of meeting and engaging people where they are. It requires deliberate movement and direction toward where people live and work. Chaplains dedicate time on their calendar several times a week for MBWA in order to be among those they serve. Some Christian chaplains refer to this as incarnational ministry.

Ministry of presence   The silence of simply being present, still, and available. Just as God was heard in the "still, small voice," a chaplain's loudest message may be through a ministry of presence. Care comes in the ministry of presence. Care comes in the silence where no words can bring comfort. Care comes by staying with people. Care does not require words. It requires presence. Providing a simple, empathic, listening ear is a primary pastoral act.

Orthodoxy   A specific faith group's authorized doctrine.

Orthopraxy   A specific faith group's authorized practices. Some practices may not be authorized by the chaplain's employer.

Pluralistic environment   A setting wherein a plurality of religious traditions exists side by side in the context of chaplaincy.

Proselytizing   Using coercion to persuade someone to follow or convert to a particular religion.

Provision   A chaplain capability of providing and personally conducting ministry for those aligned with a chaplain's faith group.

Religious ministry professional   A pastor, minister, priest, rabbi, or other clergy endorsed to represent a religious organization and to conduct its religious observances or ceremonies. This person is a fully qualified member of the professional clergy for those religious organizations.

Religious organization   An entity that is organized and functions primarily to perform religious ministries to a lay constituency and that has met the religious-purposes test of section 501(c)(3) of title 26, United States Code (Internal Revenue Code), and holds current status as a section 501(c)(3) Schedule "A" organization.

Total institution   Term coined by famed sociologist Erving Goffman to signify a place of work or residence that seeks to deliver a full range of resources with the intent of balancing work and life needs. Many people who are separated from their wider community for a defined period of time tend to live in a highly administered context where the food they receive and the rooms they sleep in are determined by the parent organization. Examples include residential colleges, hospitals, military installations, all-inclusive resorts, cruise ships, and prisons.

Notes

Introduction

1. Alejandra Molna, "As Americans Become Less Religious, the Role of Chaplains May Grow," *Washington Post*, November 29, 2019, https://www.washington post.com/religion/as-americans-become-less-religious-the-role-of-chaplains-may -grow/2019/11/29/18ca2368-12c5-11ea-bofc-62cc38411ebb_story.html.

2. This helpful ministry-task framework was developed by Naomi K. Paget and Janet R. McCormack in *The Work of the Chaplain* (Valley Forge, PA: Judson, 2006).

Chapter 1

1. All Scripture quotations come from the English Standard Version, unless otherwise indicated.

2. Frederick Buechner, *Wishful Thinking: A Seeker's ABC* (New York: HarperCollins, 1973), 119.

3. Os Guinness, *The Call: Finding and Fulfilling the Central Purpose of Your Life* (Nashville: Nelson, 2003), 29.

4. Guinness, *The Call*, 42.

5. Guinness, *The Call*, 45.

6. N. T. Wright, *Paul: A Biography* (San Francisco: HarperOne, 2018), 66.

7. Gordon MacDonald, *Building Below the Waterline: Shoring Up the Foundations of Leadership* (Peabody, MA: Hendrickson, 2011), 46, 48, 176, 178.

8. Gordon MacDonald, "Leader's Insight: When Leaders Implode," *CT Pastors* (blog), *Christianity Today*, November 6, 2006, https://www.christianitytoday.com/pastors/2006 /november-online-only/cln61106.html.

9. G. S. Prentzas, *The Brooklyn Bridge* (New York: Chelsea House Publishers, 2009), 58.

10. MacDonald, *Building Below the Waterline*, 2.

11. N. T. Wright, *Paul*, 195.

12. Emma Green, "Finding Jesus at Work," *Atlantic*, February 17, 2016, https://www .theatlantic.com/business/archive/2016/02/work-secularization-chaplaincies/462987/.

13. Richard G. Hutcheson Jr., *The Churches and the Chaplaincy* (Atlanta: John Knox, 1975), 41–44.

14. John Paul Wright, "The University as a Total Institution," *Quillette* (blog), January 2, 2017, https://quillette.com/2017/01/02/the-university-as-a-total-institution/.

15. George Ritzer and Allan Liska, "'McDisneyization' and 'Post-tourism': Complemen-

tary Perspectives on Contemporary Tourism," in *New Directions and Alternative Tourism*, ed. Stephen Williams (London: Routledge, 2004), 65–82.

16. Simon Sinek, *Leaders Eat Last: Why Some Teams Pull Together and Others Don't* (New York: Portfolio, 2014).

17. Over half of active duty enlisted personnel are twenty-five years of age or younger, according to US Department of Defense, "2016 Demographics: Profile of the Military Community," Military OneSource (website), accessed April 16, 2020, https://download.military onesource.mil/12038/MOS/Reports/2016-Demographics-Report.pdf.

18. In 2018 there were 12.3 million college and university students under age twenty-five, according to National Center for Education Statistics, "Fast Facts: Back to School Statistics," NCES (website), accessed April 16, 2020, https://nces.ed.gov/fastfacts/display .asp?id=372.

19. Of all first-time camping participants, 27 percent were children between the ages of six and twelve, and 26 percent were young adults between the ages of twenty-five and thirty-four, according to the Coleman Company, Inc., and the Outdoor Foundation, "2017 American Camper Report," Outdoor Industry Association (website), accessed April 16, 2020, https://outdoorindustry.org/wp-content/uploads/2015/03/2017-Camping -Report__FINAL.pdf.

20. The US Department of Veterans Affairs reports that the average age of a veteran is fifty-eight, with the largest group of veterans between the ages of forty-five and sixty-four and 37.1 percent of the population being sixty-five years or older. "The Veteran Population," National Center for Veterans Analysis and Statistics (website), accessed April 16, 2020, https://www.va.gov/VETDATA/docs/SurveysAndStudies/VETPOP.pdf.

21. Clifford M. Drury, *The History of the Chaplain Corps, United States Navy*, vol. 1 (Washington, DC: US Government Printing Office, 1949), 90–92.

22. Naomi K. Paget and Janet R. McCormack, *The Work of the Chaplain* (Valley Forge, PA: Judson, 2006), 14–34.

23. "Chrism Mass: Homily of Pope Francis, Saint Peter's Basilica, Holy Thursday, March 28, 2013," Holy See (website), accessed April 16, 2020, http://w2.vatican.va/con tent/francesco/en/homilies/2013/documents/papa-francesco_20130328_messa-crismale .html.

24. Elijah felt this way in 1 Kings 19:10: "I have been very jealous for the LORD, the God of hosts. For the people of Israel have forsaken your covenant, thrown down your altars, and killed your prophets with the sword, and I, even I only, am left, and they seek my life, to take it away."

25. "Malingering," Psychology Today (website), updated March 20, 2019, https://www .psychologytoday.com/conditions/malingering.

26. Scott Michael Rank, ed., "When Patton Enlisted the Entire Third Army to Pray for Fair Weather," History on the Net (website), updated November 23, 2016, https://www .historyonthenet.com/when-patton-enlisted-the-entire-third-army-to-pray-for-fair -weather.

27. Paget and McCormack, *Work of the Chaplain*, 27.

28. Dr. Janet McCormack (director of the chaplaincy and pastoral counseling programs and associate professor of chaplaincy and pastoral counseling at Denver Seminary), in discussion with the author, August 3, 2015.

29. Attributed to Saint Francis of Assisi but source unconfirmed. As far as scholars can

tell, he never actually wrote this. Yet it is a famous quote to illustrate his life as someone who lived the gospel and also preached.

30. "Traditions & History," Yale University (website), updated August 3, 2015, https://www.yale.edu/about-yale/traditions-history.

31. William H. S. Demarest, *A History of Rutgers College, 1766–1924* (New Brunswick, NJ: Rutgers College, 1924), 75.

32. Richard M. Budd, *Serving Two Masters: The Development of American Military Chaplaincy, 1860–1920* (Lincoln: University of Nebraska Press, 2002), 13.

33. Budd, *Serving Two Masters*, 13.

34. Budd, *Serving Two Masters*, 13–14.

35. Prepare/Enrich: Embrace the Journey, https://www.prepare-enrich.com/.

Chapter 2

1. Board of Chaplaincy Certification, "Certification Frequently Asked Questions," accessed April 16, 2020, http://bcci.professionalchaplains.org/content.asp?pl=25&contentid=26.

2. A full list of endorsers is found at "Endorsements," Office of the Under Secretary for Personnel and Readiness (website), US Department of Defense, https://prhome.defense.gov/M-RA/MPP/AFCB/Endorsements/.

3. "But some men joined him and believed, among whom also were Dionysius the Areopagite and a woman named Damaris and others with them" (Acts 17:34).

4. Paul G. Hiebert, "Conversion, Culture and Cognitive Categories," *Gospel in Context* 1, no. 4 (1978): 24–29, https://danutm.files.wordpress.com/2010/06/hiebert-paul-g-conversion-culture-and-cognitive-categories.pdf.

5. Hiebert, "Conversion," 6.

6. See Acts 15 and decisions made by the Council of Jerusalem.

7. Seth Godin, "The Tribes We Lead," filmed February 2009, TED video, 17:20, https://www.ted.com/talks/seth_godin_the_tribes_we_lead/transcript.

8. Bryce Covert, "Americans Work Too Much Already," *Nation* (blog), September 28, 2018, https://www.thenation.com/article/americans-work-too-much-already/.

9. Mark Abadi, "11 American Work Habits Other Countries Avoid at All Costs," *Business Insider*, March 8, 2018, https://www.businessinsider.com/unhealthy-american-work-habits-2017-11.

10. Developed in Warren's book *The Purpose-Driven Church: Growth without Compromising Your Message and Mission* (New York: HarperCollins, 1995).

11. Dave Logan, John King, and Halee Fischer-Wright, *Tribal Leadership: Leveraging Natural Groups to Build a Thriving Organization* (New York: Harper Business, 2011), 241.

12. C. S. Lewis, *Mere Christianity* (New York: HarperCollins, 2001), 83.

13. *Encyclopaedia Britannica Online*, s.v. "chaplain," accessed December 19, 2019, https://www.britannica.com/topic/chaplain.

14. C. H. Van Tyne, "Influence of the Clergy, and of Religious and Sectarian Forces, on the American Revolution," *American Historical Review* 19, no. 1 (1913): 44–64, https://doi.org/10.2307/1834806.

15. J. T. Headley, *The Chaplains and Clergy of the Revolution* (New York: Scribner, 1864), 72.

16. Headley, *Chaplains and Clergy*, 73.

17. Joint Chiefs of Staff, "Joint Guide 1-05 for Religious Affairs in Joint Operations," Joint Chiefs of Staff (website), updated February 1, 2018, https://www.jcs.mil/Portals/36/Documents/Doctrine/jdn_jg/jg1_05.pdf.

18. "Rules for the Regulation of the Navy of the United Colonies, 28 November–December 1775," *Founders Online*, National Archives (website), accessed April 16, 2020, https://founders.archives.gov/documents/Adams/06-03-02-0076-0009.

19. Clifford M. Drury, *The History of the Chaplain Corps, United States Navy*, vol. 1 (Washington, DC: US Government Printing Office, 1949), 63.

20. US Department of Defense, "DD Form 2088, Statement of Ecclesiastical Endorsement, January 2019" (website), accessed May 16, 2020, https://www.esd.whs.mil/Portals/54/Documents/DD/forms/dd/dd2088.pdf.

21. The Houston Police Officers' Union established a 24/7 intercessory prayer operation in their designated room in May 2017. See Tom Kennedy, "HPOU Prayer Room Running at a Steady Pace, Praying for HPD Officers, Other Law Enforcement," Houston Police Officers' Union, May 2017, https://hpou.org/hpou-prayer-room-running-at-a-steady-pace-praying-for-hpd-officers-other-law-enforcement/.

22. "Mosaics Adorn Church Facade at Stanford," *San Francisco Call* 94, no. 60 (July 30, 1903), California Digital Newspaper Collection, accessed April 16, 2020, https://cdnc.ucr.edu/?a=d&d=SFC19030730.2.66&e=-------en--20--1--txt-txIN--------1.

23. "For I received from the Lord what I also delivered to you" (1 Cor. 11:23) and "For I delivered to you as of first importance what I also received" (1 Cor. 15:3).

24. "So the last will be first, and the first last" (Matt. 20:16).

25. A. L. Barry, "What about . . . Fellowship in the Lord's Supper," Lutheran Church–Missouri Synod (website), accessed April 20, 2020, https://www.google.com/url?sa=t&rct=j&q=&esrc=s&source=web&cd=2&ved=2ahUKEwiSi4bC8ojgAhVxkeAKHdWLBWUQFjABegQICRAC&url=https%3A%2F%2Fwww.lcms.org%2Fdocument.fdoc%3Fsrc%3Dlcm%26id%3D1097&usg=AOvVaw1BCkySHocRpLN47_n18zWV.

26. Joe Iovino, "An Open Table: How United Methodists Understand Communion," United Methodist Church (website), accessed April 16, 2020, https://www.umc.org/en/content/an-open-table-how-united-methodists-understand-communion.

27. In 2015 the US Supreme Court made same-sex marriages legal in all fifty states in *Obergefell v. Hodges*. However, each state retains its own separate marriage laws, which adhere to Supreme Court rulings.

28. Gordon MacDonald, *Building Below the Waterline: Shoring Up the Foundations of Leadership* (Peabody, MA: Hendrickson, 2011), 7.

Chapter 3

1. Richard G. Hutcheson Jr., *The Churches and the Chaplaincy* (Atlanta: John Knox, 1975), 25.

2. Hutcheson, *Churches and the Chaplaincy*, 25.

3. US Department of Defense, "Armed Forces Chaplain Board," Office of the Under

Secretary for Personnel and Readiness (website), accessed April 16, 2020, https://prhome .defense.gov/M-RA/Inside-M-RA/MPP/AFCB/.

4. US Department of Defense, "Faith and Belief Codes," Defense Manpower Data Center (website), July 21, 2017, https://www.dmdc.osd.mil/appj/dwp/searchResults .jsp?search=faith+and+belief+codes.

5. US Courts, "First Amendment and Religion," accessed April 16, 2020, https://www.us courts.gov/educational-resources/educational-activities/first-amendment-and-religion.

6. Rachel Clark, "903rd CCBn Soldier Participates in Hajj on Invitational Orders," US Army (website), March 17, 2011, https://www.army.mil/article/53417/903rd _ccbn_soldier_participates_in_hajj_on_invitational_orders.

7. See more in Angela Duckworth's *Grit: The Power of Passion and Perseverance* (New York: Scribner, 2016).

8. "Health," Seventh-day Adventist Church (website), accessed April 30, 2020, https:// www.adventist.org/people/health/.

9. Greg Flynn, "It's Official: Army Beard Dreams Cut Short for Soldiers," *Task & Purpose*, November 27, 2017, https://taskandpurpose.com/army-beards-soldiers.

10. Matthew Cox, "14 Sikh High Schoolers Get Waivers to Enter Army Basic with Beard, Turban," Military.com, May 2, 2019, https://www.military.com/daily-news/2019 /05/02/14-sikh-high-schoolers-get-waivers-enter-army-basic-beard-turban.html.

11. Meghann Myers, "A Soldier Just Got Authorization to Wear a Beard Because of His Norse Pagan Faith," *Navy Times*, April 25, 2018, https://www.navytimes.com/news/your -army/2018/04/25/this-soldier-just-got-authorization-to-wear-a-beard-because-of-his -norse-pagan-faith/.

12. J. D. Simkins, "Army Denies Soldier's Request to Grow Beard in Observance of Flying Spaghetti Monster Religion," *Army Times*, May 23, 2019, https://www.armytimes.com /off-duty/military-culture/2019/05/23/army-denies-soldiers-request-to-grow-beard-in -observance-of-flying-spaghetti-monster-religion/.

13. Michele Chabin, "Measles Outbreaks Are Sickening Ultra-Orthodox Jews. Here's Why Many of Them Go Unvaccinated," *Washington Post*, April 3, 2019, https://www .washingtonpost.com/religion/2019/04/03/measles-outbreaks-are-sickening-ultra -orthodox-jews-heres-why-many-them-go-unvaccinated/.

14. Lena H. Sun, "New York City Orders Mandatory Shots in Toughest U.S. Action to Date against Measles," *Washington Post*, April 9, 2019, https://www.washingtonpost.com /health/2019/04/09/new-york-orders-measles-vaccinations-brooklyn-amid-outbreak -mayor-says/.

15. Assistant Secretary of Defense Memorandum Dated April 25, 1997, "Sacramental Use of Peyote by Native American Service Members," US Department of Defense, Office of the Under Secretary for Personnel and Readiness (website), May 5, 1997, https:// prhome.defense.gov/Portals/52/Documents/RFM/Readiness/DDRP/docs/1997.04.25%20 Sacramental%20Use%20of%20Peyote%20by%20Native%20American%20Service%20 Members.pdf.

16. Permitted but not required. See *Cutter v. Wilkinson*, 544 U.S. 709 (2005).

17. Federal Bureau of Investigation, "FBI Chaplains: Bringing the Light in the Darkest Hours," FBI News (website), March 5, 2018, https://www.fbi.gov/news/stories/fbi -chaplains.

18. US Public Health Service, "Surgeon General's Honor Guard Drill and Ceremonies

Manual," US Public Health Service Commissioned Corps (website), November 6, 2017, https://dcp.psc.gov/CCMIS/PDF_docs/USPHS%20SGHG%20Drill%20and%20Ceremo nies%20Manual.pdf.

19. "The Saga of the Four Chaplains," Four Chaplains Memorial Foundation (website), accessed April 16, 2020, http://www.fourchaplains.org/the-saga-of-the-four-chaplains/.

20. Stephen Chavez, "Cooperation without Compromise," *Adventist Review: Online Edition*, last modified in 2000, accessed April 16, 2020, https://www.adventistreview.org /archives/2000-1545/story1.html.

21. US Department of Justice, "Ministry of BOP Chaplains," Federal Bureau of Prisons (website), updated November 18, 2004, https://www.bop.gov/policy/technical/5360_02 .pdf.

Chapter 4

1. Sarah Pulliam Bailey, "Christianity Is Declining at a Rapid Pace, but Americans Still Hold Positive Views about Religion's Role in Society," *Washington Post*, November 15, 2019, https://www.washingtonpost.com/religion/2019/11/15/christianity-is-declining-rapid -pace-americans-still-hold-positive-views-about-religions-role-society/.

2. Larry Shannon-Missal, "Americans' Belief in God, Miracles and Heaven Declines," *Harris Poll* (blog), December 16, 2013, https://theharrispoll.com/new-york-n-y-december -16-2013-a-new-harris-poll-finds-that-while-a-strong-majority-74-of-u-s-adults-do -believe-in-god-this-belief-is-in-decline-when-compared-to-previous-years-as-just-over/.

3. "More Young People Are Moving Away from Religion, but Why?," NPR (website), January 15, 2013, https://www.npr.org/2013/01/15/169342349/more-young-people-are-moving -away-from-religion-but-why.

4. Michael Lipka, "A Closer Look at America's Rapidly Growing Religious 'Nones,'" *Pew Research Center* (blog), May 13, 2015, https://www.pewresearch.org/fact-tank/2015/05/13 /a-closer-look-at-americas-rapidly-growing-religious-nones/.

5. Michael Lipka and Claire Gecewicz, "More Americans Now Say They're Spiritual but Not Religious," *Pew Research Center* (blog), September 6, 2017, https://www.pewresearch .org/fact-tank/2017/09/06/more-americans-now-say-theyre-spiritual-but-not-religious/.

6. US Department of Defense, "Faith and Belief Codes," Defense Manpower Data Center (website), March 28, 2020, https://www.dmdc.osd.mil/appj/dwp/searchResults .jsp?search=faith+and+belief+codes.

7. Christina Walker, "Hospital Chaplains Are Bridging the Gap between Patients and Grieving Families Who Can't Stay by Their Bedside during the Coronavirus Pandemic," CNN, April 26, 2020, https://www.cnn.com/2020/04/26/us/hospital-chaplains -coronavirus/index.html.

8. M. Craig Barnes, *The Pastor as Minor Poet: Texts and Subtexts in the Ministerial Life* (Grand Rapids: Eerdmans, 2008), 46.

9. Gerard Egan and Robert J. Reese, *The Skilled Helper: A Problem-Management and Opportunity-Development Approach to Helping* (Mason, OH: Cengage Learning, 2018).

10. These ideas are summarized in "The Egan Model and SOLER," Counselling Central (website), November 8, 2018, https://www.counsellingcentral.com/the-egan-model -and-soler/. Also see Patrick J. M. Nelson, "An Easy Introduction to Egan's Skilled Helper Solution Focused Counselling Approach," Highgate Counselling Centre (website), ac-

cessed April 16, 2020, http://highgatecounselling.org.uk/members/certificate/CT1W3%20 Paper%202.pdf.

11. "Common Qualifications and Competencies for Professional Chaplains," Association of Professional Chaplains (website), last modified 2017, http://www.professional chaplains.org/files/2017%20Common%20Qualifications%20and%20Competencies%20 for%20Professional%20Chaplains.pdf.

12. Brené Brown, *The Gifts of Imperfection: Let Go of Who You Think You're Supposed to Be and Embrace Who You Are* (Center City, MN: Hazelden Publishing, 2010), 71.

13. I am deeply grateful to Chaplain Thomas R. Verner for developing these helpful questions. They are tried and true.

14. There are a number of daunting case studies and accompanying discussion questions to help prepare chaplains and church leaders to move into the chaos of crisis rather than merely doing damage control after the problem is disclosed. Please see Kenneth L. Swetland, *Facing Messy Stuff in the Church: Case Studies for Pastors and Congregations* (Grand Rapids: Kregel Academic & Professional, 2005).

15. Dallas Willard, *Renovation of the Heart* (Colorado Springs: NavPress, 2012), 38.

16. Barnes, *Pastor as Minor Poet*, 46.

17. W. Brad Johnson and William L. Johnson, *The Minister's Guide to Psychological Disorders and Treatments* (New York: Routledge, 2014). This is a thorough yet succinct guide to everything a minister might need to know about the most common psychological disorders and the most useful mental health treatments.

18. Neel Burton, "The 10 Personality Disorders," *Psychology Today* (blog), May 29, 2012, http://www.psychologytoday.com/blog/hide-and-seek/201205/the-10-personality -disorders.

19. Christopher Lane, "The Surprising History of Passive-Aggressive Personality Disorder," *Theory & Psychology* 19, no. 1 (February 2009): 55–70, https://doi.org/10.1177 /0959354308101419.

20. Charles Stone, *People-Pleasing Pastors: Avoiding the Pitfalls of Approval-Motivated Leadership* (Downers Grove, IL: IVP Books, 2014), 8.

21. Andy Stanley, "The Upside of Tension," Global(x) Leadership, April 12, 2018, YouTube video, 33:10, https://www.youtube.com/watch?v=AzHiz-zxjJ8.

22. "Cognitive Behavioral Therapy," Psychology Today (website), accessed April 23, 2020, https://www.psychologytoday.com/basics/cognitive-behavioral-therapy.

23. "What Is Cognitive Behavioral Therapy?," American Psychological Association (website), accessed April 23, 2020, https://www.apa.org/ptsd-guideline/patients -and-families/cognitive-behavioral.

24. M. McKay, Martha Davis, and Patrick Fanning, *Thoughts and Feelings: The Art of Cognitive Stress Intervention* (Oakland, CA: New Harbinger Publications, 1981). These styles of thinking (or cognitive distortions) were gleaned from the work of several authors, including Albert Ellis, Aaron Beck, and David Burns, among others.

25. David Brooks, *The Second Mountain: The Quest for a Moral Life* (New York: Random House, 2019), 32.

26. Brooks, *The Second Mountain*, 32.

27. Andrew Wu, Jing-Yu Wang, and Cun-Xian Jia, "Religion and Completed Suicide: A Meta-Analysis," *PLOS ONE* 10, no. 6 (June 25, 2015), https://doi.org/10.1371/journal.pone .0131715.

28. Karen Mason, *Preventing Suicide: A Handbook for Pastors, Chaplains, and Pastoral Counselors* (Downers Grove, IL: IVP Books, 2014), 177.

29. Mason, *Preventing Suicide*, 168.

30. LivingWorks, https://www.livingworks.net/.

31. QPR Institute: Practical and Proven Suicide Prevention Training, http://www.qprinstitute.com.

32. Yellow Ribbon Suicide Prevention Program, https://yellowribbon.org/.

33. Centers for Disease Control and Prevention, "Suicide Risk and Protective Factors," CDC: Violence Prevention (website), last modified September 3, 2019, https://www.cdc.gov/violenceprevention/suicide/riskprotectivefactors.html.

34. Philip S. Wang, Patricia A. Berglund, and Ronald C. Kessler, "Patterns and Correlates of Contacting Clergy for Mental Disorders in the United States," *Health Services Research* 38, no. 2 (April 2003): 647–73, https://doi.org/10.1111/1475-6773.00138.

35. See chap. 3 of Mason's *Preventing Suicide*.

36. US Navy Chaplain Corps, "Confidential Communications to Navy Chaplains Fact Sheet," Department of the Navy (website), updated February 2016, https://www.navy.mil/local/crb/arc/docs/ConfidentialCommunicationsFactsheet-February2016.pdf.

37. US Department of Health & Human Services, "Summary of the HIPAA Privacy Rule," Office for Civil Rights (website), updated May 3, 2019, https://www.hhs.gov/sites/default/files/privacysummary.pdf.

38. US Department of Health & Human Services, "Mandatory Reporters of Child Abuse and Neglect," Children's Bureau (website), updated April 2019, https://www.childwelfare.gov/pubPDFs/manda.pdf.

39. US Department of Health & Human Services, "Clergy as Mandatory Reporters of Child Abuse and Neglect," Children's Bureau (website), updated April 2019, https://www.childwelfare.gov/pubPDFs/clergymandated.pdf.

40. US Navy Chaplain Corps, "Confidential Communications to Navy Chaplains Fact Sheet."

41. US Navy Chaplain Corps, "Confidential Communications to Navy Chaplains Fact Sheet."

Chapter 5

1. Dean C. Ludwig and Clinton O. Longenecker, "The Bathsheba Syndrome: The Ethical Failure of Successful Leaders," *Journal of Business Ethics* 12, no. 4 (April 1, 1993): 265–73, https://doi.org/10.1007/BF01666530.

2. "Senate Chaplain Prays for Divine Intervention in Gov't Shutdown," *CBS This Morning*, October 8, 2013, YouTube video, 3:02, https://www.youtube.com/watch?v=5qyJAm9ju3A.

3. Kelsey Dallas, "Q&A: Why the Senate Chaplain Calls Spirituality a 'National Security Issue,'" *Deseret News*, February 4, 2019, https://www.deseret.com/2019/2/5/20664977/q-a-why-the-senate-chaplain-calls-spirituality-a-national-security-issue.

4. See "Association of Professional Chaplains Code of Ethics," Association of Professional Chaplains (website), updated September 24, 2000, General Principles and Values 110.15, http://www.professionalchaplains.org/Files/professional_standards/professional_ethics/apc_code_of_ethics.pdf.

5. "Common Qualifications and Competencies for Professional Chaplains," Association of Professional Chaplains (website), last modified 2017, section 4, qualification OL4, http://www.professionalchaplains.org/files/2017%20Common%20Qualifications%20 and%20Competencies%20for%20Professional%20Chaplains.pdf.

6. Thomas L. Friedman, *The World Is Flat 3.0: A Brief History of the Twenty-First Century* (New York: Picador, 2007).

7. Edwin F. O'Brien, "The Role of Military Chaplains," Catholic News Service, October 25, 2007, http://www.catholicculture.org/culture/library/view.cfm?recnum=7949.

8. O'Brien, "Role of Military Chaplains."

9. Stephen Beale, "Trump's Catholic Warriors," *National Catholic Register*, January 31, 2017, https://www.ncregister.com/daily-news/trumps-catholic-warriors.

10. Kayshel Trudell, "Air Force Graduates First Fully Religiously Accommodated Sikh Airman," Air Force Recruiting Service, September 30, 2019, http://www.recruiting .af.mil/News/ArticleDisplay/tabid/4412/Article/1976078/air-force-graduates-first-fully -religiously-accommodated-sikh-airman-from-secur.aspx.

11. *Congressional Record*, vol. 150, Proceedings and Debates of the 108th Congress (Washington, DC: Government Printing Office, 2004), https://www.congress.gov/crec /2004/10/06/CREC-2004-10-06-pt1-PgS10469-2.pdf.

12. See 130.13, "Association of Professional Chaplains Code of Ethics," Association of Professional Chaplains (website), updated September 24, 2000, http://www.professional chaplains.org/Files/professional_standards/professional_ethics/apc_code_of_ethics .pdf.

13. US Department of Defense, "Are Service Members Permitted to Freely Practice Their Religious Beliefs?" FAQ (website), updated March 25, 2019, https://www.defense .gov/ask-us/faq/Article/1774638/are-service-members-permitted-to-freely-practice-their -religious-beliefs/.

14. Dr. Janet McCormack, in discussion with the author, August 3, 2015.

15. Mark D. Roberts, "Praying in the Name of Jesus," *Patheos* (blog), 2011, https://www .patheos.com/blogs/markdroberts/series/praying-in-the-name-of-jesus/.

16. McCormack, in discussion with the author, August 3, 2015.

Chapter 6

1. Emma Green, "Finding Jesus at Work," *Atlantic*, February 17, 2016, https://www .theatlantic.com/business/archive/2016/02/work-secularization-chaplaincies/462987/.

2. I became a certified strengths coach four years ago and frequently use this tool as an invitational gateway toward knowing people within an organization. See more about CliftonStrengths at http://www.gallup.com/cliftonstrengths/.

3. Michael D. Watkins, *The First 90 Days: Proven Strategies for Getting Up to Speed Faster and Smarter* (Boston: Harvard Business Review Press, 2013), 37.

4. Ken Sampson, *Resiliency: 31 Ways to Build Spiritual Resilience* (Harlan, IA: Guideposts Outreach Publications, 2011).

5. Gordon MacDonald, *Ordering Your Private World* (Nashville: Nelson, 2003), 45.

6. Isadora Alman, "Ninety Minute Therapy Sessions," *Psychology Today* (blog), July 6, 2015, https://www.psychologytoday.com/blog/sex-sociability/201507/ninety-minute -therapy-sessions.

7. Tom Gjelten, "'We Can't Anoint the Sick': Faith Leaders Seek New Approaches to Pastoral Care," NPR, "All Things Considered," March 23, 2020, https://www.npr .org/2020/03/23/820119972/we-can-t-anoint-the-sick-faith-leaders-seek-new-approaches -to-pastoral-care.

8. Timothy Keller, *The Reason for God: Belief in an Age of Skepticism* (New York: Dutton, 2008), 193–94.

9. Dietrich Bonhoeffer, *Life Together: A Discussion of Christian Fellowship*, trans. John W. Doberstein (New York: Harper & Row, 1954), 120.

10. Bonhoeffer, *Life Together*, 118, 119.

11. Pirkei Avot (Ethics of Our Fathers), chapter 1, Mishna 6, https://dafyomireview .com/avot.php?d=8.

12. W. Brad Johnson and Charles R. Ridley, *The Elements of Mentoring: The 65 Key Elements of Mentoring* (New York: St. Martin's, 2008), xix.

13. W. Brad Johnson and David G. Smith, "Real Mentorship Starts with Company Culture, Not Formal Programs," *Harvard Business Review*, December 30, 2019, https://hbr.org /2019/12/real-mentorship-starts-with-company-culture-not-formal-programs.

14. Lois J. Zachary, *Creating a Mentoring Culture: The Organization's Guide* (San Francisco: Jossey-Bass, 2005), 3

15. Johnson and Ridley, *The Elements of Mentoring*, 46.

Appendix A

1. Carey Cash, *A Table in the Presence* (Nashville: W. Publishing Group, 2004), 219.

2. See "Chaplains: Divine Services," 10 USC §8221 (2018), https://uscode.house.gov /view.xhtml?req=granuleid:USC-prelim-title10-section8221&num=0&edition=prelim.

3. Pete Kilner, "Love Is at the Heart of Effective Leadership," *Army Magazine* 68, no. 12 (December 2018), https://www.ausa.org/issues/army-magazine-vol-68-no-12-december -2018.

4. E. B. Stolzenberg et al., *The American Freshman: National Norms Fall 2018* (Los Angeles: UCLA Higher Education Research Institute, 2019), https://heri.ucla.edu/publications -tfs.

Bibliography

Abadi, Mark. "11 American Work Habits Other Countries Avoid at All Costs." *Business Insider*, March 8, 2018. https://www.businessinsider.com/unhealthy -american-work-habits-2017-11.

Adsit, Chris. *The Combat Trauma Healing Manual: Christ-Centered Solutions for Combat Trauma*. Newport News, VA: Military Ministry Press, 2008.

Alcoholics Anonymous: The Story of How Many Thousands of Men and Women Have Recovered from Alcoholism. 4th ed. Alcoholics Anonymous World Services, 2002.

Alman, Isadora. "Ninety Minute Therapy Sessions." *Psychology Today* (blog), July 6, 2015. https://www.psychologytoday.com/blog/sex-sociability/201507 /ninety-minute-therapy-sessions.

American Psychological Association. "What Is Cognitive Behavioral Therapy?" APA (website). Accessed April 16, 2020. https://www.apa.org/ptsd-guide line/patients-and-families/cognitive-behavioral.

Assistant Secretary of Defense Memorandum Dated April 25, 1997. "Sacramental Use of Peyote by Native American Service Members." Office of the Under Secretary for Personnel and Readiness (website). May 5, 1997. https:// prhome.defense.gov/Portals/52/Documents/RFM/Readiness/DDRP /docs/1997.04.25%20Sacramental%20Use%20of%20Peyote%20by%20 Native%20American%20Service%20Members.pdf.

"Association of Professional Chaplains Code of Ethics." Association of Professional Chaplains (website). Updated September 24, 2000. http://www.pro fessionalchaplains.org/Files/professional_standards/professional_ethics /apc_code_of_ethics.pdf.

Bailey, Sarah Pulliam. "Christianity Is Declining at a Rapid Pace, but Americans Still Hold Positive Views about Religion's Role in Society." *Washington Post*, November 15, 2019. https://www.washingtonpost.com/religion/2019/11/15 /christianity-is-declining-rapid-pace-americans-still-hold-positive-views -about-religions-role-society/.

Barnes, M. Craig. *The Pastor as Minor Poet: Texts and Subtexts in the Ministerial Life*. Grand Rapids: Eerdmans, 2008.

Beckner, Thomas. *Correctional Chaplains: Keepers of the Cloak*. Orlando: Cappella, 2012.

Bergen, Doris L. *The Sword of the Lord: Military Chaplains from the First to the Twenty-First Century*. Notre Dame: University of Notre Dame Press, 2004.

Board of Chaplaincy Certification. "Certification Frequently Asked Questions." Accessed April 16, 2020. http://bcci.professionalchaplains.org/content .asp?pl=25&contentid=26.

Bonhoeffer, Dietrich. *Life Together: A Discussion of Christian Fellowship*. Translated by John W. Doberstein. New York: Harper & Row, 1954.

Brooks, David. *The Second Mountain: The Quest for a Moral Life*. New York: Random House, 2019.

Brown, Brené. *The Gifts of Imperfection: Let Go of Who You Think You're Supposed to Be and Embrace Who You Are*. Center City, MN: Hazelden Publishing, 2010.

Budd, Richard M. *Serving Two Masters: The Development of American Military Chaplaincy, 1860–1920*. Lincoln: University of Nebraska Press, 2002.

Buechner, Frederick. *Wishful Thinking: A Seeker's ABC*. New York: HarperCollins, 1973.

Burton, Neel. *The Meaning of Madness*. N.p.: Acheron, 2015.

———. "The 10 Personality Disorders." *Psychology Today* (blog), May 29, 2012. http://www.psychologytoday.com/blog/hide-and-seek/201205/the-10 -personality-disorders.

Carroll, Andrew. *Grace under Fire: Letters of Faith in Times of War*. Colorado Springs: Waterbrook, 2007.

Carter, Stephen L. *Integrity*. New York: Harper Perennial, 1996.

Cash, Carey. *A Table in the Presence*. Nashville: W. Publishing Group, 2004.

Centers for Disease Control and Prevention. "Suicide Risk and Protective Factors." CDC: Violence Prevention (website). Last modified September 3, 2019. https://www.cdc.gov/violenceprevention/suicide/riskprotective factors.html.

Chabin, Michele. "Measles Outbreaks Are Sickening Ultra-Orthodox Jews. Here's Why Many of Them Go Unvaccinated." *Washington Post*, April 3, 2019. https://www.washingtonpost.com/religion/2019/04/03/measles-out breaks-are-sickening-ultra-orthodox-jews-heres-why-many-them-go-un vaccinated/.

Chavez, Stephen. "Cooperation without Compromise." *Adventist Review: Online Edition*. Last modified in 2000. Accessed April 16, 2020. https://www.ad ventistreview.org/archives/2000-1545/story1.html.

Childs, James M., Jr. *Ethics in the Community of Promise: Faith, Formation, and Decision*. Minneapolis: Augsburg Fortress, 2006.

Cole, Thomas R. *The Journey of Life: A Cultural History of Aging in America.* New York: Cambridge University Press, 1992.

Coleman Company, Inc., and The Outdoor Foundation, The. "2017 American Camper Report." Outdoor Industry Association (website). Accessed April 16, 2020. https://outdoorindustry.org/wp-content/uploads/2015 /03/2017-Camping-Report__FINAL.pdf.

"Common Qualifications and Competencies for Professional Chaplains." Association of Professional Chaplains (website). Last modified 2017. http://www .professionalchaplains.org/files/2017%20Common%20Qualifications%20 and%20Competencies%20for%20Professional%20Chaplains.pdf.

Covert, Bryce. "Americans Work Too Much Already." *Nation* (blog), September 28, 2018. https://www.thenation.com/article/americans-work-too-much -already/.

Cox, Matthew. "14 Sikh High Schoolers Get Waivers to Enter Army Basic with Beard, Turban." Military.com. May 2, 2019. https://www.military.com /daily-news/2019/05/02/14-sikh-high-schoolers-get-waivers-enter-army -basic-beard-turban.html.

Crary, David. "More US Firms Are Boosting Faith-Based Support for Employees." *Business Insider* (website). February 11, 2020. https://www.busi nessinsider.com/more-us-firms-are-boosting-faith-based-support-for -employees-2020-2.

Crick, Robert. *Outside the Gates: The Need for Theology, History, and Practice of Chaplaincy Ministries.* New York: HigherLife Publishing, 2012.

Counselling Central. "The Egan Model and SOLER." Accessed April 16, 2020. https://www.counsellingcentral.com/the-egan-model-and-soler/.

Dallas, Kelsey. "Q&A: Why the Senate Chaplain Calls Spirituality a 'National Security Issue.'" *Deseret News*, February 4, 2019. https://www.deseret.com /2019/2/5/20664977/q-a-why-the-senate-chaplain-calls-spirituality-a -national-security-issue.

DeGroat, Chuck. *Toughest People to Love: How to Understand, Lead, and Love the Difficult People in Your Life.* Grand Rapids: Eerdmans, 2014.

Demarest, William H. S. *A History of Rutgers College, 1766–1924.* New Brunswick, NJ: Rutgers College, 1924.

Drury, Clifford M. *The History of the Chaplain Corps, United States Navy.* Vol. 1. Washington, DC: US Government Printing Office, 1949.

Duckworth, Angela. *Grit: The Power of Passion and Perseverance.* New York: Scribner, 2016.

Egan, Gerard, and Robert J. Reese. *The Skilled Helper: A Problem-Management and Opportunity-Development Approach to Helping*. Mason, OH: Cengage Learning, 2018.

Egan, Kerry. *On Living*. New York: Riverhead Books, 2017.

Ekblad, Bob. *Reading the Bible with the Damned*. Louisville: Westminster John Knox, 2005.

Federal Bureau of Investigation. "FBI Chaplains: Bringing the Light in the Darkest Hours." FBI News (website). March 5, 2018. https://www.fbi.gov/news /stories/fbi-chaplains.

Federation of Fire Chaplains: https://ffc.wildapricot.org.

Flynn, Greg. "It's Official: Army Beard Dreams Cut Short for Soldiers." *Task & Purpose*, November 27, 2017. https://taskandpurpose.com/army-beards -soldiers.

Francis. "Chrism Mass: Homily of Pope Francis, Saint Peter's Basilica, Holy Thursday, March 28, 2013." Holy See (website). Accessed April 16, 2020. http:// w2.vatican.va/content/francesco/en/homilies/2013/documents/papa -francesco_20130328_messa-crismale.html.

Friedman, Thomas L. *The World Is Flat 3.0: A Brief History of the Twenty-First Century*. New York: Picador, 2007.

"From George Washington to Robert Dinwiddie, 29 April 1757." *Founders Online*. National Archives. Accessed April 16, 2020. https://founders.archives.gov /documents/Washington/02-04-02-0080.

Gawande, Atul. *Being Mortal: Medicine and What Matters in the End*. New York: Metropolitan Books, 2015.

Gentzler, Richard H., Jr. *Designing an Older Adult Ministry*. Nashville: Discipleship Resources, 2000, 2006.

Gibbs, Eddie. *The Journey of Ministry: Insights from a Life of Practice*. Downers Grove, IL: IVP Books, 2012.

Gilmartin, Kevin. *Emotional Survival for Law Enforcement: A Guide for Officers and Their Families*. Tucson, AZ: E-S Press, 2002.

Gjelten, Tom. "'We Can't Anoint the Sick': Faith Leaders Seek New Approaches to Pastoral Care." NPR, "All Things Considered," March 23, 2020. https://www .npr.org/2020/03/23/820119972/we-can-t-anoint-the-sick-faith-leaders -seek-new-approaches-to-pastoral-care.

Godin, Seth. "The Tribes We Lead." Filmed February 2009. TED video, 17:20. https://www.ted.com/talks/seth_godin_the_tribes_we_lead/transcript.

Green, Emma. "Finding Jesus at Work." *Atlantic*, February 17, 2016. https://www .theatlantic.com/business/archive/2016/02/work-secularization-chap laincies/462987/.

Guinness, Os. *The Call: Finding and Fulfilling the Central Purpose of Your Life.* Nashville: Nelson, 2003.

Headley, J. T. *The Chaplains and Clergy of the Revolution.* New York: Scribner, 1864.

Hiebert, Paul G. "Conversion, Culture and Cognitive Categories." *Gospel in Context* 1, no. 4 (1978): 24–29. https://danutm.files.wordpress.com/2010/06 /hiebert-paul-g-conversion-culture-and-cognitive-categories.pdf.

Hutcheson, Richard G., Jr. *The Churches and the Chaplaincy.* Atlanta: John Knox, 1975.

International Conference of Police Chaplains. http://www.icpc4cops.org.

International Critical Incident Stress Foundation. https://icisf.org.

Iovino, Joe. "An Open Table: How United Methodists Understand Communion." United Methodist Church (website). Accessed April 16, 2020. https://www .umc.org/en/content/an-open-table-how-united-methodists-understand -communion.

Johnson, W. Brad, and Charles R. Ridley. *The Elements of Mentoring: The 65 Key Elements of Mentoring.* New York: St. Martin's, 2008.

Johnson, W. Brad, and William L. Johnson. *The Minister's Guide to Psychological Disorders and Treatments.* New York: Routledge, 2014.

Joint Chiefs of Staff. "Joint Guide 1-05 for Religious Affairs in Joint Operations." Joint Chiefs of Staff (website). Updated February 1, 2018. https://www.jcs .mil/Portals/36/Documents/Doctrine/jdn_jg/jg1_05.pdf.

Keller, Timothy. *The Reason for God: Belief in an Age of Skepticism.* New York: Dutton, 2008.

———. *Walking with God through Pain and Suffering.* New York: Riverhead Books, 2013.

Kennedy, Tom. "HPOU Prayer Room Running at a Steady Pace, Praying for HPD Officers, Other Law Enforcement." Houston Police Officers' Union. May 2017. https://hpou.org/hpou-prayer-room-running-at-a-steady-pace -praying-for-hpd-officers-other-law-enforcement/.

Kimble, Melvin A., Susan H. McFadden, James W. Ellor, and James J. Seeber, eds. *Aging, Spirituality, and Religion.* Minneapolis: Fortress, 1995.

Kirschman, Ellen. *I Love a Cop: What Police Families Need to Know.* Rev. ed. New York: Guilford, 2018.

Koenig, Harold G., and Andrew J. Weaver. *Counseling Troubled Older Adults: A Handbook for Pastors and Religious Caregivers.* Nashville: Abingdon, 1997.

Lamb, Wally. *Couldn't Keep It to Myself: Wally Lamb and the Women of York Correctional Institution.* New York: Harper Perennial, 2003.

Lamott, Anne. *Traveling Mercies: Some Thoughts on Faith.* New York: Anchor Books, 2000.

Lane, Christopher. "The Surprising History of Passive-Aggressive Personality Disorder." *Theory & Psychology* 19, no. 1 (February 2009): 55–70. https://doi.org/10.1177/0959354308101419.

Lartey, Emmanuel Y. *Pastoral Theology in an Intercultural World.* Eugene, OR: Wipf & Stock, 2013.

Lee, Cameron, and Kurt Fredrickson. *That Their Work Will Be a Joy: Understanding and Coping with the Challenges of Pastoral Ministry.* Eugene, OR: Wipf & Stock, 2012.

Lewis, C. S. *Mere Christianity.* New York: HarperCollins, 2001.

Lipka, Michael. "A Closer Look at America's Rapidly Growing Religious 'Nones.'" *Pew Research Center* (blog), May 13, 2015. https://www.pewresearch.org/fact-tank/2015/05/13/a-closer-look-at-americas-rapidly-growing-religious-nones/.

Lipka, Michael, and Claire Gecewicz. "More Americans Now Say They're Spiritual but Not Religious." *Pew Research Center* (blog), September 6, 2017. https://www.pewresearch.org/fact-tank/2017/09/06/more-americans-now-say-theyre-spiritual-but-not-religious/.

Logan, Dave, John King, and Halee Fischer-Wright. *Tribal Leadership: Leveraging Natural Groups to Build a Thriving Organization.* New York: Harper Business, 2011.

Ludwig, Dean C., and Clinton O. Longenecker. "The Bathsheba Syndrome: The Ethical Failure of Successful Leaders." *Journal of Business Ethics* 12, no. 4 (April 1, 1993): 265–73. https://doi.org/10.1007/BF01666530.

MacDonald, Gordon. *Building Below the Waterline: Shoring Up the Foundations of Leadership.* Peabody, MA: Hendrickson, 2011.

———. "Leader's Insight: When Leaders Implode." *CT Pastors* (blog). *Christianity Today*, November 6, 2006. https://www.christianitytoday.com/pastors/2006/november-online-only/cln61106.html.

———. *Ordering Your Private World.* Nashville: Nelson, 2003.

Mace, Nancy L., and Peter V. Rabins. *The 36-Hour Day: A Family Guide to Caring for Persons with Alzheimer Disease, Related Dementias, and Memory Loss.* 5th ed. Baltimore: Johns Hopkins University Press, 2011.

Mahedy, William P. *Out of the Night: The Spiritual Journey of Vietnam Veterans.* Knoxville, TN: Radix, 2004.

Mason, Karen. *Preventing Suicide: A Handbook for Pastors, Chaplains, and Pastoral Counselors.* Downers Grove, IL: IVP Books, 2014.

McKay, M., Martha Davis, and Patrick Fanning. *Thoughts and Feelings: The Art of Cognitive Stress Intervention.* Oakland, CA: New Harbinger Publications, 1981.

Molna, Alejandra. "As Americans Become Less Religious, the Role of Chaplains May Grow." *Washington Post*, November 29, 2019. https://www.washing tonpost.com/religion/as-americans-become-less-religious-the-role-of -chaplains-may-grow/2019/11/29/18ca2368-12c5-11ea-b0fc-62cc38411e bb_story.html.

Montilla, R. Esteban, and Ferney Medina. *Pastoral Care and Counseling with Latino/as*. Minneapolis: Fortress, 2006.

"Mosaics Adorn Church Facade at Stanford." *San Francisco Call* 94, no. 60 (July 30, 1903). California Digital Newspaper Collection. Accessed April 16, 2020. https://cdnc.ucr.edu/?a=d&d=SFC19030730.2.66&e=-------en--20--1--txt -txIN--------1.

Mouw, Richard J. *He Shines in All That's Fair: Culture and Common Grace*. Grand Rapids: Eerdmans, 2002.

———. *Uncommon Decency: Christian Civility in an Uncivil World*. Downers Grove, IL: IVP Books, 2010.

Myers, Meghann. "A Soldier Just Got Authorization to Wear a Beard Because of His Norse Pagan Faith." *Navy Times*, April 25, 2018. https://www.navytimes .com/news/your-army/2018/04/25/this-soldier-just-got-authorization-to -wear-a-beard-because-of-his-norse-pagan-faith/.

National Center for Education Statistics. "Fast Facts: Back to School Statistics." NCES (website). Accessed April 16, 2020. https://nces.ed.gov/fastfacts /display.asp?id=372.

Nelson, Patrick J. M. "An Easy Introduction to Egan's Skilled Helper Solution Focused Counselling Approach." Highgate Counselling Centre (website). Accessed April 16, 2020. http://highgatecounselling.org.uk/members/cer tificate/CT1W3%20Paper%202.pdf.

Nouwen, Henri J. M. *In the Name of Jesus: Reflections on Christian Leadership*. New York: Crossroad, 1992.

———. *The Road to Daybreak: A Spiritual Journey*. New York: Doubleday, 1988.

———. *The Wounded Healer*. New York: Image Books, 1979.

NPR Staff. "More Young People Are Moving Away from Religion, but Why?" NPR (website), January 15, 2013. https://www.npr.org/2013/01/15/169342349 /more-young-people-are-moving-away-from-religion-but-why.

O'Brien, Edwin F. "The Role of Military Chaplains." Catholic News Service, October 25, 2007. http://www.catholicculture.org/culture/library/view.cfm ?recnum=7949.

Paget, Naomi K., and Janet R. McCormack. *The Work of the Chaplain*. Valley Forge, PA: Judson, 2006.

Patterson, Kerry. *Crucial Conversations: Tools for Talking When Stakes Are High.* New York: McGraw-Hill, 2011.

Peterson, Eugene. *Five Smooth Stones for Pastoral Work.* Grand Rapids: Eerdmans, 1992.

———. *The Pastor: A Memoir.* New York: HarperOne, 2012.

———. *Under the Unpredictable Plant: An Exploration in Vocational Holiness.* Grand Rapids: Eerdmans, 1994.

Pew Research Center. "Americans Have Positive Views about Religion's Role in Society, but Want It out of Politics." *Pew Research Center's Religion & Public Life Project* (blog), November 15, 2019. https://www.pewforum .org/2019/11/15/americans-have-positive-views-about-religions-role-in -society-but-want-it-out-of-politics/.

Prentzas, G. S. *The Brooklyn Bridge.* New York: Chelsea House Publishers, 2009.

Rank, Scott Michael, ed. "When Patton Enlisted the Entire Third Army to Pray for Fair Weather." History on the Net (website). Updated November 23, 2016. https://www.historyonthenet.com/when-patton-enlisted-the-entire -third-army-to-pray-for-fair-weather.

Ritzer, George, and Allan Liska. "'McDisneyization' and 'Post-tourism': Complementary Perspectives on Contemporary Tourism." In *New Directions and Alternative Tourism,* edited by Stephen Williams, 65–82, vol. 4 of *Tourism: The Experience of Tourism.* London: Routledge, 2004.

Roberts, Mark D. "Praying in the Name of Jesus." *Patheos* (blog), 2011. https:// www.patheos.com/blogs/markdroberts/series/praying-in-the-name-of -jesus/.

"Rules for the Regulation of the Navy of the United Colonies, 28 November– December 1775." *Founders Online,* National Archives (website). Accessed April 16, 2020. https://founders.archives.gov/documents/Adams/06-03 -02-0076-0009.

"Saga of the Four Chaplains, The." Four Chaplains Memorial Foundation (website). Accessed April 16, 2020. http://www.fourchaplains.org/the-saga-of -the-four-chaplains/.

Sampson, Ken. *Resiliency: 31 Ways to Build Spiritual Resilience.* Harlan, IA: Guideposts Outreach Publications, 2011.

Sellner, Edward. *Mentoring: The Ministry of Spiritual Kinship.* Cambridge, MA: Cowley Publications, 2002.

"Senate Chaplain Prays for Divine Intervention in Gov't Shutdown." *CBS This Morning,* October 8, 2013. YouTube video, 3:02. https://www.youtube.com /watch?v=5qyJAm9ju3A.

Shannon-Missal, Larry. "Americans' Belief in God, Miracles and Heaven Declines." *Harris Poll* (blog), December 16, 2013. https://theharrispoll.com /new-york-n-y-december-16-2013-a-new-harris-poll-finds-that-while -a-strong-majority-74-of-u-s-adults-do-believe-in-god-this-belief-is-in -decline-when-compared-to-previous-years-as-just-over/.

Simkins, J. D. "Army Denies Soldier's Request to Grow Beard in Observance of Flying Spaghetti Monster Religion." *Army Times*, May 23, 2019. https:// www.armytimes.com/off-duty/military-culture/2019/05/23/army-denies -soldiers-request-to-grow-beard-in-observance-of-flying-spaghetti-mons ter-religion/.

Sinek, Simon. *Leaders Eat Last: Why Some Teams Pull Together and Others Don't.* New York: Portfolio, 2014.

Sittser, Gerald L. *A Grace Disguised: How the Soul Grows through Loss.* Expanded ed. Grand Rapids: Zondervan, 2004.

Skerker, Michael, David Whetham, and Don Carrick, eds. *Military Virtues.* Havant, UK: Howgate Publishing, 2019.

Smedes, Lewis B. *Mere Morality: What God Expects from Ordinary People.* Grand Rapids: Eerdmans, 1989.

Stolzenberg, E. B., M. K. Eagan, E. Romo, E. J. Tamargo, M. C. Aragon, M. Luedke, and N. Kang. *The American Freshman: National Norms Fall 2018.* Los Angeles: UCLA Higher Education Research Institute, 2019. https://heri.ucla .edu/publications-tfs.

Stone, Charles. *People-Pleasing Pastors: Avoiding the Pitfalls of Approval-Motivated Leadership.* Downers Grove, IL: IVP Books, 2014.

Sulmasy, Daniel P. "Terri Schiavo and the Roman Catholic Tradition of Forgoing Extraordinary Means of Care." *Journal of Law, Medicine & Ethics* 33, no. 2 (June 1, 2005): 359–62. https://doi.org/10.1111/j.1748-720X.2005.tb00500.x.

Sun, Lena H. "New York City Orders Mandatory Shots in Toughest U.S. Action to Date against Measles." *Washington Post*, April 9, 2019. https://www .washingtonpost.com/health/2019/04/09/new-york-orders-measles -vaccinations-brooklyn-amid-outbreak-mayor-says/.

Swetland, Kenneth L. *Facing Messy Stuff in the Church: Case Studies for Pastors and Congregations.* Grand Rapids: Kregel, 2005.

Swinton, John. *Dementia: Living in the Memories of God.* Grand Rapids: Eerdmans. 2012.

Trudell, Kayshel. "Air Force Graduates First Fully Religiously Accommodated Sikh Airman." Air Force Recruiting Service, September 30, 2019. http:// www.recruiting.af.mil/News/ArticleDisplay/tabid/4412/Article/1976078 /air-force-graduates-first-fully-religiously-accommodated-sikh-airman -from-secur.aspx.

US Courts. "First Amendment and Religion." Accessed April 16, 2020. https:// www.uscourts.gov/educational-resources/educational-activities/first -amendment-and-religion.

US Department of Defense. "Are Service Members Permitted to Freely Practice Their Religious Beliefs?" FAQ (website). Updated March 25, 2019. https:// www.defense.gov/ask-us/faq/Article/1774638/are-service-members -permitted-to-freely-practice-their-religious-beliefs/.

———. "Armed Forces Chaplain Board." Office of the Under Secretary for Personnel and Readiness (website). Accessed April 16, 2020. https://prhome .defense.gov/M-RA/Inside-M-RA/MPP/AFCB/.

———. "DD Form 2088, Statement of Ecclesiastical Endorsement, January 2019." Accessed May 16, 2020. https://www.esd.whs.mil/Portals/54/Documents /DD/forms/dd/dd2088.pdf.

———. "Endorsements." Office of the Under Secretary for Personnel and Readiness (website). Accessed April 16, 2020. https://prhome.defense.gov /M-RA/MPP/AFCB/Endorsements/.

———. "Faith and Belief Codes." Defense Manpower Data Center (website). March 28, 2020. https://www.dmdc.osd.mil/appj/dwp/searchResults.jsp ?search=faith+and+belief+codes.

———. "2016 Demographics: Profile of the Military Community." Military One-Source (website). Accessed April 16, 2020. https://download.militaryone source.mil/12038/MOS/Reports/2016-Demographics-Report.pdf.

US Department of Health & Human Services. "Clergy as Mandatory Reporters of Child Abuse and Neglect." Children's Bureau (website). Updated April 2019. https://www.childwelfare.gov/pubPDFs/clergymandated.pdf.

———. "Mandatory Reporters of Child Abuse and Neglect." Children's Bureau (website). Updated April 2019. https://www.childwelfare.gov/pubPDFs /manda.pdf.

———. "Summary of the HIPPA Privacy Rule." Office for Civil Rights (website). Updated May 3, 2019. https://www.hhs.gov/sites/default/files/privacy summary.pdf.

US Department of Justice. "Ministry of BOP Chaplains." Federal Bureau of Prisons (website). Updated November 18, 2004. https://www.bop.gov/policy /technical/5360_02.pdf.

US Department of Veterans Affairs. "The Veteran Population." National Center for Veterans Analysis and Statistics (website). Accessed April 16, 2020. https://www.va.gov/VETDATA/docs/SurveysAndStudies/VETPOP.pdf.

US Equal Employment Opportunity Commission. "Religious Discrimination."

Laws, Regulations, Guidance & MOUs (website). Accessed April 16, 2020. https://www.eeoc.gov/laws/types/religion.cfm.

US Navy Chaplain Corps. "Confidential Communications to Navy Chaplains Fact Sheet." Department of the Navy (website). Updated February 2016. https://www.navy.mil/local/crb/arc/docs/ConfidentialCommunications Factsheet-February2016.pdf.

US Public Health Service. "Surgeon General's Honor Guard Drill and Ceremonies Manual." US Public Health Service Commissioned Corps (website). November 6, 2017. https://dcp.psc.gov/CCMIS/PDF_docs/USPHS%20 SGHG%20Drill%20and%20Ceremonies%20Manual.pdf.

Vanier, Jean. *Becoming Human.* Toronto: House of Anansi, 2008.

Vanier, Jean, and John Swinton. *Mental Health: The Inclusive Church Resource.* London: Darton, Longman & Todd, 2014.

Van Tyne, C. H. "Influence of the Clergy, and of Religious and Sectarian Forces, on the American Revolution." *American Historical Review* 19, no. 1 (1913): 44–64. https://doi.org/10.2307/1834806.

Walker, Christina. "Hospital Chaplains Are Bridging the Gap between Patients and Grieving Families Who Can't Stay by Their Bedside during the Coronavirus Pandemic." CNN, April 26, 2020. https://www.cnn.com/2020/04/26 /us/hospital-chaplains-coronavirus/index.html.

Wang, Philip S., Patricia A. Berglund, and Ronald C. Kessler. "Patterns and Correlates of Contacting Clergy for Mental Disorders in the United States." *Health Services Research* 38, no. 2 (April 2003): 647–73. https://doi.org/10 .1111/1475-6773.00138.

Warren, Rick. *The Purpose-Driven Church: Growth without Compromising Your Message and Mission.* New York: HarperCollins, 1995.

Watkins, Michael D. *The First 90 Days: Proven Strategies for Getting Up to Speed Faster and Smarter.* Boston: Harvard Business Review Press, 2013.

Weaver, Sarah Jane. "Policy Changes Announced for Members in Gay Marriages, Children of LGBT Parents." Church of Jesus Christ of Latter-day Saints (website). April 4, 2019. https://www.churchofjesuschrist.org/church /news/policy-changes-announced-for-members-in-gay-marriages -children-of-lgbt-parents?lang=eng.

Willard, Dallas. *Renovation of the Heart.* Colorado Springs: NavPress, 2012.

Wimberly, Edward P. *African American Pastoral Care.* Rev. ed. Nashville: Abingdon, 2008.

Wright, John Paul. "The University as a Total Institution." *Quillette* (blog), January 2, 2017. https://quillette.com/2017/01/02/the-university-as-a-total -institution/.

Wright, N. T. *Paul: A Biography*. San Francisco: HarperOne, 2018.

Wu, Andrew, Jing-Yu Wang, and Cun-Xian Jia. "Religion and Completed Suicide: A Meta-Analysis." *PLOS ONE* 10, no. 6 (June 25, 2015). https://doi.org/10.1371/journal.pone.0131715.

Zachary, Lois J. *Creating a Mentoring Culture: The Organization's Guide*. San Francisco: Jossey-Bass, 2005.

Index

access, religious, 98–99, 233
accommodation, 233. *See also* religious accommodation
adviser, the chaplain as, 5, 45, 139–59; biblical basis for prophetic voice of the chaplain, 139–44; civic ceremonies and public prayer, 153–58; cross-cultural competencies, 150–52; decision making in organizations, 144–50; definition of advisement and adviser, 5, 6, 45, 144–53; discussion questions, 158–59; ethical review and medical ethics boards, 145–46, 149; legal review by in-house legal counsel, 145, 147; as moral agents, 146–47; organ transplant decisions, 146; religious accommodations, 148, 149–50; risks when advising senior leadership, 141–44; sample questions to guide conversations, 152–53; speaking truth to organizational leadership, 140–44, 148–49; virtues of advisers, 143
advocacy. *See* pastoral advocacy
agnostics, 105–7, 119
Alcoholics Anonymous, 208
American Correctional Chaplains Association (ACCA), 52
American Protestant Correctional Chaplains Association (APCCA), 52
American Red Cross, 215
American Revolution, 64–65
Americans with Disabilities Act (ADA), 205
apparel, religious, 50, 83–84, 89
Association for Clinical Pastoral Education (ACPE), 52, 137
Association of Professional Chaplains

(APC), 51, 52, 137, 233; Code of Ethics, 143, 155
atheists, 105–7, 119, 208–9
Atlantic, 23, 161
autism, 205

Baha'i dietary observances, 82
Baham, Caryn, 192
baptisms, 34, 67–68, 69–70, 94, 97, 218
Barnes, Craig, 109, 121
Barry, John D., 225
"Bathsheba Syndrome," 142
Being Mortal (Gawande), 146
biblical basis for chaplaincy, 13–21; being intentional through movement and direction, 14–15; embracing diversity and inclusion through connection and compassion, 15–17; Jesus's ministry and model of three foundational pillars, 14–21; Old Testament priests, 13–14; Paul's Areopagus address, 16, 53; Paul's counsel to his captors at sea, 140–41; prophet Hushai's advice to Absalom, 139–40; prophetic voice of chaplain as adviser to an institution, 139–44; prophet Nathan's rebuke of King David, 141–42; in Proverbs, 139; seeking transformation through presence and practical service, 17–21; story of Jesus and the Samaritan woman at the well, 14–16
bioethics boards, 146
Black, Barry, 142–43
blessing of the fleet, 153–54
blessing of the hands, 153
board-certified chaplain (BCC), 189, 233
Board of Chaplaincy Certification, Inc. (BCCI), 51, 143, 233